PRACTICAL OBJECT-ORIENTED DESIGN WITH UML

Mark Priestley
University of Westminster

The McGraw-Hill Companies

London · Burr Ridge, IL · New York · St Louis · San Francisco
Auckland · Bogotá · Caracas · Lisbon · Madrid · Mexico
Milan · Montreal · New Delhi · Panama · Paris · San Juan
São Paulo · Singapore · Sydney · Tokyo · Toronto

Published by
McGRAW-HILL Publishing Company
Shoppenhangers Road, Maidenhead, Berkshire, SL6 2QL, England
Telephone: +44 (0)1628 502500
Fax: +44 (0)1628 770224
Website: `http://www.mcgraw-hill.co.uk`

Cataloguing in Publication Data is available from the British Library

First published as 'Practical Object-oriented Design' , 1996, by McGraw-Hill
This edition: ISBN 0-07-709599-5

Cataloging-in-Publication Data is available from the Library of Congress

Publisher: Alfred Waller
Commissioning Editor: Elizabeth Robinson
Produced by: Steven Gardiner Limited
Cover Design: Ripe Design Company (`http://www.ripe.org.uk`)

Website: `http://www.mcgraw-hill.co.uk/textbooks/priestley`
Author's website: `http://www.wmin.ac.uk/~priestm`

12345 CUP 98765

Typeset by Mark Priestley
and printed and bound in Great Britain by The University Press, Cambridge.

Printed on permanent paper in compliance with ISO Standard 9706.

CONTENTS

PREFACE

Mr Palomar's rule had gradually altered: now he needed a great variety of models, perhaps interchangeable, in a combining process, in order to find the one that would best fit a reality that, for its own part, was always made of many different realities, in time and in space.

Italo Calvino

This book is a revised edition of my earlier book *Practical Object-Oriented Design*. It shares the same aims as the earlier book, namely to provide a practical introduction to design which will be of use to people with experience of programming who want to learn how to express the design of object-oriented programs more abstractly.

The most significant change from the earlier book is that the notation used is now that of UML, the Unified Modeling Language. UML is to a large extent an evolutionary development of the OMT language used in the earlier book, so this change has not necessitated great changes in the structure and content of the book.

As with the earlier book, much emphasis is placed on clearly explaining the constructs and notation of the design language, and demonstrating the close relationship between the design and the implementation of object-oriented programs. Unlike questions of methodology and process, these issues are treated rather superficially in many books. If they are not clearly understood, however, it is difficult to make meaningful use of a notation such as UML.

In addition, the book addresses a number of pragmatic issues which are often omitted from design books, such as the integration of a design with an existing framework, the use of patterns in design, dealing with persistent data, and the physical design of object-oriented programs.

UML is a much larger and more complex language than OMT, and when learning it there is a danger of being overwhelmed by details of the notation. In order to avoid this, the book uses a subset of UML that is sufficient to express all the significant features of medium-sized object-oriented programs. The most significant omissions are any coverage of concurrency, activity diagrams, and anything other than a brief mention of component and deployment diagrams. These aspects of the language are obviously important for 'industrial-strength' applications of UML, but these lie somewhat outside the experience of the intended audience of this book.

The Java language is used for programming examples. In order to ensure maximum portability, the use of the language has been kept as straightforward as possible and the Java 1.0 event model is used in preference to later, more complex, models. For the benefit of readers who prefer to use C++, the book's web site will provide alternative versions of those sections of the book which are specific to the Java language.

STRUCTURE OF THE BOOK

Following an introductory chapter, Chapter 2 introduces the basic concepts of object modelling in the context of a simple programming example. Chapters 3 to 5 contain a more extended example of the use of UML in designing a diagram editor application, while chapters 6 to 8 present the most important UML notations systematically.

Chapters 2 to 5 introduce many features of UML in the context of extended examples before a more systematic presentation of the language is given in chapters 6 to 8. However, the diagram editor case study in chapters 3 to 5 is not referred to in the text of chapters 6 to 8, so readers who prefer to cover the language systematically before looking at its use can move directly from chapter 2 to chapter 6, returning later to chapters 3 to 5.

Chapters 9 to 13 are more or less independent of each other and can be read in any order. Chapter 9 covers the use of constraints with UML, and the OCL language. Chapter 10 presents systematic techniques for the implementation of designs, building on some basic material presented in Chapter 5. Chapter 11 covers some miscellaneous issues including the relationship between logical and physical design, and the impact of non-functional requirements on a design, and Chapter 12 discusses some important principles of object-oriented design, and the popular area of design patterns. A case study is presented in Chapter 13, and it is planned that further case studies will be available from the book's web site.

FURTHER RESOURCES

A web page for this book has been set up, providing access to the source code for the case studies used in the book, solutions to selected exercises, additional case studies and other related material. It can be found at the following URL:

```
http://www.mcgraw-hill.co.uk/textbooks/priestley
```

A instructor's manual, including suggested solutions to all exercises, is available to *bona fide* academics. Information on how to obtain the manual can be found on the publisher's web site.

ACKNOWLEDGEMENTS

In the preparation of this book, my most significant debt is to the readers of the earlier book who have taken the trouble to communicate to me their opinions. I have much appreciated this steady trickle of, on the whole, positive feedback. It is in the nature of publishing that the only concrete way I have of expressing my gratitude is to hope that you will all immediately buy this new book, and find it just as useful.

The enthusiasm of Elizabeth Robinson for this new edition was instrumental in motivating me to complete the book, and I would also like to thank the anonymous reviewers of the manuscript for their helpful comments. Thanks also to Alison, for providing some breaks that neither of us really needed, and a big thank you to Rosemary, Felix and Alasdair.

INTRODUCTION TO UML

According to its designers, UML, the Unified Modeling Language, is 'a general-purpose visual modeling language that is used to specify, visualize, construct and document the architecture of a software system'. This chapter explains how models are used in the software development process, and the role of a language such as UML. The high-level structure of UML is described, together with an informal account of its semantics and the relationship between design notations and code.

1.1 MODELS AND MODELLING

The use of models in the development of software is extremely widespread. This section explains two characteristic uses of models, to describe real-world applications and also the software systems that implement them, and then discusses the relationships between these two types of model.

Models of programs

Software is often developed in the following manner. Once it has been determined that a new system is to be built, an informal description is written stating what the software should do. This description, sometimes known as a *requirements specification*, is often prepared in consultation with the future users of the system, and can serve as the basis for a formal contract between the user and the supplier of the software.

The completed requirements specification is then passed to the programmer or project team responsible for writing the software; they go away and in relative isolation produce a program based on the specification. With luck, the resulting program will be produced on time, within budget, and will satisfy the needs of the people for whom the original proposal was produced, but in many cases this is sadly not the case.

In an attempt to address some of these problems, much effort has been devoted to analysing the process by which software is developed, and many methods have been proposed suggesting how it could be done better. Processes can be illustrated graphically; for example, the diagram in Figure 1.1 depicts the rudimentary process outlined in the previous paragraph.

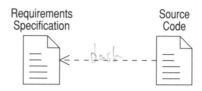

Figure 1.1 A primitive model of software development

In this diagram the icons represent the two different documents involved in the development of the system, namely the original specification and the source code itself. The dashed arrow states that the code depends on the requirements specification in the sense that the functionality provided by the system should be that specified in the requirements. In many real developments the situation is less clear-cut than this: it is a common experience to find that writing code or seeing a prototype system running changes one's view of what a proposed system should do.

The description of the desired system from which a development process starts can take many forms. Very often a written specification forms the starting point of the development. Such a specification might be either a very informal outline of the required system, or a highly detailed and structured functional specification. In small developments the initial system description might not even be written down, but only exist as the programmer's informal understanding of what is required. In yet other cases a prototype system may have been developed in conjunction with the future users, and this could then form the basis of subsequent development work. In the discussion above all these possibilities are included in the general term 'requirements specification', but this should not be taken to imply that only a written document can serve as a starting point for development.

It should also be noted that Figure 1.1 does not depict the whole of the software life cycle. In this book, the term 'software development' is used in rather a narrow sense, to cover only the design and implementation of a software system, and many other important aspects of software engineering are ignored. A complete project plan would also cater for crucial activities such as project management, requirements analysis, quality assurance and maintenance.

When a small and simple program is being written by a single programmer, there is little need to structure the development process any more than has been done above. Experienced programmers can keep the data and subroutine structures of such a program clear in their minds while writing it, and if the behaviour of the program is not what is expected they can make any necessary changes directly to the code. In certain situations this is an entirely appropriate way of working.

With larger programs, however, and particularly if more than one person is involved in the development, it is usually necessary to introduce more structure into the process. Software development is no longer treated as a single unstructured activity, but is instead broken up into a number of subtasks, each of which usually involves the production of some intermediate piece of documentation.

Figure 1.2 illustrates a software development process which is slightly more complex than the one shown in Figure 1.1. The programmer is no longer writing code based on the requirements specification alone, but has first of all produced a structure chart showing how the overall functionality of the program is split into a number of subroutines, and illustrating the calling relationship between the subroutines.

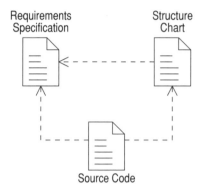

Figure 1.2 A more complex software development process

Figure 1.2 shows that the structure chart depends on the information contained in the requirements specification, and both the specification and the structure chart are used to write the final code. The programmer might be using the structure chart to clarify the overall architecture of the program, and referring to the specification when coding individual subroutines to check up on specific details of the required functionality.

The intermediate descriptions or documents that are produced in the course of developing a piece of software are known as *models*. The structure chart mentioned in Figure 1.2 is an example of a model in this sense. A model gives an abstract view of a system, highlighting certain important aspects of its design and ignoring large amounts of low-level detail. As a result, models are much easier to understand than the complete code of the system and are often used to illustrate aspects of a system's overall structure or architecture. An example of the kind of structure that is meant is provided by the subroutine calling structure documented in the structure chart above.

As larger and more complex systems are developed, and as the number of people involved in the development team increases, more formality needs to be introduced into the process. One aspect of this increased complexity is that a wider range of models is used in the course of a development. Indeed, software design could almost be defined as the construction of a series of models describing important aspects of the system in more and more detail, until sufficient understanding of the requirements is gained to enable coding to begin.

The use of models is therefore central to software design, and provides two important benefits which help to deal with the complexity involved in developing almost any significant piece of software. Firstly, models provide succinct descriptions of important aspects of a system that may be too complex to be grasped as a whole. Secondly, models provide a valuable means of communication, both between different members of the development team, and also between the team and outsiders such as the client. This book describes the models that are used in object-oriented design and gives illustrations of their use.

Models of applications

Models are also used in software development to help in understanding the application area being addressed by a system, before the stages of system design and coding are reached. Such models are sometimes referred to as *analysis models* as opposed to the *design models* discussed above. The two types of model can be differentiated by the fact that unlike design models, analysis models do not make any explicit reference to the proposed software system or its design, but aim instead to capture certain aspects and properties of the 'real world'.

In general terms, analysis and design models fulfil the same needs and provide the same sorts of benefit. Both software systems and the real-world systems that they are supporting or interacting with tend to be highly complex and very detailed. In order to manage this complexity, descriptions of systems need to emphasize structure rather than detail, and to provide an abstract view of the system. The exact nature of this abstract view will depend on the purposes for which it is produced, and in general several such views, or models, will be needed to give an adequate overall view of a system.

Characteristically, analysis models describe the data handled in an application and the various processes by which it is manipulated. In traditional analysis methods, these models are expressed using diagrams such as logical data models and data flow diagrams. It is worth noticing that the use of analysis models to describe business processes predates and is independent of the computerization of such processes. For example, organization charts and diagrams illustrating particular production processes have been used for a long time in commerce and industry.

Relationship between analysis and design models

It is likely that both analysis and design models, as defined above, will be produced in the course of the development of any significant software system. This raises the question of what relationship exists between them.

The process of system development has traditionally been divided into a number of phases. An analysis phase, culminating in the production of a set of analysis models, is followed by a design phase, which leads to the production of a set of design models. In this scenario, the analysis models are intended to form the input to the design phase, which has the task of creating structures which will support the properties and requirements stated in the analysis models.

One problem with this division of labour is that very different types of language and notation have often been used for the production of analysis and design models. This leads to a process of translation when moving from one phase to the next. Information contained in the analysis models must be reformulated in the notation required for the design models.

Clearly, there is a danger that this process will be both error-prone and wasteful. Why, it has been asked, go to the trouble of creating analysis models if they are going to be replaced by design models for the remainder of the development process? Also, given that notational differences exist between the two types of model, it can be difficult to be certain that all the information contained in an analysis model has been accurately extracted and represented in the design notation.

One promise of object-oriented technology has been to remove these problems by using the same kinds of model and modelling concepts for both analysis and design. In principle, the idea is that this will remove any sharp distinction between analysis and design models. Clearly, design models will contain low-level details that are not present in analysis models, but the hope is that the basic structure of the analysis model will be preserved and be directly recognizable in the design model. Apart from anything else, this might be expected to remove the problems associated with the transfer between analysis and design notations.

A consequence of using the same modelling concepts for analysis and design is to blur the distinction between these two phases. The original motivation behind this move was the hope that software development could be treated as a seamless process: analysis would identify relevant objects in the real-world system, and these would be directly represented in software. In this view, design is basically a question of adding specific implementation details to the underlying analysis model, which would be preserved unchanged throughout the development process. The plausibility of this view will be considered in more detail in Section 2.10 once the object model has been discussed in more detail.

The purpose of this book is to explain the modelling concepts used by object-oriented methods, and to show how models can be expressed in the notation defined by UML. The focus of the book is on design and the use of design models in the development of software, but the same modelling concepts apply equally well to the production of analysis models. Analysis is a skill distinct from design, and there is much to learn about the techniques for carrying it out effectively, but the resulting analysis models can be perfectly well expressed using the notation presented in this book.

1.2 METHODOLOGIES

Software development, then, is not simply a case of sitting down at a terminal and typing in the program code. In most cases the complexity of the problem to be solved requires that intermediate development steps are taken, and that a number of abstract models of the program structure are produced. These points apply equally well to developments involving only one programmer and to conventional team developments.

Over the years, many different strategies for developing software have been tried out, and those that have been found particularly successful or widely applicable have been formalized and published as _methodologies_. In software engineering circles, the term 'methodology' is often used (or misused) simply to mean a suggested strategy or method for developing software systems. Diagrams such as Figures 1.1 and 1.2, which show a number of the artefacts produced in the course of a development and the relationships between them, illustrate some of the essential aspects of a methodology. A description of an industrial-strength methodology, however, would be a great deal more complicated than either of those diagrams.

Methodologies usually offer guidance on at least two important aspects of software development. Firstly, a methodology defines a number of models that can be used to help design a system. As explained in the previous section, a model describes a particular aspect of a system at an abstract level, and therefore enables discussions of the design of the system to proceed at a high level without becoming involved too soon in details of coding. A methodology will also define a set of formal notations in which the recommended models can be written down and documented. Often these formal notations are graphical, thus giving rise to the wide use of diagrams in software development. The models together with the notation in which the models are documented are sometimes referred to as the _language_ defined by the methodology.

As well as defining a language, a methodology imposes some constraints on the order in which things must be done in the course of a development. These constraints are implied by the arrows in Figures 1.1 and 1.2 and they comprise the _process_ defined by the methodology. The process defined by a methodology is often defined much less formally than the language, and usually a large amount of flexibility is envisaged, allowing the methodology to be used in a wide variety of situations, for applications with differing requirements, and even with programmers who may be disinclined to design a program before writing it.

The process defined by a methodology can be thought of as defining an outline schedule or plan for a project. Each stage in such a process defines a particular 'deliverable work product', and the forms of these deliverables are usually specified by the language of the methodology. Although this approach can be taken to extremes, it is clear that as well as helping in the technical aspects of software development, the use of a methodology can be of great assistance in project management.

Classification of methodologies

Great similarities can be observed among many published methodologies, and based on these it is possible to group methodologies into a number of broad classes. The similarities arise from the fact that different methodologies can be based on a common understanding of how to describe the underlying structure of software systems. As a result, related methodologies will often recommend the use of very similar models in development. Sometimes, of course, the relationship between two models can be obscured by the fact that different notation is used for them. These surface differences can hide but do not remove the underlying structural similarities.

A well-known example of a class of methodologies is the so-called *structured methods*, including structured analysis, structured design and their many variants. The characteristic model used by these methodologies is the data flow diagram, which illustrates how data is passed between the different processes in a system. Structured methods picture a software system as being made up of a collection of data which can be processed by a number of functions external to the data. These methodologies are particularly appropriate for the design of data rich systems, and are often used in the development of systems destined for implementation on relational databases.

A different class of methodologies consists of those described as *object-oriented*. Although there are similarities between the notation used in some object-oriented and structured methodologies, the object-oriented methods are based on a completely different understanding of the basic structure of software systems. This understanding is embodied in the *object model* described in Chapter 2.

Although notational details differ widely, there is a high level of agreement among different object-oriented methodologies about the kinds of model that can usefully be applied when carrying out an object-oriented development. Because of this, it is quite possible to talk about object-oriented design in a generic manner, without being constrained by the definitions of one methodology. It is important to use a consistent and clearly defined notation, however, and in this book that of the Unified Modeling Language will be used.

1.3 THE UNIFIED MODELING LANGUAGE

The Unified Modeling Language (UML) is, as its name suggests, a unification of a number of earlier object-oriented modelling languages. The three principal designers of UML had each previously published their own methods, and the explicit purpose of UML was to integrate the insights of these three methods. This integration was aided by the common framework, in the form of the object model, shared by the original methods, and also no doubt by the fact that the three individuals concerned ended up working for the same company.

Because of its impressive pedigree, and assisted by its adoption as a standard by the Object Management Group, UML generated a lot of interest in the software industry even before its publication in a definitive form, and it can be expected to be the dominant language used in object-oriented modelling for the foreseeable future.

UML marks a significant departure from earlier methodologies in clearly and explicitly differentiating the language used to document a software design from the process used to produce it. As its name states, UML defines a language only, and as such provides no description or recommendations relating to the process of development. This eminently sensible approach recognizes that there is very little consensus in the software industry about process, and a growing recognition that the choice of process is crucially affected by the nature of the product and the environment in which the development will take place. UML is intended to be a well-defined language which can be productively used with a wide range of different processes.

The remainder of this section discusses some of the basic high-level concepts of UML, and describes the ways in which UML classifies models and presents them to software developers.

Views

UML is informed by a vision of the structure of software systems known as the *4+1 view model*. The UML version of this model is shown in Figure 1.3. As this figure clearly indicates, the model gets its name from the fact that a system's structure is described in five views, one of which, the use case view, has a special role to play in integrating the contents of the other four views.

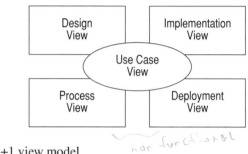

Figure 1.3 The 4+1 view model

The five views shown in Figure 1.3 do not correspond to particular formal constructs or diagrams that can be described in UML. Rather, each view corresponds to a particular perspective from which the system can be examined. Different views highlight different aspects of the system which are of interest to particular groups of stake holders. A complete model of the system can be formed by merging the information found in all five views, but for particular purposes it may be sufficient to consider only the information contained in a subset of the views.

The *use case view* defines the system's external behaviour and is of interest to end users, analysts and testers. This view defines the requirements of the system, and therefore constrains all the other views, which describe certain aspects of the system's design or construction. This is why the use case view has a central role and is often said to drive the development process.

The *design view* describes the logical structures which support the functional requirements expressed in the use case view. It consists of definitions of program components, principally classes, together with specifications of the data they hold, and their behaviour and interactions. The information contained in this view is of particular interest to programmers, as the details of how the system's functionality will be implemented are described in this view.

The *implementation view* describes the physical components out of which the system is to be constructed. These are distinct from the logical components described in the design view, and include such things as executable files, libraries of code and databases. The information contained in this view is relevant to activities such as configuration management and system integration.

The *process view* deals with issues of concurrency within the system, and the *deployment view* describes how physical components are distributed across the physical environment, such as a network of computers, that the system runs in. These two views address non-functional requirements of the system such as fault-tolerance and performance issues. The process and deployment views are relatively undeveloped in UML, compared in particular with the design view which contains much of the notation that would informally be thought of as design-related.

Models

A model in UML terms is defined as a 'semantically closed abstraction of a system'. This means that a model should be complete in the sense that the entire system is covered by the model. However, a model is an abstraction, so not every detail of the system need be included in every model.

Different models of a system may be produced at different levels of abstraction. For example, as explained in Section 1.1, it is common to define analysis and design models of a system at different stages of the development process. It then becomes important to define the relationship between these models, and to ensure their mutual consistency.

Model elements

Models are composed of *model elements*. These are the 'atoms' of modelling, and UML defines a wide range of different types of model element, including such familiar concepts as classes, operations and function calls. A model is a structure built up of a number of interrelated model elements.

If a CASE tool is being used to support development, it will maintain a database storing all the information that has been declared about the model elements known to the system. The sum total of this information, the entire contents of the database, makes up a complete model of the system.

Diagrams

A model is normally presented to a designer as a set of *diagrams*. Diagrams are graphical representations of collections of model elements. Different types of diagram present different information, typically about either the structure or behaviour of the model elements they depict. Each diagram type has rules stating what kinds of model elements can appear in diagrams of that type, and how they are to be shown.

UML defines nine distinct diagram types, which are listed in Table 1.1 together with an indication of the views that each is characteristically associated with.

When learning UML it is natural to place emphasis on learning the details of the various types of diagram. Conceptually, however, a diagram should be thought of as simply presenting to the user certain aspects of the underlying system model. If a CASE tool is being used, for example, a diagram provides a convenient way of examining some of the information stored in its database.

Table 1.1 UML's diagram types

	Diagram	View
1	Use case diagram	Use case view
2	Object diagram	Use case and design views
3	Sequence diagram	Use case and design views
4	Collaboration diagram	Use case and design views
5	Class diagram	Design view
6	Statechart diagram	Design view
7	Activity diagram	Design view
8	Component diagram	Implementation view
9	Deployment diagram	Deployment view

UML diagrams are largely graphical in form, because most people find such representations easier to work with than purely textual representations. Graphical notations are rather limited, however, in terms of what they can easily express, so it is common to supplement UML with a textual specification language such as the Object Constraint Language, which is described in Chapter 9.

1.4 DESIGN MODELS AND CODE

A system design and the source code that implements it should, at least in principle, be closely related and consistent with each other. Figure 1.4 shows some of the relationships that exist between design, code and the completed system.

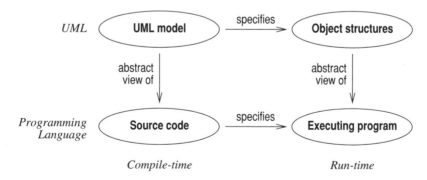

Figure 1.4 Relationships between models and code

One significant distinction that is made in Figure 1.4 is that between *compile-time* and *run-time* artefacts. Source code programs, written in languages such as Java or C++, are documents which define the behaviour that we want a program to exhibit, and must be compiled and executed before they have any effect. UML design diagrams are also documents which specify a system, but ones which may not be able to be directly translated into executable code.

Source code and design diagrams therefore share the property of specifying aspects of a desired system, but they differ in expressing this at different levels of abstraction. Almost by definition, a program gives a complete description of a system: the code that executes is simply a translation of what is defined in the source code of the system. Design models, on the other hand, omit much of the detail that is found in code, and in particular much procedural detail.

However, it is not unreasonable to view a source program as being simply a very concrete design model, as the purpose and nature of the two types of artefact are very similar. This point is particularly clear in the case of object-oriented languages, in which much program structure is expressed using exactly the same concepts as appear in object-oriented design languages.

Programs, then, define the run-time properties of executing systems. When writing ← a program, programmers often try to visualize the behaviour of the code they are writing by thinking of the effects that their program will have when it runs. However, it is unusual for programmers to think in terms of the raw addresses and binary data that is being manipulated by the machine. Instead, they tend to work with an abstract model of what is happening when a program runs.

In particular, programmers in object-oriented languages tend to use abstract models of program execution which talk in terms of objects being created and destroyed as a program runs, and objects knowing about other objects and being able to communicate with them. These abstract models are called *object structures* in Figure 1.4. The arrow on the right-hand side of the diagram shows that object structures are abstractions of what really happens when a program runs, in the same sort of way as a design diagram is an abstraction of the information contained in a source program.

The significance of all this is that object structures, the abstract models that we use to understand programs, are also used as a semantic foundation for UML's design models, as indicated by the top arrow in Figure 1.4. This means that in a very real sense design models and programs are describing exactly the same thing, and explains how design models can be translated into code with some hope of preserving the properties specified in the design. It also means that UML can largely be understood in terms of concepts which are familiar from programming.

Two conclusions can be drawn from this discussion. Firstly, the diagrams defined in a language such as UML are not just pictures, but have a definite meaning in terms of what they specify about the run-time properties of systems. In this respect, diagrams are just like programs, but more abstract.

Secondly, the model that is used for explaining the meaning of UML notations is very similar to the models that object-oriented programmers use to help them visualize the behaviour of the programs they are writing. Thus UML and object-oriented languages have the same semantic foundations, which means that it is relatively easy to implement a design, or conversely to document an existing program, with some confidence that the two representations of the system are consistent.

Chapter 2 describes the object model in detail, shows ways of defining object structures in UML, and explains how diagrams can be used to visualize the properties of programs.

1.5 THE SOFTWARE DEVELOPMENT PROCESS

UML is a modelling language, not a process, but its designers clearly have strong ideas about what sort of development process is most suitable for use on projects using UML and other object-oriented techniques.

Traditionally, a *linear* or 'waterfall' model of the software development process has been proposed. In such a model, activities are carried out in order, and the results of one stage are carried forward to serve as the starting point for work in the following stage. A small example of this is the characterization of analysis and design 'phases' that was discussed in Section 1.1.

In much of the literature on object-oriented design, however, the assumption of an underlying linear process is contradicted by the recognition that system development very often actually proceeds in an *iterative* manner. This means that it is acknowledged that earlier steps in the process must be revisited when the work done there needs to be corrected or modified.

An iterative model allows a welcome and necessary degree of flexibility to enter the software development process, and is a more accurate reflection of the way much software is in fact developed. On the other hand, changing a piece of work that was completed at an earlier stage in the process can cause changes to cascade throughout the entire project, and in general the earlier in the process the initial change is made, the greater the knock-on effects will be.

Considerations like this might suggest that linear software development processes should be followed wherever possible. Empirical research suggests, however, that except in very simple or well understood cases, systems are never developed by progressing through a simple sequence of steps such as those outlined above.

One prominent reason for this is that a linear process assumes that a system's requirements are fixed and do not change throughout the development process. This is a very unrealistic assumption. In many cases, system development starts without a clear idea of what the system should do. This can either be because the users do not clearly understand what they want, or because a completely new type of product is being developed. Worse still, the experience of seeing a system take shape often suggests many other ways in which the system could be used, thus generating new requirements. In this way, the very process of developing a system often causes instability in the requirements.

Another factor undermining the linear development process is the fact that software design is still a rather experimental activity. Design decisions are often taken without a full understanding of the effect that they will have on subsequent development, and it is inevitable that in some cases decisions will turn out to have been mistaken. In these cases it is necessary to be able to backtrack, and to explore the possibility of alternative approaches, something that is not allowed for in strictly linear models.

In practice, then, systems are rarely developed according to the strict linear process specified by traditional design methodologies. There will always be iteration in the process, where earlier stages in the work, right back to the requirements, are revisited and altered or corrected later in the development.

Some writers have taken this further, and suggested that software should be developed in an evolutionary or *incremental* manner, where certain core functionality is implemented initially, and a complete system is gradually 'grown' by adding more and more functionality to it until a complete implementation is obtained. It has even been suggested that every project needs a unique development process defined for it.

Nevertheless, when a completed system is being documented there are strong reasons for *pretending* that a linear process has been followed. Documentation of a system should concentrate on describing the structure of what has been produced in such a way someone new to the system can quickly come to understand its functionality, its design, and the rationale for the various design decisions that were made. In such a description it can be very helpful to present first the requirements, then the system's architecture, and then the details of its implementation in a manner very reminiscent of the traditional stages of the life cycle.

In the case studies and examples presented in this book, this style of presentation will be used, even though it is very far from being an accurate reflection of how the programs were in fact developed.

1.6 SUMMARY

- Most non-trivial software developments use some methodology, even if only a very informal one. This normally implies the production of models to help understand the structure and design of the system.
- Methodologies define both a language and a process. The language defines the models to be used and the notation for expressing them. The process states what order to produce the models in.
- UML is a language for expressing object-oriented design models. It is not a complete methodology, though its authors consider it to be suitable for use with an iterative and incremental development process.
- UML defines a number of views of a system, which represent properties of the system from various perspectives and relative to various purposes.
- Information contained in a model is communicated in graphical form, using various types of diagram.
- Design models and source code share a common semantic foundation, the object model. This ensures that it is possible to maintain a close relationship between the design and the code of a system.

1.7 EXERCISES

1.1 Do you agree that it is desirable, or even possible, to separate the study of a design language from that of a process that uses the language? Does the same answer hold for programming languages?

1.2 Try to illustrate the details of a methodology you are familiar with using diagrams similar to Figures 1.1 and 1.2.

1.3 Read the introductions to the UML Reference Guide and User Guide, and then write a short account of what the creators of UML understand by an incremental and iterative development process.

1.4 Consider the relative merits of graphical and textual instructions and documentation for the following tasks:

    (*a*) programming a video recorder;

    (*b*) changing a wheel on a car;

    (*c*) getting to a friend's house that you have never visited before;

    (*d*) cooking a new and complex recipe;

    (*e*) describing the structure of the organization that you work within.

Can you identify any common features of the tasks you have identified as being most suitable for graphical support? Does the activity of software design share these features?

2

MODELLING WITH OBJECTS

Object-oriented programming and design languages share a common understanding of what software is and how programs work. The *object model* is the common computational model shared by UML and object-oriented programming languages. Programming and design languages express facts about programs at different levels of abstraction, but our understanding of both types of language is based on the abstract description of running programs provided by this model.

This chapter describes the essential features of the object model, introducing them in the context of a simple application. The notation provided by UML for illustrating these concepts is presented, and the chapter also illustrates how they can be implemented, thus making clear the close connections between design and programming languages.

2.1 THE OBJECT MODEL

The object model is not a specific model in UML, but rather a general way of thinking of the structure of object-oriented programs, the framework of concepts that are used to explain all object-oriented design and programming activity. As the name suggests, the object model asserts that the best way to understand an executing program is as a collection of *objects*.

Individual objects are responsible for maintaining part of a system's data and also for implementing aspects of its overall functionality. At the very least, objects will contain functions to access and update the data that they contain. Objects therefore combine two fundamental aspects of computer programs, namely data and processing, that are often kept separate in other approaches to software design. Objects tend to be highly dynamic: as a system evolves and the data stored by the system changes, objects are frequently created and destroyed to reflect these alterations.

An individual object only implements a small fragment of a system's functionality. The global behaviour of the system is generated by the interaction of a number of distinct objects. The objects in a system must therefore be linked together in such a way as to permit communication between them. By means of this interaction, objects can cooperate to support behaviour that transcends the data or processing capabilities of individual objects.

In summary, then, the underlying approach to software proposed by the object model is to view an executing object-oriented program as being a *dynamic network of intercommunicating objects*.

A program is thought of as a graph, or network, whose structure can change from moment to moment. Objects form the nodes in this graph, and the arcs connecting the objects are known as *links*. The objects are discrete packages comprising a small subset of the program's data, together with the functions which operate on that data. Objects can be created and destroyed at run-time, and the topology of the object network can also be changed at run-time. The structure of the network is therefore *dynamic*.

The links between objects also serve as communication paths which enable objects to interact by sending *messages* to other objects. Messages are analogous to function calls: they are requests to the receiving object to carry out some operation, and can be accompanied by data parameterizing the message. In this way, computation can take place in the network.

The role of the object model

The object model provides the semantic foundation for UML's design models. The meaning of any design construct or notation in UML can be explained by rephrasing it in terms of assertions about a set of connected and intercommunicating objects. *Static* models describe the kinds of connections that can exist between objects and the possible topologies the resulting object network can have. *Dynamic* models describe the messages that can be passed between objects and the effect that receiving a message has on an object.

At the same time, the object model provides a very natural way of thinking about the run-time properties of object-oriented programs. A 'network of objects' is only a slight abstraction of a computer's memory in which objects occupy memory at certain addresses and can store references to other objects that are also in memory.

This dual role of the object model establishes a direct link between UML design notations and actual programs, and explains why UML is a suitable language for designing and documenting the design of object-oriented programs.

A stock control example

In manufacturing environments a common requirement is to keep track of the stock of parts held, and the way in which these parts are used. In this chapter we will illustrate the object model with a simple program which models different kinds of parts and the ways in which these parts are used to construct assemblies of arbitrary complexity.

The program will have to manage information describing the different kinds of part known to the system. This sort of information might be available in a firm's catalogue, for example. For the purposes of this example, we will assume that we are interested in the following three pieces of information about each part.

1. Its catalogue reference number (an integer).
2. Its name (a string).
3. The cost of an individual part (a floating point value).

Parts can be assembled into more complex structures called *assemblies*. An assembly can contain any number of parts, and can have a hierarchical structure. In other words, an assembly can be made up of a number of subassemblies, each of which in turn is composed of parts and possibly further subassemblies of its own.

A program which maintained this information could then be used for a number of purposes, such as maintaining catalogue and inventory information, recording the structure of manufactured assemblies, and supporting various operations on assemblies, such as calculating the total cost of the parts in an assembly, or printing a listing of all the parts in an assembly. In this chapter we will consider a simple query function which will find out the cost of the materials in an assembly by adding up the costs of all the parts it contains.

2.2 OBJECTS

The data and functionality in an object-oriented system is distributed among the objects that exist while the system is running. Each individual object maintains part of the system's data, and provides a range of operations which permit other objects in the system to perform a specified range of manipulations on that data. One of the hard tasks of object-oriented design is deciding how to split up a system's data into a set of objects which will interact successfully to support the required overall functionality.

A frequently applied rule of thumb for the identification of objects is to represent real-world objects from the application domain by objects in the model. One of the major tasks of the stock control system is to keep track of all the physical parts held in stock by the manufacturer. A natural starting point, therefore, is to consider representing each of these parts as an object in the system.

In general there will be lots of part objects, each describing a different part and so perhaps storing different data, but each having the same structure. The common structure of a set of objects which represent the same kind of entity is described by a *class*, and each object of that kind is said to be an *instance* of the class. As a first step in the design of the stock management system, then, we are proposing that a 'part' class is defined.

Once a candidate class has been identified, we can consider what data should be held by instances of that class. A natural suggestion in the case of parts is that each object should contain the information that the system must hold about that part: its name, number and cost. This suggestion is reflected in the following implementation.

```
public class Part
{
  public Part(String nm, long num, double cst) {
    name   = nm ;
    number = num ;
    cost   = cst ;
  }

  public String getName()   { return name ; }
  public long   getNumber() { return number ; }
  public double getCost()   { return cost ; }

  private String name ;
  private long   number ;
  private double cost ;
}
```

Classes are defined at compile-time, whereas objects are created at run-time, as instances of classes. Execution of the following statement results in the creation of a new object: an area of memory is allocated for the object and then suitably initialized. Once the new object is created, a reference to it is stored in the variable 'myScrew'.

```
Part myScrew = new Part("screw", 28834, 0.02) ;
```

Graphical notation for depicting individual objects and the data held in them is defined by UML. The object created by the line of code above is illustrated in Figure 2.1. The object is represented by a rectangle divided into two compartments. The upper compartment contains the object's name followed by the name of its class, both underlined. At least one of these names must be present in every object icon. Class names are normally chosen to start with an upper-case letter and object names with a lower-case letter.

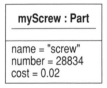

Figure 2.1 A part object

Data is held in objects as the values of *attributes*. An attribute resembles a variable contained inside an object: it has a name, and a data value can be associated with the attribute. This data value can change as the system evolves. The lower compartment of an object icon contains the names and values of the object's attributes. This compartment is optional, and can be omitted if for current purposes it is not necessary to show the values of an object's attributes on a diagram.

2.3 OBJECT PROPERTIES

A common characterization of objects states that an object is something which has state, behaviour and identity. These notions are explained in more detail below, together with the related notion of encapsulation. The various terms are also related to those features of a class definition that implement them.

State

The first significant feature of objects is that they act as containers for data. In Figure 2.1, this property of objects is pictured by including the data inside the icon representing the object. In a pure object-oriented system all the data maintained by the system is stored in objects: there is no notion of global data or of a central data repository as there is in other models.

The aggregate of the data values contained in an object's attributes is often referred to as the object's *state*. As these data values will change as a system evolves, it follows that an object's state can change too. In object-oriented programming languages, an object's state is specified by a number of fields defined in the object's class. For example, the three attributes shown in Figure 2.1 correspond to the three fields defined in the part class shown in Section 2.2.

Behaviour

In addition to storing data, each object provides an interface consisting of a number of operations. Normally some of these operations will provide access and update functions for the data stored inside the object, but others will be more general and implement some aspect of the system's global functionality.

Operations are not shown on object icons in UML. The reason for this is that an object provides exactly the operations that are defined by its class. As a class can have many instances, each of which provides the same operations, it would be redundant to show the operations for each object. In this respect, an object's behaviour differs from its state as, in general, different instances of the same class will store different data, and hence have a different state.

In programming languages, an object's operations are defined in its class, as a set of methods. The set of operations defined by an object defines that object's *interface*. For example, the interface of the part class defined in Section 2.2 consists of a constructor, and access functions to return the data stored in an object's fields.

Identity

A third aspect of the definition of objects is that every object is distinguishable from every other object. This is the case even if two objects contain exactly the same data and provide exactly the same set of operations in their interface. For example, the following lines of code create two objects which have the same state.

```
Part screw1 = new Part("screw", 28834, 0.02) ;
Part screw2 = new Part("screw", 28834, 0.02) ;
```

The object model assumes that every object is provided with a unique *identity* which serves as a kind of label to distinguish the object from all others. An object's identity is an intrinsic part of the object model and is distinct from any of the data items stored in the object.

Designers do not need to define a special data value to distinguish individual instances of a class. Sometimes, however, an application domain will contain real data items which are unique to individual objects, such as identification numbers of various kinds, and these data items will often be modelled as attributes. In cases where there is no such data item, however, it is not necessary to introduce one simply for the purpose of distinguishing objects.

In object-oriented programming languages, the identity of an object is usually represented by its address in memory. As it is impossible for two objects to be stored at the same location, all objects are guaranteed to have a unique address, and hence the identities of any two objects will be distinct.

Object names

UML allows objects to be given names, which are distinct from the name of the class the object is an instance of. These names are internal to the model, and allow an object to be referred to elsewhere in a model. They do not correspond to any data item that is stored in the object; rather, a name should be thought of as providing a convenient alias for an object's identity.

In particular, an object's name is distinct from the name of a variable that happens to hold a reference to the object. When illustrating objects it is often convenient, as in Figure 2.1, to use as an object's name the name of a variable containing a reference to that object. However, more than one variable can hold references to the same object, and a single variable can refer to different objects at different times, so it would be easy for this convention, if widely applied, to lead to confusion.

Encapsulation

Objects are normally understood to *encapsulate* their data. This means that data stored inside an object can only be manipulated by the operations belonging to that object, and consequently that an object's operations cannot directly access the data stored in a different object.

In many object-oriented languages, a form of encapsulation is provided by the access control mechanisms of the language. For example, the fact that the data members of the part class in Section 2.2 are declared to be 'private' means that they can only be accessed by operations belonging to objects of the same class. Notice that this class-based form of encapsulation is weaker than the object-based form which allows no object to have access to the data of any other object, not even that belonging to objects of the same class.

2.4 AVOIDING DATA REPLICATION

Although it is attractively straightforward and simple, it is unlikely that the approach to modelling parts adopted in Section 2.2 would be satisfactory in a real system. Its major disadvantage is that the data describing parts of a given type is *replicated*: it is held in part objects, and if there are two or more parts of the same kind it will be repeated in each relevant part object. There are at least three significant problems with this.

Firstly, it involves a high degree of redundancy. There may be thousands of parts of a particular type recorded by the system, all sharing the same reference number, description and cost. If this data was stored for each individual part, a significant amount of storage would be used up unnecessarily.

Secondly, the replication of the cost data in particular can be expected to lead to maintenance problems. If the cost of a part changed, the cost attribute would need to be updated in every affected object. As well as being inefficient, it is difficult to ensure in such cases that every relevant object has been updated, and that no objects representing parts of a different kind have been updated by mistake.

Thirdly, the catalogue information about parts needs to be stored permanently. In some situations, however, no part objects of a particular type may exist. For example, this might be the case if none had yet been manufactured. In this case, there would be nowhere to store the catalogue information. It is unlikely to be acceptable, however, that catalogue information can only be stored when parts exist to associate it with.

A better approach to designing this application would be to store the shared information that describes parts of a given type in a separate object. These 'descriptor' objects do not represent individual parts. Rather, they represent the information associated with a *catalogue entry* that describes a type of part. Figure 2.2 illustrates the situation informally.

For each distinct type of part known to the system, there should be a single catalogue entry object which holds the name, number and cost of parts of that type. Part objects no longer hold any data. To find out about a part it is necessary to refer to the catalogue entry object that describes it.

This approach solves the problems listed above. Data is stored in one place only, so there is no redundancy. It is straightforward to modify the data for a given type of part: if the cost of a type of part changed, only one attribute would have to be updated, namely the cost attribute in the corresponding catalogue entry object.

Finally, there is no reason why a catalogue entry object cannot exist even if no part objects are associated with it, thus addressing the problem of how part information can be stored prior to the creation of any parts.

2.5 LINKS

The design of the stock control program now includes objects of two distinct classes. Catalogue entry objects hold the static information that applies to all parts of a given type, whereas each part object represents a single physical part.

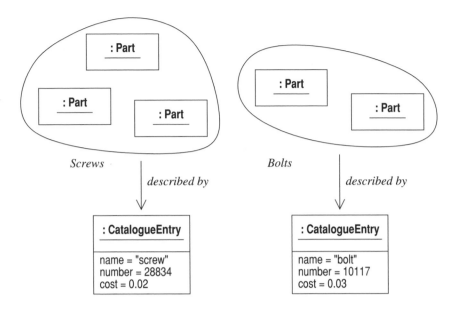

Figure 2.2 Parts described by catalogue entries

There is a significant relationship between these objects, in that a part object can only sensibly be considered in conjunction with the relevant catalogue entry object. The relationship between the two is that the entry describes the part.

A relationship between objects is in UML known as a *link*. Links are shown graphically as lines connecting the two related objects. Figure 2.3 shows two objects which represent individual screws linked to the object that defines the catalogue entry for screws, and hence describes their properties.

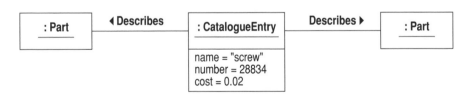

Figure 2.3 Links between objects

Links can be labelled with a term describing the particular relationship being modelled. These labels are optional and are often omitted where there is no chance of confusion. Labels are often verbs and, in conjunction with the class names of the linked objects, are chosen to suggest a natural English rendition of the meaning of the link, in this case that 'a catalogue entry describes a part'. A small arrowhead next to a link name indicates the direction in which the relationship should be read, and use of this convention allows more freedom in the way that diagrams are laid out.

Object diagrams

An *object diagram* is a diagram which shows objects and links between them. Figure 2.3 is a very simple example of an object diagram. Object diagrams give a 'snapshot' of the structure of the data in a system at a given moment.

In a structure of linked objects, information is modelled in two distinct ways. Some data is held explicitly as attribute values in objects, but other information is held purely structurally, by means of links. For example, the fact that a part is of a given type is represented by the link between the part object and the appropriate catalogue entry: there is no data item in the system which explicitly records the type of a part.

Implementation of links

Most programming languages do not define a way of directly implementing of links. The simplest approach is usually to represent the link inside the linked objects by providing some way in which an object can know which other objects it is linked to.

Depending on the language being used, and the properties of the link being implemented, there are many different ways of doing this. A simple strategy is for objects to hold references to the objects they are linked to. For example, the following implementation of the part and catalogue entry classes allows each part to maintain a reference to the catalogue entry that describes it.

```java
public class CatalogueEntry
{
  public CatalogueEntry(String nm, long num, double cst) {
    name   = nm ;
    number = num ;
    cost   = cst ;
  }

  public String getName()   { return name ; }
  public long   getNumber() { return number ; }
  public double getCost()   { return cost ; }

  private String name ;
  private long   number ;
  private double cost ;
}

public class Part
{
  public Part(CatalogueEntry e) {
    entry = e ;
  }

  private CatalogueEntry entry ;
}
```

This implementation states that when a part is created, a reference to the appropriate catalogue entry object must be provided. The rationale for this is that it is meaningless to create a part of an unknown or unspecified type. The following lines of code show how to create two objects, a catalogue entry and a corresponding part. The constructor of the part class ensures that the part object is linked to the catalogue entry object after it is created.

```
CatalogueEntry screw
   = new CatalogueEntry("screw", 28834, 0.02) ;
Part screw1 = new Part(screw) ;
```

Navigability

The implementation of the part class given above includes a field to store a reference to a catalogue entry object, but the catalogue entry class contains no fields referring to parts. This means that it is possible for a part object to access its catalogue entry object, by using the embedded reference, but that there is no way of directly retrieving the set of parts that are linked to a given catalogue entry object.

This introduces an asymmetry into the relationship which was not present in the links shown in Figure 2.3. Although this may seem like a shortcoming in the implementation of the links, it often turns out that it is in fact unnecessary to implement links in both directions, and that significant simplifications in an implementation can be obtained by not doing so.

The fact that it is only possible to follow references from parts to catalogue entries is expressed by saying that the link can be *navigated* in one direction only. Navigability is shown on object diagrams by adding an arrowhead to a link, as shown in Figure 2.4, to show the direction in which it is traversed. If a link has no arrowheads, the assumption is that it can be navigated in either direction.

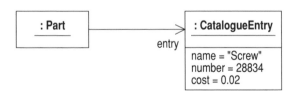

Figure 2.4 Navigability

Figure 2.4 also shows an alternative way of labelling a link. Rather than giving the link itself a name, a label can be attached to either end of the link: such labels are known as *role names*. A role name is in effect the name by which the object next to the role name is known to the object at the other end of the link. A useful convention, therefore, is to use the names of the fields used to implement links as role names, as in this case. The name of the field in the part class that holds the reference to the catalogue entry is used as the role name at the catalogue entry end of the link.

2.6 MESSAGE PASSING

One possible application of the stock control program is to find the cost of an assembly based on the cost of its component parts. In order to implement this functionality, we will need to provide a query function of some sort which will enable us to find out the cost of individual parts. The basic mechanism in the object model for making enquiries of an object, or indeed any other sort of request for information or action, is to *send a message* to it.

Messages are sent from one object to another. Links between objects are used as communication channels for messages, and messages are shown on object diagrams as labelled arrows adjacent to links. In Figure 2.5 a client object is shown sending a message to a part object asking it for its cost. Messages are written using a familiar 'function call' notation.

Figure 2.5 Sending a message

The client object in Figure 2.5 has an object name but no class name. The cost message could be sent to a part by objects of many different classes, if necessary, and the class of the sender of the message is irrelevant to understanding the message and the part object's response to it. It is therefore convenient to omit the class of the client from object diagrams, like Figure 2.5, which illustrate particular interactions.

When an object receives a message, it will normally respond in some way. In Figure 2.5 the expected response is that the part object will return its cost to the client object that sent it the query. However, the cost is not stored as the value of an attribute in the part object, so it cannot simply look up the value and return it.

This highlights a characteristic feature of object-oriented systems, namely that the data in such a system is distributed across a network of linked objects. Some data is held as attribute values within objects, whereas other data may be held in other objects to which an object is linked.

In this case, the attribute value representing the cost of the part is stored in the catalogue entry object that is linked to the part object. When a cost message is received, a part object must therefore send a further message to the catalogue entry object linked to it in order to retrieve the required data item, which can then be returned to the client object. The complete interaction is shown in Figure 2.6.

In Figure 2.6 the two messages have been given different names in order to emphasize their difference. In general, when responding to a message an object can send any number of messages to any objects that it is linked to, and these messages need not have any obvious relationship to the message that was received.

Figure 2.6 also illustrates UML's notation for showing return values from messages. The value returned is written before the message name and separated from it by the assignment symbol ':='. As Figure 2.5 shows, this notation can simply be omitted when the return value is not being shown, or when no value is returned.

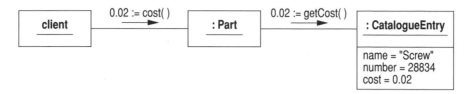

Figure 2.6 Finding the cost of a part

Implementation of message passing

The semantics of the messages shown above are simply those of normal procedural function calls. When an object sends a message to another object, the flow of control in the program passes from the sender to the object receiving the message. The object that sent the message waits until control returns before continuing with its own processing. It follows that a straightforward way to implement the sending of a message is by calling a method in the object to which the message is sent.

For example, in order to support the 'getCost' message shown in Figure 2.5, objects of the catalogue entry class must provide a corresponding operation which returns the value of the cost attribute. This has already been defined as a method in the catalogue entry class, as follows.

```
public class CatalogueEntry
{
  public double getCost() {
    return cost ;
  }

  private double cost ;
}
```

Figure 2.6 shows that the 'getCost' message is sent by the part object in response to receiving a 'cost' message. This implies that there should be a 'cost' method in the part class. Furthermore, in order to capture the fact that the 'getCost' message is sent in response to to the 'cost' message, the implementation of the 'cost' method should call the 'getCost' method in the linked catalogue entry object, as shown below. If a client object now calls the 'cost' method, the 'getCost' method will in turn be called, thus implementing the interaction shown in Figure 2.6.

```
public class Part
{
  public double cost() {
    return entry.getCost() ;
  }

  private CatalogueEntry entry ;
}
```

2.7 POLYMORPHISM

As well as maintaining details of individual parts, the stock control program must be capable of recording how they are put together into assemblies. A simple assembly, containing a strut and two screws, is shown in Figure 2.7. Notice that irrelevant attributes of the catalogue entry class have simply been left out of this diagram.

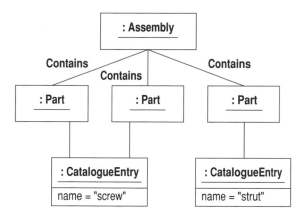

Figure 2.7 A simple assembly

In Figure 2.7 the information about which parts are contained in the assembly is represented by the links connecting the part objects to the assembly object. If these links are to be implemented in the same way as those in Section 2.5, an assembly object must hold references to all the part objects in the assembly.

One way of achieving this is for the assembly object to contain a data structure capable of storing references to several objects, together with methods to add and remove references from this data structure. Depending on the detailed needs of the system it may or may not be necessary to implement these links so that they can be navigated in either direction. This will not be considered further here: we shall assume that these links can only be navigated from an assembly to the parts it contains.

It is not enough, however, for an assembly to be modelled simply as a collection of parts. Assemblies often have a hierarchical structure, whereby parts may be assembled into subassemblies, and subassemblies put together with other subassemblies and parts to make higher level assemblies, to any required degree of complexity. A simple example of this is shown in Figure 2.8, which assumes, slightly implausibly, that the strut and one screw are combined into a subassembly to which a second screw is added to complete the final assembly.

In order to achieve a hierarchical structure an assembly must be able to contain both parts and other assemblies. This means that, unlike Figure 2.7, where the links labelled 'contains' all connected an assembly object to a part object, in Figure 2.8 they can also connect an assembly object to another assembly object. In this case, it is clearly important to know which assembly is being contained by the other. This is shown in Figure 2.8 by means of arrowheads associated with the labels on the links.

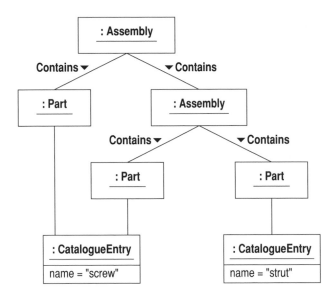

Figure 2.8 A hierarchical assembly

Like many programming languages, UML is strongly typed. Links which are labelled in the same way are considered to be of the same type, and strong typing requires that links of the same type should connect the same types of object. For example, in Figure 2.7 this requirement is satisfied: every link labelled 'contains' connects an instance of the assembly class to an instance of the part class.

It appears, however, that this requirement is violated in Figure 2.8, where some of the 'contains' links connect an instance of the assembly class not to a part object but to a different object of the assembly class. In other words, the objects at the 'contained' end of these links are not constrained to belong to a single class, but can belong to one of a range of classes. This situation is an example of *polymorphism*: this word means 'many forms', and suggests that in some situations objects of more than one class can be connected by links of the same type.

UML, being strongly typed, does not allow links to connect objects of arbitrary classes. For polymorphic links like those shown in Figure 2.8, it is necessary to specify the range of classes which can participate in the links. This is normally done by defining a more general class and stating that the more specific classes that we wish to link are specializations of the general class.

In the stock control program, we are trying to model situations where assemblies can be made up of components, each of which could be either a subassembly or an individual part. We can therefore specify that the 'contains' links connect assembly objects to *component* objects which, by definition, are either part objects or other assembly objects, representing subassemblies. These decisions, and in particular the existence of the component class, cannot be shown on object diagrams, however, but only on *class diagrams*. A class diagram for the stock control program will be briefly discussed in Section 2.9.

Implementation of polymorphism

In order to achieve polymorphism in object-oriented languages the mechanism of *inheritance* is used. A component class can be defined, and the part and assembly classes defined to be subclasses of this class, as shown below.

```
public abstract class Component { }

public class Part extends Component { }

public class Assembly extends Component
{
  private Vector components = new Vector() ;

  public void add(Component c) {
    components.addElement(c) ;
  }
}
```

In Figure 2.8, polymorphism is manifested in the links that connect assemblies to their components. The assembly class above implements this link in the way suggested earlier, by storing in a suitable data structure references to the objects representing the components of the assembly. The function 'add' in the assembly class allows a reference to a component to be added into this data structure.

At run-time the actual objects that are created and linked to an assembly will be instances of the part and assembly classes, not of the component class itself. However, the semantics of inheritance in languages like Java mean that references to subclasses can be used wherever a reference to a superclass is specified. In this case, this means that references to both parts and assemblies can be passed as parameters to the add function, as both of these classes are subclasses of the component class, which specifies the type of the function's parameter.

The implementation of the assembly class is potentially even more polymorphic than this, as it uses the Java library class 'Vector', which can hold references to objects of any kind, to store the component references. The restriction to components is enforced by the type of the parameter of the 'add' method, which provides the only way that clients can add components to the assembly.

Abstract classes

Unlike the part and assembly classes, we never expect to create instances of the component class. Parts and assemblies correspond to real objects or constructions in the application domain. The component class, however, is a representation of a *concept*, namely the fact that parts and assemblies can be considered as specific examples of a more general notion of component. The reason for introducing the component class into the model was not to enable the creation of component objects, but rather to specify that parts and assemblies are in certain circumstances interchangeable.

Classes like 'Component' which are introduced primarily to specify relationships between other classes in the model, and not to support the creation of new types of objects, are known as *abstract classes*. As shown in the example above, some programming languages allow classes to be explicitly defined as abstract.

2.8 DYNAMIC BINDING

If an assembly object is passed a message asking for its cost, it can satisfy this request by asking its components for their cost and then returning the sum of the values it is returned. Components which are themselves assemblies will send similar messages to their components. Components which are simple parts, however, will send a 'getCost' message to the linked catalogue entry object, as shown in Figure 2.6.

Figure 2.9 shows all the messages that would be generated if the assembly object at the top of the hierarchy in Figure 2.8 were sent a 'cost' message. Notice how in an object-oriented program a single request can easily give rise to a complex web of interactions between the objects in the system.

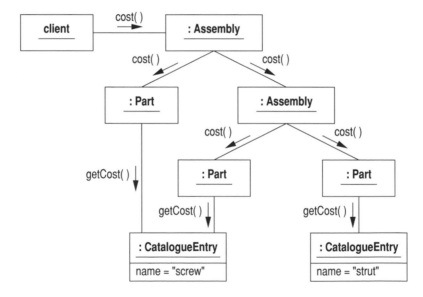

Figure 2.9 Message passing in the hierarchy

In this interaction, assembly objects work out their cost by sending the same message, namely 'cost', to all their components. As explained above, the actual processing that is carried out when this message is received will depend on whether it has been sent to an assembly or a part object. The object sending the message does not know, and in fact need not know, whether a particular component is a part or an assembly. It simply sends the message and relies on the receiving object interpreting it in an appropriate manner.

This behaviour is known as *dynamic*, or *late*, *binding*: essentially, it is the receiver, not the sender, of a message who decides what code is executed as a result of the message being sent. In polymorphic situations, the type of the receiver of a message may not be known until run-time, and hence the code to be executed in response to messages can only be selected at run-time.

In Java, this behaviour is obtained simply by declaring the cost function in the component class and then redefining it in the part and assembly classes to provide the required functionality for each of those classes, as shown in the following extracts from the relevant classes. Other languages have different ways of providing late binding: in C++, for example, the mechanism of virtual functions must be used.

```
public abstract class Component
{
  public abstract double cost () ;
}

public class Part extends Component
{
  public double cost() {
    return entry.getCost() ;
  }
}

public class Assembly extends Component
{
  private Vector components = new Vector() ;

  public double cost() {
    double total = 0.0 ;
    Enumeration enum = components.elements() ;
    while (enum.hasMoreElements()) {
      total += ((Component) enum.nextElement()).cost() ;
    }
    return total ;
  }
}
```

2.9 CLASS DIAGRAMS

The preceding sections have shown a number of object diagrams illustrating the stock control program. Each of these diagrams provides a snapshot of the system state at run-time: they show the objects that exist at a given instant together with the links between them. Object diagrams can also show messages, in which case what is being illustrated is the flow of control through the objects in the system in the course of executing a particular interaction.

In contrast, the source code for the program does not directly show the run-time properties of the program. From the code it is impossible to tell how many objects might be created when the program is run, or how they will be linked. Rather, the code describes various structures, of data and behaviour, that will be instantiated when the program is run.

Object diagrams are useful for visualizing program execution, but it is usually only possible to show a small sample of a program's possible states diagrammatically. To provide a manageable summary the complete structure and behaviour of a system it is necessary to describe it at a more abstract level, as the source code for the program does. UML provides a wide range of notations for summarizing the overall design of a system and in practice these are more important as permanent design documentation than the illustrative object diagrams.

One important type of diagram is the *class diagram*: as the name implies, such a diagram shows classes, together with information about the possible relationships between them. A class diagram for the program discussed in this chapter is shown in Figure 2.10. This diagram summarizes much of the information that is contained in the source code presented in this chapter.

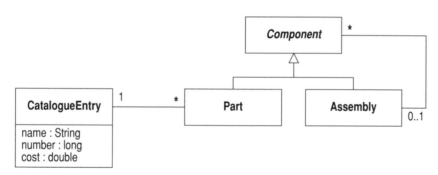

Figure 2.10 A class diagram for the stock control program

The details of UML's class diagram notation will be fully explained in Chapter 6, but it is not too hard to see how Figure 2.10 displays the main structural features of the stock management program. Firstly, the diagram shows, as rectangular icons, the four classes required in the implementation of the bill of materials program. The UML representations of objects and classes are deliberately made similar: the most significant difference is the underlining of the class name to indicate an object.

The class diagram shows the abstract component class, which did not appear on the object diagrams because no instances of the class were ever created. The fact that the part and assembly classes are specialized subclasses of this class is shown by means of an arrow pointing from them to the more general component class.

The data held in objects is represented in Figure 2.10 by giving the name and type of the attributes belonging to each instance of the class. This resembles the way in which attributes are shown in object icons, except that here the type of an attribute is specified rather than a particular data value.

Classes are connected if it is possible to link instances of those classes. The relationship between classes, which is technically known as an *association*, also gives some information about how many links are permitted. Figure 2.10 states that a catalogue entry can be linked to many parts, but that each part is linked to exactly one catalogue entry, and also that an assembly can consist of any number of components, but that a component need not be contained within an assembly.

2.10 THE APPLICABILITY OF THE OBJECT MODEL

The previous sections have illustrated the basic features of the object model, and the close connection between the concepts of the object model and those of object-oriented programming languages has been emphasized. The object model is used at all stages of the software development life-cycle, however, from requirements analysis onwards, and it is important to examine its suitability for these activities.

It is often said that the object-oriented viewpoint is inspired by our everyday way of looking at the world. We do in fact perceive the world as consisting of objects which have various properties, interact with each other, and behave in various characteristic ways, and the object model is said to be a reflection of this common sense view. It is sometimes further claimed that, as a result of this, modelling with objects is very easy, and that the objects required in a software system can be found simply by examining the real-world domain being modelled.

It is certainly the case that in some systems there is a fairly direct correspondence between some of the real-world objects being modelled and some of the software objects, but this analogy cannot be taken as a terribly helpful guide to building object-oriented systems. The overriding aims in designing software are to produce systems which are correct, easily maintainable, easy to modify and reuse, and which make efficient use of resources.

In general, however, there is little reason to expect that simply copying the objects perceived in the real world will result in software which has these desirable properties. For example, the straightforward representation of parts as part objects in Section 2.2 was shown in Section 2.4 to lead to significant problems of efficiency and maintainability, and there was even some doubt as to whether it could meet the functional requirements of the system. Another typical example of poor design arising from overemphasizing the properties of real-world objects is given in Section 12.5.

Furthermore, the message passing mechanism used for communication between objects in the object model does not seem to represent accurately the way that many events happen in the real world. For example, consider a situation where two people, not looking where they are going, bump into each other. It is very counterintuitive to think of this as a situation where one of the people sends a 'bump' message to the other. Rather it seems that an event has taken place in which each person is an equal and unintentional participant. For this kind of reason, some object-oriented analysis methods recommend modelling the real world in terms of objects and events, and only introducing messages relatively late on in the design process.

Clearly there are cases where real-world objects, and in particular agents, can be thought of as sending messages to other objects. The most significant strengths of the object model arise not from its suitability as a technique for modelling the real world, however, but from the fact that programs and software systems which have an object-oriented structure are more likely to possess a number of desirable properties of software, such as being easy to understand and maintain.

Object-orientation is most helpfully understood as a particular approach to the problem of how to relate data and processing in software systems. All software systems have to handle a given set of data and provide the ability to manipulate and process that data. In traditional procedural systems the data and the functions that process the data are separated. The system's data is thought of as being stored in one place, and the functionality required by an application is provided by a number of operations which have free access to any part of the data, while remaining essentially separate from it. Each operation has the responsibility of picking out the bits of data that it is interested in from the central repository.

An observation that can immediately be made about this kind of structure is that most operations will only use a small fraction of the total data of the system, and that most pieces of data will only be accessed by a small number of operations. What object-orientation attempts to do is to split up the data repository, and integrate pieces of data with the operations that directly manipulate them.

This approach can provide a number of significant technical advantages over more traditional structures. In terms of ease of understanding, however, the benefits of object-oriented design seem to arise not from the fact that the object model is particularly faithful to the structure of the real world, but rather from the fact that operations are localized together with the data that they affect, rather than being part of a large and complex global structure.

2.11 SUMMARY

- Object-oriented modelling languages are based on an abstract *object model* which views a running system as being a dynamic network of interacting objects. This model also provides an abstract interpretation of the run-time properties of object-oriented programs.
- Objects contain data and a set of operations to manipulate that data. Every object is distinguishable from every other object, irrespective of the data held or operations provided. These properties of objects are known as the *state*, *behaviour* and *identity* of an object.
- A *class* describes a set of objects which share the same structure and properties. These objects are known as the *instances* of the class.
- Objects typically prevent external objects from having access to their data, which is then said to be *encapsulated*.
- *Object diagrams* show a set of objects, at run time, together with the links between them. Objects can be named, and the values of their attributes can be shown.

- Objects cooperate by sending *messages* to other objects. When an object receives a message it executes one of its operations. Sending the same message to different objects can result in different operations being executed.
- Interactions between objects, in the form of messages, can be shown on object diagrams, together with parameters and return values.
- *Class diagrams* provide an abstract summary of the information shown on a set of object diagrams. They show the same kind of information as is typically found in a system's source code.
- A rule of thumb that is often used in object-oriented modelling is to base a design on the objects found in the real world. The properties of designs arrived at in this way need to be evaluated carefully, however.

2.12 EXERCISES

2.1 Assume that the following lines of code are executed.

```
CatalogueEntry frame
  = new CatalogueEntry("Frame", 10056, 49.95) ;
CatalogueEntry screw
  = new CatalogueEntry("Screw", 28834, 0.02) ;
CatalogueEntry spoke
  = new CatalogueEntry("Spoke", 47737, 0.95) ;

Part screw1 = new Part(screw) ;
Part screw2 = new Part(screw) ;

Part theSpoke = new Part(spoke) ;
```

(*a*) Draw a diagram showing the objects that have been created, their data members and the links between them.

(*b*) The following code creates an assembly object and adds to it some of the objects created earlier.

```
Assembly a = new Assembly() ;
a.add(screw1) ;
a.add(screw2) ;
a.add(theSpoke) ;
```

Draw a diagram showing the objects involved in the assembly a after these lines have executed, and the links between them.

(*c*) Execution of the following line of code can be shown as a cost() message being sent to the assembly a.

```
a.cost() ;
```

Add onto your diagram the messages that would be sent between objects during execution of this function.

2.2 On a single diagram, illustrate the following using the UML notation for objects, links and messages.

(*a*) An object of class `Window`, with no attributes shown.

(*b*) An object of class `Rectangle` with attributes *length* and *width*. Assume that the rectangle class supports an operation to return the area of a rectangle object.

(*c*) A link between the window and rectangle objects, modelling the fact that the rectangle defines the screen coordinates of the rectangle.

(*d*) The window object sending a message to the rectangle asking for its area.

2.3 Suppose that an environmental monitoring station contains three sensors, namely a thermometer, a rain gauge and a humidity reader. In addition, there is an output device, known as a printer, on which the readings from these three sensors are shown. Readings are taken and transcribed onto the printer every five minutes. This process is known as 'taking a checkpoint'.

Draw an object diagram showing a plausible configuration for these objects, and include on the diagram the messages that might be generated in the system every time a checkpoint is taken. Assume that a checkpoint is initiated by a message sent from a timer object to the monitoring station.

Does your diagram clearly show the order in which messages are sent? If not, how might this be shown?

2.4 A workstation currently has three users logged into it, with account names A, B and C. These users are running four processes, with process IDs 1001, 1002, 1003 and 1004. User A is running processes 1001 and 1002, B is running process 1003 and C is running process 1004.

(*a*) Draw an object diagram showing objects representing the workstation, the users and processes, and links to represent the relationships of a process running on a workstation and a user owning a process.

(*b*) Consider an operation which lists information about the processes that are currently running on a workstation. It can either report on all the current processes or, if invoked with a suitable argument, those for a single specified user. Discuss what messages would need to be passed between the objects shown in part (*a*) in order to implement this operation.

2.5 Draw an object diagram representing the objects and relationships implied by the following description of certain aspects of a library system.

A library holds the following books, among many others: 'History of World War 2', 'The Adventures of Robin Hood' and two copies of 'Harry Potter and the Philosopher's Stone'. Felix and Alasdair are registered users of the library. Alasdair currently has the 'The Adventures of Robin Hood' out on loan, and Felix has borrowed the 'History of World War 2' and one copy of 'Harry Potter and the Philosopher's Stone'.

2.6 One of the operations the library system must provide is the ability to send reminder letters to those borrowers who have overdue books on loan. Extend your model of the library system to store the date by which a borrowed book is to be returned, considering carefully which object should store this piece of data. Show on the diagram the messages that would be generated in response to an initial request to print out all the necessary reminders.

2.7 An alternative design for the program discussed in this chapter might propose doing away with the part and catalogue entry classes and instead representing each different type of part by a distinct class. The model could, for example, contain 'screw', 'strut' and 'bolt' classes. The reference number, description and cost of each type of part would be stored as static data members in the relevant class, and individual parts would simply be instances of this class.

(*a*) What difference would this change make to the storage requirements of the program?

(*b*) Define the assembly class for this new design. What assumptions do you have to make to ensure that assemblies can contain parts of different types?

(*c*) It is likely that new types of parts will have to be added to the system as it evolves. Explain how this can be done, first in the original design presented in this chapter, and second in the alternative design being considered in this question.

(*d*) In the light of these considerations, which of the two design proposals do you think is preferable, and in which circumstances?

2.8 Suppose that a new requirement is defined for the stock control system, to maintain a count of the number of parts or each type that are in stock and not currently being used in assemblies. Decide where this data should be kept, and draw messages on a suitable object diagram to show how the count is decremented every time a part is added to an assembly.

2.9 A 'parts explosion' for an assembly is a report which shows, in some suitable format, a complete list of all the parts in an assembly. Extend the stock management program to support the printing of a parts explosion for an assembly. Illustrate your design by including messages on an object diagram representing a typical assembly, such as the one shown in Figure 2.8.

2.10 In Section 2.5 it was stated that it would be an error to create a part object without linking it to a suitable catalogue entry object. However, the constructor of the part class that was presented in that section did not enforce this constraint, as it did not check whether the catalogue entry reference passed to it was not null. If it was null, a part object would be created that was not linked to any catalogue entry. Extend the constructor defined there to deal with this problem in a sensible way.

3

DIAGRAM EDITOR: USE CASE VIEW

In the following three chapters, a design for a simple diagram editor will be presented. This chapter describes the use case view, defining and analysing a set of use cases which document the editor's functionality, Chapter 4 covers the design view, which gives an abstract specification of the software to be built, and Chapter 5 considers the implementation view and the issues involved in turning the design into a working piece of software.

3.1 STATEMENT OF REQUIREMENTS

The diagram editor is an interactive program which allows the user to create simple graphical diagrams built up out of elements such as boxes and lines. The following initial statement of requirements is taken from the book *Designing Object-Oriented Software*, by Rebecca Wirfs-Brock and others (1991).

> The drawing editor is an interactive graphics editor. With it, users can create and edit drawings composed of lines, rectangles, ellipses and text.
>
> Tools control the mode of operation of the editor. Exactly one tool is active at any one time.
>
> Two kinds of tools exist: the selection tool and creation tools. When the selection tool is active, existing drawing elements can be selected with the cursor. One or more drawing elements can be selected and manipulated; if several drawing elements are selected, they can be manipulated as if they were a single element. Elements that have been selected in this way are referred to as the *current selection*. The current selection is indicated visually by displaying the control points for the element. Clicking on and dragging a control point modifies the element with which the control point is associated.

When a creation tool is active, the current selection is empty. The cursor changes in different ways according to the specific creation tool, and the user can create an element of the selected kind. After the element is created, the selection tool is made active and the newly created element becomes the current selection.

The text creation tool changes the shape of the cursor to that of an I-beam. The position of the first character of the text is determined by where the user clicks the mouse button. The creation tool is no longer active when the user clicks the mouse button outside the text element. The control points for a text element are at the four corners of the region within which the text is formatted. Dragging the control points changes this region.

The other creation tools allow the creation of lines, rectangles and ellipses. They change the shape of the cursor to that of a crosshair. The appropriate element starts to be created when the mouse button is pressed, and is completed when the mouse button is released. These two events create the start point and the stop point.

The line creation tool creates a line from the start point to the stop point. These are the control points of a line. Dragging a control point changes the end point.

The rectangle creation tool creates a rectangle such that these points are diagonally opposite corners. These points and the other corners are the control points. Dragging a control point changes the associated corner.

The ellipse creation tool creates an ellipse fitting within the rectangle defined by the two points described above. The major radius is one half the width of the rectangle, and the minor radius is one half the height of the rectangle. The control points are at the corners of the bounding rectangle. Dragging a control point changes the associated corner.

This specification refers to the editor as a 'drawing editor'. However, given the nature of the editor's output, the term 'diagram editor' seems more appropriate and will be used throughout the remainder of this book.

The specification states nothing about the environment in which the diagram editor will run. We will assume that the program should provide a graphical display of the diagram being created, and that a mouse and keyboard will be used as input devices.

In this chapter and the two following, the design and implementation of a version of this diagram editor will be discussed. Figure 3.1 shows a screen shot of the completed program running as a Java applet. Complete code for this applet can be downloaded from the web site accompanying this book.

The control bar at the top of the applet contains two buttons which enable the user to create a new diagram and to view alternate diagrams. The drop-down list enables the user to select one of the available tools, and the final button gives the option, which is only implicit in the specification above, of deleting elements.

The diagram that the user is working on is shown in the main window of the applet. In the situation shown in Figure 3.1 the user has created three shapes, a rectangle, a line and an ellipse. The current tool is a selection tool, and the user has selected and is moving the ellipse. The control points of the ellipse can be seen at the corners of its bounding rectangle.

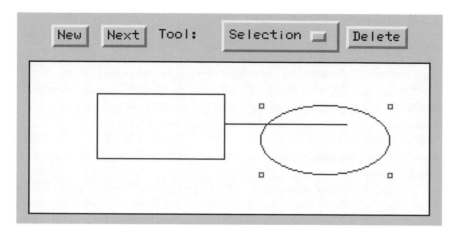

Figure 3.1 The diagram editor

3.2 THE USE CASE VIEW

Among the different possible views of a system, the *use case view* is considered to be central to UML. The use case view describes the externally visible behaviour of the system. Insofar as software development begins with a consideration of the requirements of the proposed system, therefore, the use case view establishes the forces that will drive and constrain subsequent development.

The use case view presents a structured view of a system's functionality. It does this by defining a number of *actors*, which model the roles that users can play when interacting with the system, and describing the *use cases* that those actors can participate in. A use case describes one way in which a user can interact with a system. The use case view contains a set of use cases which should define the complete functionality of the system as seen from the user's perspective.

In principle, the use case view should be comprehensible to clients, end users, domain experts, testers, and anybody else whose involvement with the system does not require detailed knowledge of its structure and implementation. The use case view does not describe the organization or structure of a software system. Its role is to impose a constraint on designers, who must come up with a structure which will provide the functionality specified in the user case view.

Actors

A use case describes a single type of interaction between a system and its users. However, systems often have different categories of users, who are able to perform different subsets of the system's functionality. For example, multi-user systems often define a role known as the 'system administrator': this individual has access to a specialized range of functionality that is not available to ordinary users, such as defining new users, or taking back-ups of the system.

The different roles that people can fill when they interact with a system are known as *actors*. Use case analysis begins by identifying the different actors involved in a system. Actors often correspond to a particular level of access to a system, defined by the range of system functions that can be performed. In other cases, the actors are not so rigidly defined, but correspond simply to groups of people with different interests in the system.

In general there is not a one-to-one correspondence between the actors defined for a system and its real users. One person could interact with a system as two different actors, for example by logging on to the system using passwords which give different access privileges. Conversely, there may be many real people corresponding to a single actor. Actors need not even be human users. For example, the computers in a network may communicate directly with each other, and it would be quite possible for a remote computer to qualify as an actor in a particular system.

From the point of view of its actors, the diagram editor is particularly simple. It is intended as a simple stand-alone, single user application. Anyone using the editor has access to all its functionality, and the system has no interfaces with other programs or machines. The use case model needs therefore to define only a single actor which will from now on be referred to as the *user*.

Use cases

The specification given in Section 3.1 describes what users can do with the diagram editor. The following list summarizes these operations, giving an example of what might be meant by an operation in cases where the specification is vague.

1. Create diagrams.
2. Create text and graphical elements.
3. Edit diagrams, for example by deleting elements.
4. Select existing elements.
5. Manipulate diagram elements, for example by moving them.
6. Modify diagram elements, by dragging a control point to resize them.

Each of these operations will be described in more detail and presented as a use case. Even within a single use case, however, the details of the interaction between the user and the editor can vary significantly. For example, before dragging a control point the user has to click the mouse button over the displayed control point. If the user clicks the mouse button at a position where no control point is displayed, however, nothing will happen. This possibility represents an exception, or a variation on the normal course of events in this use case.

In general, then, the definition of a use case consists of a basic course of events, and a number of alternative and exceptional courses of events. The basic course describes the normal, straightforward way in which things happen, whereas the alternative courses describe what happens when the user makes a non-standard or alternative choice, or when an error occurs.

For example, in the use case describing how new elements are created, the basic course of events would describe the straightforward use of the system to add a new element to the diagram. A situation where the user chooses to abandon the creation process half-way through, for example, would be described by an alternative course of events belonging to the same use case.

A use case is therefore a description of a whole class of interactions. Each time an actor performs a use case, what is actually done will vary in some particulars from what is done on other occasions, even though in some general sense the overall intention behind the interaction remains the same. Furthermore, different instantiations of a use case can often be grouped into distinct families, namely those described by the basic and the various exceptional courses of events.

When constructing use cases, and also in later stages of the design process, it is helpful to consider sequences of interactions that might actually take place between an actor and the system. Each such sequence corresponds to a single instance of a user interacting with the system in the way defined by a particular use case. These sequences are known as *scenarios*, and are often described informally at an early stage in the design process.

The relationship between use cases and scenarios is rather like that between classes and objects. A use case may have many scenarios instantiating it, each of which gives a concrete example of the more abstract pattern defined by the use case.

Use case diagrams

A *use case diagram* summarizes in graphical form the different actors and use cases in a system, and shows which actors can participate in which use cases. An initial use case diagram for the diagram editor is given in Figure 3.2, showing the use cases which were identified in the informal statement of requirements.

The simplest forms of use case diagram, like Figure 3.2, simply show actors, use cases and the relationships between them. Actors are represented by a stylized icon of a person, and use cases by ovals containing the name of the use case. Where an actor participates in a particular use case, this relationship is shown by a line connecting the actor to the relevant use case.

UML allows more structure to be included in a use case diagram by defining various types of relationship between use cases. For example, it is possible to make explicit behaviour that is common to more than one use case, and to formalize its inclusion in other use cases. A more sophisticated use case diagram for the diagram editor is presented at the end of this chapter.

In the following sections, each of the use cases for the diagram editor will be considered in turn. Where necessary, scenarios for each use case will be considered, and an informal account of the complete use case will be given.

Once its functionality is understood, a *realization* of each use case will be defined, specifying a set of interacting objects that would provide an implementation of the use case. In this way we will gradually build up an understanding of the objects, classes and interactions required for the design of diagram editor.

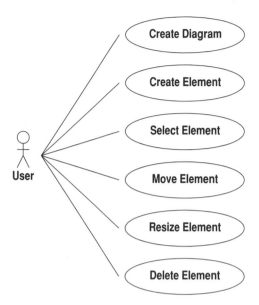

Figure 3.2 Initial use case diagram for the diagram editor

3.3 CREATING NEW DIAGRAMS

The specification of the diagram editor does not give details about how diagrams are created and managed. We will make the following assumptions.

> The editor presents the user with a work space within which one diagram can be displayed at a time. When it is started up, the work space contains a new, empty diagram. An option is provided to allow the user to create new diagrams; when a new diagram is created it is displayed in the work space, and the diagram that was there before is hidden. The diagram that is currently visible in the work space is known as the *active* or *current* diagram. An option is provided enabling the user to cycle through the set of diagrams making each one active in turn.

> Following the rule of thumb introduced in Section 2.2, which suggests that domain concepts can often be modelled as objects, we can consider modelling each diagram by an instance of a diagram class. The basic responsibility of these objects will be to record which elements appear on the diagram. The initial state of the editor, then, will include a single diagram object, corresponding to the 'new, empty diagram' mentioned above.
> An important fact about this and any other diagram is that it is one of the diagrams being manipulated by the diagram editor. To model this fact, it is natural to introduce an object representing the diagram editor itself. One of the responsibilities of this object is to keep track of the diagrams that the user has created. The relationship between the diagram editor and a diagram that it is currently managing can be represented by means of a link between the two objects, as shown in Figure 3.3.

Figure 3.3 The relationship between a diagram and the diagram editor

When the user creates additional diagrams, further diagram objects will be added to Figure 3.3 and linked to the diagram editor. This raises the question of how the editor knows which diagram is the currently active one. Links of the type shown in Figure 3.3 link the diagram editor to all the current diagrams, and hence cannot be used to distinguish the currently active diagram from the others.

A standard solution to problems of this kind is to introduce an additional type of link to connect the diagram editor to the currently active diagram. An example of such a link is shown in Figure 3.4. It is labelled with a role name which indicates that the diagram connected to it is the diagram that is currently being displayed by the editor.

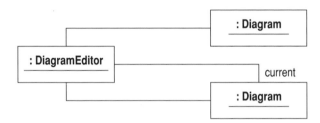

Figure 3.4 Identifying the current diagram

To create a complete picture of the initial state of the diagram editor, an additional link identifying the current diagram should be added between the two objects shown in Figure 3.3. Where there is only one diagram, of course, there is no ambiguity about which diagram is active. Nevertheless, we have taken the decision to identify the current diagram by means of this link, and so for consistency it must always be present.

3.4 USE CASE REALIZATION

Once defined, use cases can be used to guide further development of the system. One way in which this is done is by defining *realizations* of use cases. A realization of a use case describes a collection of interacting objects which will support the functionality required by the use case. Providing realizations of a system's use cases is a first step in moving from an external description of a system's functionality to a more detailed design of its internal structure.

Use case realizations are specified in UML using *interaction diagrams*, of which there are two types. The first type, known as *collaboration diagrams*, was used informally in Chapter 2 to illustrate the behaviour of the stock control program. *Sequence diagrams* are an alternative type of interaction diagram, and will be used to document the realization of the use cases in this chapter.

The two forms of interaction diagram are more or less equivalent, and provide alternative ways of presenting the same information. Many people find that sequence diagrams provide a clearer illustration of the order in which various events take place, so where this aspect of an interaction is of particular importance, sequence diagrams are often used.

The following scenario describes a typical course of events that might occur when a user wishes to create a new diagram.

1. The user interacts with some user interface component, such as a menu item or a tool bar button, to signal the request to the system.
2. In response, the system creates a new diagram object.
3. The new diagram is made the currently active diagram.
4. The editor's display is updated to display the newly created diagram.

It is often useful to separate the specific functionality of an application from more generic concerns, such as the way in which input and output will be managed. In this chapter, we will assume that input from the user is captured by user interface code and translated into application-specific messages that are sent to the diagram editor. Furthermore, we will not consider how the current diagram is displayed or how this display is updated in response to the user's actions. A more detailed consideration of input and output is given in Chapter 5.

Sequence diagrams

Given these simplifying assumptions, a possible realization of the scenario described informally above is shown as a sequence diagram in Figure 3.5.

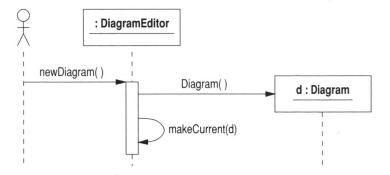

Figure 3.5 Creating a new diagram

The interaction starts at the top of the diagram, and time flows down the diagram from top to bottom. At the very top of the diagram relevant objects that exist at the start of the interaction are shown. In this case, these are an instance of the actor representing the user, and the diagram editor object itself. Other diagrams that exist but do not participate in this interaction are not shown on the diagram.

Each object or instance shown has a *lifeline*, represented as a dashed line extending below its icon. The lifeline shows the period of time during which the object exists. In this case, both the user and the diagram editor object exist for the complete duration of the interaction.

According to the assumptions made above, when the user requests that a new element is created, a message to this effect will be sent to the diagram editor object. Messages are shown on sequence diagrams as arrows going from one object's lifeline to another. Figure 3.5 ignores the processing that will be performed by the user interface code in handling the user's actions, and simply shows a message labelled 'newDiagram' being sent from the user to the diagram editor.

When the diagram editor receives this message, a new *activation* is started, shown as an elongated rectangle on the diagram editor's lifeline. An activation corresponds to the period of time during which an object is active processing a message. Showing activations on sequence diagrams makes it easy to see where the flow of control is within an interaction, and how one message can be sent while an object is processing another.

In response to the 'newDiagram' message, the first thing the diagram editor does is actually to create the new diagram. This new object is shown at its point of creation, with its lifeline continuing below it. Messages that cause the creation of new objects are a slightly special case. They are often known as *constructors*, and differ in various ways from normal operations or methods. UML models this difference by showing creation messages terminating at the icon representing the new object rather than at its lifeline. Figure 3.5 assumes that the constructor has the same name as the class, a convention followed by a number of languages.

Finally, the diagram editor has to record that the new diagram now becomes the current diagram. This process will probably involve resetting some internal attribute and not require any communication with any other object. Accordingly, it is modelled in Figure 3.5 as a message sent by the diagram editor to itself. In a sense this message is superfluous, as it generates no interactions between objects. It is included to draw attention to an important part of the realization of this use case.

The diagram object in Figure 3.5 has a *name*, 'd'. It is useful to name objects on object and sequence diagrams when they have to be referred to elsewhere on the diagram. In Figure 3.5 the name is used as a parameter for the 'makeCurrent' message. This makes it clear that the diagram being made current is precisely the one that has just been created.

3.5 CREATING NEW ELEMENTS

One of the advantages of the use case technique is that it forces a designer to come up with a very clear and detailed description of the interactions between the system and the user, and to make explicit many things which are vague or missing from the original specification. This is often achieved by writing some scenarios describing concrete instances of the use case before attempting a complete definition of a use case. The following scenario describes the creation of a rectangle element.

1. If necessary, the user makes a rectangle tool active.
2. The user moves the cursor a number of times.
3. The user presses the mouse button.
4. The user moves the cursor a number of times. A faint image of a rectangle is drawn; opposite corners of the rectangle are defined by the position at which the mouse button was pressed and the current position of the cursor.
5. The user releases the mouse button and the new rectangle is displayed on the screen.

This scenario first specifies that the user is responsible for selecting the required creation tool; although obvious, this is not explicitly stated in the original requirements, which simply say 'when a creation tool is active'. One piece of functionality that was not mentioned in the requirements is added in this scenario: when the user is moving the mouse to locate the stop point a faint image of the rectangle is drawn on the screen, to help the user judge when the required stop point has been reached.

This scenario also introduces a slight incompatibility with the original specification, which states that after an element is created the selection tool becomes active and the newly created element is selected. The scenario does not specify this, however. A justification for this change is that users will often want to create a large number of elements, one after the other. It would be very tiresome if after each creation the selection tool became active and had to be deactivated before proceeding. In a real development, of course, this change would need to be discussed with the customer for whom the system was being developed.

It is clear from the specification that scenarios describing the creation of ellipses or lines would be almost identical to the one given above for creating a rectangle. All these graphical elements are initially defined by two points, and the scenario simply describes the means by which the user indicates these points to the system.

The pattern of interaction described in the specification for creating a text element is very different, however. Because of this difference, it would seem to be appropriate to split the use case 'create element' into two more specialized use cases, namely 'create graphical element' and 'create text element'.

Despite the differences between these two new use cases, they are both in a sense contained within the general use case 'create an element'. If we were simply required to create an element, it would not matter which kind of element was created, or which use case was executed. Another way of phrasing this is to say that wherever the 'create element' use case is mentioned, we could substitute either 'create graphical element' or 'create text element', and it would not affect the correctness of what was being said. The general case is useful for times when we do not care or do not need to specify which type of element is under discussion.

This notion of being able to substitute one entity for another is widespread in UML. The corresponding relationship is given the name *generalization* and is represented graphically by an open-headed arrow. Figure 3.6 shows the generalization relationships between the three use cases discussed here. Notice that the arrow always points to the more general entity in the relationship. The inverse of generalization is *specialization*, so the use case 'create text element', for example, would be referred to as a specialization of 'create element'.

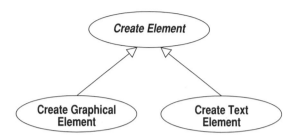

Figure 3.6 Generalization between use cases

Once the two sub-cases shown in Figure 3.6 have been defined, there is nothing more to be said about the general case. If an element is created, then either a graphical or a text element is created: there is no third possibility. This means that there is no special behaviour associated with the general use case, and no possibility of executing it on its own. We recognize this by describing it as an *abstract* use case, and writing its name in a sloping font, as shown in Figure 3.6.

An informal description of the use case for creating graphical elements is given in Table 3.1. The use case describes the general case of creating a graphical element, not just the specific case of the rectangle considered above. It is clear from the specification of the editor that identical interactions are involved in the creation of all graphical elements, and therefore one use case will serve to describe all of them.

Table 3.1 Use case for creating a graphical element

Name	Create graphical element
Description	If necessary, the user makes the appropriate creation tool active. The user moves the cursor to the desired start point of the shape and presses the mouse button. The user moves the cursor to the desired stop point; a faint image of the shape defined by the start point and current position is displayed by the editor and updated as the mouse moves. When the desired stop point is reached the user releases the mouse button. The new element is added to the current diagram.
Exceptions	None.

Use cases are a rather informal technique, and UML does not define a standard way of presenting them. In this book, use cases are presented using slightly structured English text. The different sections in the table above distinguish the important aspects of a use case, namely its name, a description of the basic course of events, and descriptions of the exceptional, or alternative, courses of events that can occur. References in the description of the basic course of events specify the points at which exceptional events can occur.

A possible realization

Figure 3.7 shows a sequence diagram depicting the objects and the interactions involved in the course of creating a rectangle. The details of this interaction will be exactly the same for other types of graphical element.

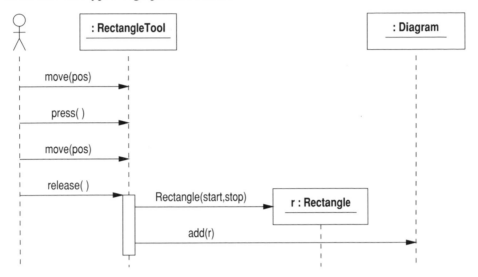

Figure 3.7 Creating a rectangle

The description of the editor makes use of the notion of *tools*. To complete any task with the editor, the user must first activate an appropriate tool, and then work with the tool in the ways that it permits. A tool will have state, recording the progress of the interaction, and it will have an operational interface through which the user can manipulate it. It therefore seems reasonable to model tools as objects.

A further aspect of the tool metaphor is that a tool, when active, must be the focus for all user input. In Figure 3.5 user input was represented by messages being sent from the user to the diagram editor. Messages which relate to the usage of a tool will simply be forwarded from the diagram editor on to the relevant tool. For simplicity, this forwarding process is omitted from Figure 3.7 which simply shows messages being passed directly from the user to the tool.

Elements certainly have state, recording their position on the diagram, and will therefore also be modelled as objects. When an element is being created, the user identifies two points, known as the 'start' and 'stop' points. An element is only fully defined when both points are known, at the very end of the interaction, and the coordinates of the two points are then passed as arguments to the constructor of the element. Once created, the new element is added to the current diagram.

Some of the messages in Figure 3.7 include a parameter 'pos', referring to the current position of the mouse cursor. This design does not assume that the cursor position is passed with press and release messages, even though many programming environments in fact provide this feature.

Sequence diagrams do not show the links between the objects involved in an interaction. These can be conveniently shown on an object diagram. Figure 3.8 shows the objects in the system and their interconnections after a single rectangle has been created and added to the current diagram. The links between the diagram editor and the tool and between the tool and the active diagram are needed to support the messages that were specified in the realization of the use case above.

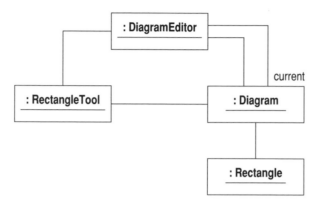

Figure 3.8 The situation after a rectangle has been created

This diagram shows that permanent links are maintained between the tool and the diagram, and between the diagram and the elements that it contains. No link is maintained between a creation tool and the element it creates, however. Once creation is complete, the tool passes all responsibility for the new element over to the diagram.

Collaboration diagrams

For comparison, Figure 3.9 shows the same interaction as Figure 3.7, but presented as a collaboration diagram rather than as a sequence diagram. As this diagram shows, collaboration diagrams are basically object diagrams with messages shown flowing along links in the diagram.

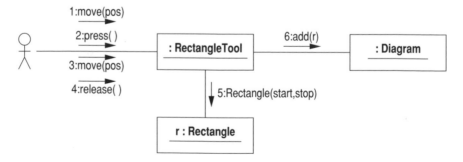

Figure 3.9 Creating a rectangle: collaboration diagram

The major differences between the two forms of interaction diagram are that the collaboration diagram shows the links between objects, but does not explicitly represent the passage of time. As a result, messages on a collaboration diagram have to be numbered to indicate their order. In Figure 3.9 a simple sequential numbering scheme is used for messages, but a more sophisticated hierarchical scheme is described in Chapter 7.

Also, objects that are created in the course of the interaction are not distinguished graphically from other objects on collaboration diagrams. As a result it is sometimes difficult to discern the point within the transaction at which they are created.

3.6 SELECTING ELEMENTS

The use case given in Table 3.2 describes how users select elements once they have been created. Elements must be selected before they can be moved, resized or deleted. The specification simply states that elements are selected by 'clicking on them with the cursor'. As well as the normal course of events implied by this description, a couple of exceptional courses need to be identified in this use case, namely the cases where the user clicks the cursor over an area of the screen where no element is displayed, or when the user clicks on an element that is already selected.

Table 3.2 Use case for selecting an element

Name	Select element
Description	If necessary, the user makes the selection tool active. The user moves the mouse cursor over an element and presses the mouse button. [Exception: *no such element*.] The element becomes selected and its control points are displayed. [Exception: *element already selected*.] The user releases the mouse button.
Exceptions	*No such element*: If the user presses the mouse button at a position on the screen where no element is displayed, no element is selected. *Element already selected*: If the user presses the mouse button over an element that is already selected, that element stays selected.

Realization of element selection

We will assume that *selection tools* are responsible for managing the process of selecting elements, in the same way as creation tools manage the process of creating new elements. Before considering the details of this interaction, it will be helpful to consider an example of the state of the system when a selection tool is active, just before the user attempts to select an element.

Figure 3.10 shows the state of the system when one element has been created and a selection tool has been activated. The diagram editor object itself has been omitted from this and subsequent diagrams, as it does not participate directly in the interactions being considered.

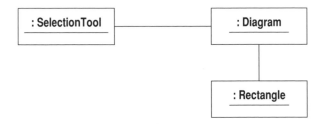

Figure 3.10 The situation before selecting an element

When the user presses the mouse button, the selection tool must determine whether there is an element at the current cursor position. The information required to answer this is held in the individual elements, so one approach would be to ask each element in turn if it contains the point at which the user clicked the mouse.

The selection tool can only make this enquiry indirectly, by sending messages to the diagram, which maintains links to all the elements displayed. One possible solution is for the selection tool to send a message to the current diagram asking for the identity of the element, if any, that is located at the current cursor position, passed as a parameter.

The diagram can satisfy this enquiry by asking each element in turn whether it contains the given point. Once the required element has been found, its identity can be returned to the selection tool which will then record that element as having been selected. Details of this interaction are shown in Figure 3.11.

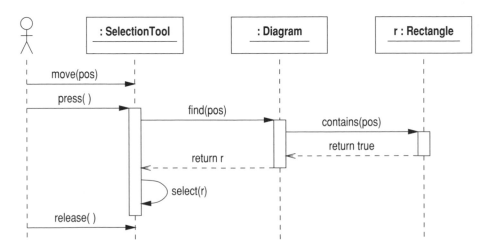

Figure 3.11 Selecting an element: the basic course of events

Figure 3.11 shows how the return of data in response to a message is shown on a sequence diagram. *Return messages* are dashed arrows going from the end of an activation back to the lifeline of the object that sent the original message. Return messages can clarify the flow of control within an interaction, but it is largely a stylistic decision whether or not to show them explicitly. One situation in which they should be shown is when data is returned to the calling object, as in Figure 3.11.

Just as the diagram editor has to record the identity of the current diagram, the selection tool has to record which elements are currently selected on the diagram. The identity of the selected elements can be identified by means of additional links connecting them to the selection tool, in much the same way as the current diagram was identified in Figure 3.4 by means of an additional link connecting it to the diagram editor. Adopting this approach, Figure 3.12 shows the system state after the rectangle in Figure 3.10 has been selected.

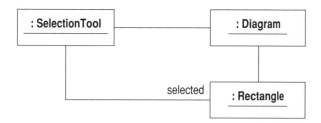

Figure 3.12 The situation after the element is selected

The exceptional cases

If the user had clicked the mouse over an empty area of the screen, the 'contains' and 'find' messages in Figure 3.11 would have returned different results, and no element would have been selected. This interaction is illustrated in Figure 3.13.

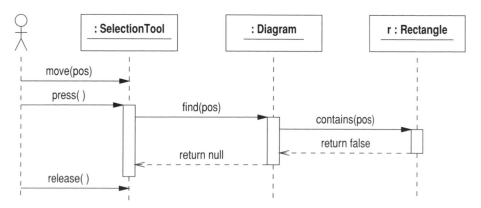

Figure 3.13 Failure to select an element

In the case where the user clicks on an element that is already selected, the interaction is exactly the same as that already shown in Figure 3.11. The only difference will occur in the processing of the 'select' message: we assume that the selection tool will detect if an element is already selected, and proceed accordingly.

3.7 DELETING ELEMENTS

The specification of the diagram editor does not mention the deletion of elements, so before producing a realization of this use case we first need to sketch out a scenario explaining how deletion takes place. One possibility is to assume that when the user indicates that elements are to be deleted, by selecting a suitable menu item or tool bar button or perhaps by pressing the delete key on the keyboard, all the currently selected elements on the diagram are deleted.

Inclusion of use cases

The complete use case for deleting elements therefore breaks down into two stages. First, the elements to be deleted are selected. This is a straightforward application of the use case for selecting elements, discussed above in Section 3.6. Once this process is complete, the user signals that deletion should take place, and behaviour specific to the delete use case occurs.

Another way of expressing this is to say that the 'select element' use case is *included* in the 'delete element' use case. In UML this relationship can be expressed graphically, as shown in Figure 3.14.

Figure 3.14 Use case inclusion

The dashed arrow in Figure 3.14 is an example of a *dependency*, the symbol used by UML for general types of relationship between model elements. The precise nature of the relationship is clarified by a label attached to the dependency, known as a *stereotype*. In this case the stereotype states that the relationship being shown is that of inclusion between use cases.

In this relationship, the use case being included is known as the *inclusion* use case, and the use case doing the including as the *base* use case. The include relationship is appropriate if a complete sequence diagram for the base case would include the sequence diagram for the inclusion case, and the interactions in the inclusion case are performed without interruption. Inclusion of use cases is a way of reusing the functionality specified in the supplier use case, in much the same way as a function call allows a program to reuse the functionality defined in a function.

Deleting an element

A sequence diagram showing the additional interactions needed for deleting elements is given in Figure 3.15. As Figure 3.14 specifies that the select element use case is included in this one, it is not necessary to write out the interactions dealing with selection of elements again. When the interaction in Figure 3.15 starts, the rectangle object is already selected: this is suggested by the object name chosen for it.

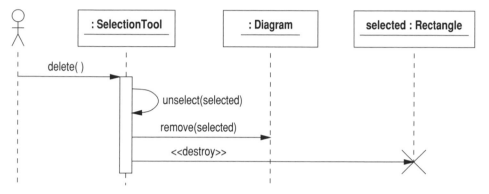

Figure 3.15 Deletion of selected elements

Before the selected element can be physically deleted, it must be removed from the diagram. In addition, as it is currently selected, it must be 'unselected': in practice this means that the selection tool must no longer store a link to the element. If these steps were omitted, the selection tool and the diagram would end up holding 'dangling references', or links to an object that has been deleted. This is a common source of programming errors.

Deletion of objects is shown in UML by sending a message to the object to be destroyed. Messages that destroy objects are labelled with the stereotype 'destroy'. The object's lifeline ends at the point of destruction, and this is highlighted by drawing a large cross at the end of the lifeline.

3.8 MOVING AND RESIZING ELEMENTS

When a selection tool is active, there are a number of different activities that the user can perform simply by clicking the mouse button. Additional elements can be selected by clicking on them, selected elements can be moved by dragging them with the mouse, and finally an individual selected element can be resized by clicking on and dragging one of its control points.

As in the use case for selecting elements, the correct choice of action in this case depends on the position of the cursor when the mouse button is pressed, and also on the current state of the editor, namely which elements are selected. If the diagram editor is to exhibit the correct functionality, the following steps should take place whenever the user presses the mouse button with the selection tool active.

1. The tool should check whether the user has clicked on a control point of an element that is already selected. In this case, subsequent moves of the mouse will cause that element to be resized, until the user releases the mouse button.
2. If the user does not click on a highlighted control point, but does click on an element, that element will become selected if it is not selected already, and subsequent mouse moves will cause all the selected element to move, until the user releases the mouse button.

Realizations of these use cases are given below.

Resizing an element

Assume that the diagram contains three elements, namely a rectangle, a line and an ellipse, and that two of these elements, the line and the rectangle, are currently selected. This initial situation is depicted in the object diagram shown in Figure 3.16.

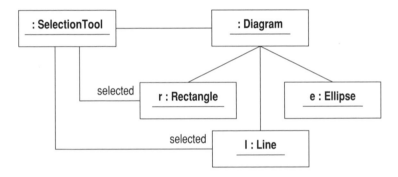

Figure 3.16 A situation with two selected elements

When the user presses the mouse button, the first thing to check is whether the cursor is currently positioned over one of the control points of a selected element. The sequence diagram in Figure 3.17 shows that the selection tool sends a message to each selected element in turn to check whether that element has a control point at the specified position. In the interaction shown, the user has clicked on one of the control points belonging to the line element.

Figure 3.17 also shows that when the user subsequently moves the mouse messages labelled 'moveControl' are sent to the element being resized, requesting that the control point being dragged by the user is moved. For this to work, the selection tool must have some way of remembering which of its selected elements is currently being resized.

This is another example of the common situation where it is necessary for an object to remember the identity of one object out of a set. In this case the element being resized has to be distinguished from the remainder of the currently selected elements. As usual, the solution is to define an additional link to identify the element being resized, as shown in Figure 3.18.

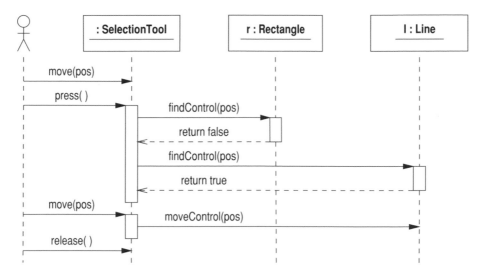

Figure 3.17 Looking for a control point

Figure 3.18 contains three different types of link, distinguished by the ways in which they are labelled. Different links will be used as communication channels for different messages. For example, the 'findControl' messages in Figure 3.17 are sent to all the currently selected elements, and so will be sent using the links labelled 'selected'. The 'moveControl' message, on the other hand, will only be sent to the element currently being resized, using the link labelled 'Resizing'.

In order for an element to respond appropriately when it receives a 'moveControl' message, it must remember which of its control points has been clicked on. In the design shown in Figure 3.17, this will be the control point that was identified just before a value of 'true' was returned to the 'findControl' message. The way in which elements record the identity of this point, and react to a 'moveControl' message will be treated as an implementation detail and not be considered further here.

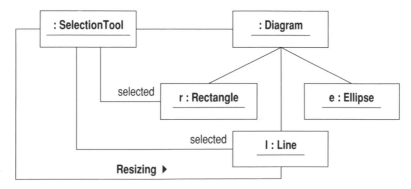

Figure 3.18 Identifying the element being resized

Moving an element

If all the selected elements return a value of false to the 'findControl' message, the selection tool reverts to the normal case of selecting an element. However, if the user then moves the mouse before releasing the mouse button, the selected element will also be moved. After the mouse button has been released, moving the mouse has no effect on the locations of the selected element.

Figure 3.19 shows the interactions involved in moving a newly selected element. This interaction is an extension of Figure 3.11 which assumes that the rectangle is the only element on the diagram and that it is not selected at the start of the interaction.

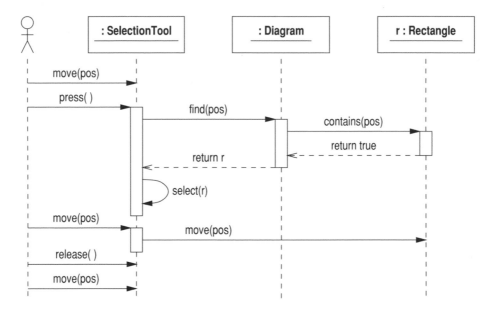

Figure 3.19 Selecting and moving an element

3.9 USE CASE EXTENSION

Figures 3.17 and 3.18 suggest that there is considerable commonality between the use cases for moving and resizing elements and the use case for selecting elements illustrated in Figure 3.11. The sequence diagram for moving an element in Figure 3.19 is the same as Figure 3.11 apart from the inclusion of a move message before the mouse button is released. In the case of resizing, there is some alternative functionality that may be executed, depending on where the mouse button is pressed.

These differences, however, mean that it would not be correct to model the relationship by saying that the use cases for moving and resizing elements include the use case for selecting elements. In neither case are the interactions in the select element use case included as an unbroken whole in the larger use case.

Instead, the relationship between the use cases can be modelled as one of *extension*, which allows optional functionality to be incorporated into use cases. The UML notation for use case extension is shown in Figure 3.20. As this diagram indicates, it is very similar to that used for inclusion.

Figure 3.20 Use case extension

To describe an extending relationship fully, the *base* use case, 'select element' in Figure 3.20, must contain two things.

1. An *extension point* indicating where the additional functionality is included. In this case, the extension point is just after the user presses the mouse button down.
2. A *condition* stating when the additional functionality is added. In this case, it is added in the situations where the user moves the mouse before releasing the mouse button.

The extension use case, 'move element' in this case, must describe the new functionality, which in this case is that when the user moves the mouse the selected element is also moved, as shown in Figure 3.19.

Resizing elements as an extension

We can also describe the use case for resizing an element as an extension of 'select element'. In this case, the extension point is at the point where the user presses the mouse button and the condition is that the user has pressed the mouse button over the control point of a selected element. The additional functionality is that subsequent moves will drag the control point and hence resize the element.

As Figure 3.21 illustrates, it is possible to label an extension relationship with details of the extension point and the condition. The extension points provided by a base use case can be listed in a section of the use case icon, and the 'extend' dependency can be labelled with the name of the extension point at which the extension is applied, written in parentheses, and the condition stating when the extension will take place, written in square brackets.

Figure 3.21 Full notation for use case extension

3.10 USE CASE DIAGRAMS

Figure 3.2 showed a simple use case diagram for the diagram editor. In the course of this chapter, the three relationships that UML defines between use cases have been introduced, namely generalization, inclusion and extension. They have been used to introduce more structure into the use case diagram, and in particular to permit a degree of reuse between use cases.

These changes are incorporated into the more complex version of the complete use case diagram shown in Figure 3.22. The actor representing users of the editor is shown twice in this diagram purely in order to simplify the layout of the diagram, and the full notation for specifying the extension relationship has not been used.

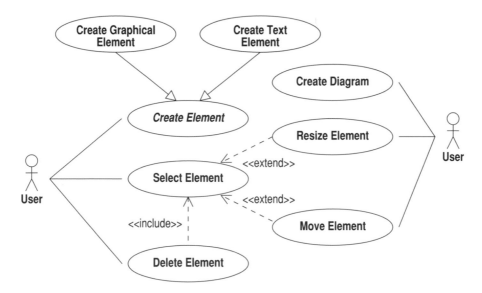

Figure 3.22 Complete use case diagram for the diagram editor

Generalization between actors

Actors as well as use cases can be related by generalization. This provides a convenient way for different levels of access to the system to be modelled and related to each other.

For example, suppose that in a shared environment ordinary users of the diagram editor were not allowed to delete elements. System administrators, however, have the ability to delete elements in addition to doing everything else that ordinary users can. This could be shown by a slight modification to the use case diagram in which system administrators are modelled as a second actor, related to ordinary users by generalization. Figure 3.23 shows a diagram illustrating this.

The meaning of this relationship is given in terms of substitution, as with use cases. In this case, this means that anything an ordinary user can do can also be done by an administrator. Additional capabilities are also defined for the more specialized actor.

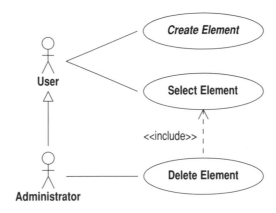

Figure 3.23 Use case diagram including actor generalization

3.11 SUMMARY

- The use case view contains actors, which describe the roles that users can play when interacting with a system, and use cases, which describe the functionality available to them.
- A use case defines a particular type of transaction between users and the system. Particular interactions, or instances of the use case, can be described in scenarios. Both scenarios and use cases are defined informally, as UML does not specify any formal notation for them.
- Scenarios can be classified into those that represent the basic course of events described by the use case, and those that represent alternative or exceptional courses of events.
- A use case diagram shows the actors and use cases involved in a system. A relationship between an actor and a use case indicates that the actor can participate in the use case.
- Use cases and actors can be related by generalization, where one use case or actor is defined as a special case of another.
- The 'include' relationship between use cases allows one use case to be wholly incorporated in another. Like a function call, this provides a mechanism whereby a use case can be reused.
- The 'extend' relationship between use cases allows optional functionality to be included in a use case. It is specified by defining an extension point and a condition which determine where and when the additional functionality is executed. This information can optionally be shown on the use case diagram.
- A realization of a use case or scenario describes a configuration of interacting objects adequate to support the functionality described.
- Sequence diagrams and collaboration diagrams shows the objects involved in an interaction and the messages that pass between them, and can be used to illustrate the realizations of use cases.

3.12 EXERCISES

3.1 Draw an object diagram similar to Figure 3.8 representing a situation where an ellipse and a rectangle have been created and added to a diagram, and a line tool has just been activated.

3.2 Draw an object diagram similar to Figure 3.8 representing the state of the diagram editor shown in Figure 3.1.

3.3 Draw an object diagram showing the diagram editor with two diagrams, the first containing a rectangle and the second containing a line and an ellipse. The first diagram is the current one, and the user has just made a selection tool active.

3.4 Draw an object diagram showing the same diagrams and elements as in the previous question, but where the second diagram is current, both elements on it are selected, and the user is currently resizing the ellipse.

3.5 In the interaction shown in Figure 3.7, the new rectangle object is created only after the user releases the mouse button. Draw an alternative sequence diagram in which the rectangle is created as soon as the user presses the mouse button on the 'start' point for the rectangle. As the user subsequently moves the mouse, the 'stop' point of the rectangle changes, and a message or messages will need to be sent to the rectangle object informing it of this. You will also need to consider at what point the rectangle is added to the diagram. What arguments can be given which might lead a designer to choose between these alternative realizations of the use case?

3.6 Consider a variation of the use case for selecting an element, described in Section 3.6, in which clicking the mouse button over an element that is already selected has the effect of *deselecting* the element. Make any changes necessary to the use case and its realization to specify this variant, and discuss which of the two use cases provides a better interface for the user of the diagram editor.

3.7 A possible shortcoming of the method of element deletion described in the text is that it interferes with the current selection of elements. Consider an alternative proposal whereby individual elements can be deleted when a selection tool is active by clicking on them with the right mouse button, say. Produce a realization of this version of the use case, and change the use case diagram for the diagram editor to take this change into account.

3.8 Draw a variation of the sequence diagram shown in Figure 3.19, where the rectangle is selected before the interaction starts and the user clicks on the rectangle, but not on one of its control points.

3.9 Draw a sequence diagram for the form of element creation specified in the requirements specification, where after an element is created, the selection tool is made active and the new element is selected.

3.10 Suppose a selection tool is active, and the user selects a rectangle tool. Draw a sequence diagram illustrating this. It must deal with the creation of the new tool, the deletion of the old tool, and unselecting all the currently selected elements.

3.11 Suppose a selection tool is active, and the user creates a new diagram. Draw a sequence diagram illustrating this. It must deal with the deletion of the existing tool and the creation of the new diagram.

3.12 Write a use case describing the creation of text elements. This will require you to be much more explicit about the detailed interactions involved than the requirements specification is. A number of scenarios should be written first, to clarify details of the interaction before the complete use case is written. Make explicit any extra assumptions about the editor's functionality that you make, and if appropriate, justify the design decisions that you have made.

When you are clear about the functionality that will be provided in the creation of text elements, draw one or more sequence diagrams illustrating a realization of the use case.

3.13 If elements overlap each other on the diagram, there will be an ambiguity if an attempt is made to select an element in the region of overlap. The specification simply asserts that the element at the place where the user clicks the mouse button will be selected. Given that more than one element can be present at a given location, however, it is necessary to explain how users can specify which is to be selected.

Write scenarios describing how users can step through all of the elements displayed at a given position until the required element, and that element only, is selected. Make suitable changes to the description of the select element use case, and to Figure 3.11 which gives a realization of this use case.

3.14 The use cases above have interpreted the reference in the specification to 'manipulating one or more elements' as meaning that the elements to be manipulated are selected each time they are required. An alternative interpretation would be to introduce a concept of a *group item*, whereby a number of simple items could be bound together and treated from then on as a single element. There would also be a need for an 'unbinding' operation to break a group element down into its constituent parts.

Write an additional paragraph for the requirements specification to define group elements, write use cases as required to specify the new interactions now available to the user, and provide a realization of this use case.

3.15 Suppose that the functionality of the diagram editor is to be extended to provide a *clipboard* feature. The clipboard is intended to support operations such as creating copies of elements on a diagram and moving or copying elements from one diagram to another. First write a number of scenarios to clarify way in which the user will interact with the clipboard functionality, and then define a number of new use cases describing the new functionality and provide realizations for them in the form of sequence diagrams.

3.16 A simple system is to be developed to support the management of exercises completed by students taking a course. Students first meet with the course tutor to register for the module, and then during the course they submit a number of pieces of work. At any point, a student can find out from the system the marks they have received for any exercises already completed. The course tutor can enter a mark for a piece of work, and print out a summary of the marks gained by all students on course. Describe suitable use cases and draw a use case diagram for this system.

3.17 Draw a use case diagram for the following library system.

The library stores various items that can be borrowed, including books and journals. Books can be borrowed by both staff and students, but only staff members can borrow journals. When a user borrows a book, their loan details are checked to ensure that they have no overdue books on loan, and have not already borrowed the maximum permitted number of books.

Users can check their own loan details at any time. Librarians are permitted to check the loan details of any user.

Library users can reserve books that are currently out on loan. If three reservations have already been made for a given book, and a further reservation is made, a new copy will be ordered by the librarian.

4

DIAGRAM EDITOR: DESIGN VIEW

The last chapter presented the use case view of the diagram editor. This described the external behaviour of the system as a structured set of use cases, but without directly defining the structure of the system. This is the role of the *design view*, which specifies a set of classes which will support the functionality of the system. The relationship between the two views is that the design view is constrained to define a structure which is adequate to provide the functionality specified in the use case view. This chapter describes the design view of the diagram editor.

4.1 THE ROLE OF THE DESIGN VIEW

The use case view of the diagram editor defined in Chapter 3 consisted essentially of a set of use cases. Sequence diagrams presented realizations of each use case as an interaction among collaborating objects. Given that this is essentially what an object-oriented system is, it might be wondered why the diagrams presented in Chapter 3 are not by themselves adequate documentation of the design.

The answer is that they are not abstract enough to serve as the only documentation of the design. Objects can be created and destroyed as a system runs and the links between existing objects change as the system evolves. This means that the object diagram describing the system's state can potentially change from moment to moment. Clearly, it is neither feasible nor desirable for a designer to draw an object diagram for every possible state of a system.

Furthermore, the particular interactions documented as realizations of the use cases were only representative examples of an extremely wide range of possible interactions. Different messages will pass between objects depending, among other things, on the behaviour of the system's users. It would not be possible to document explicitly every possible sequence of messages that could occur as the system is running.

To make this mass of details comprehensible, models with a greater degree of generality must be used. They must enable the designer to describe the constant patterns underlying the changing reality of the system and to summarize the mass of information provided by concrete object diagrams. Two major classes of model have been found to be indispensable in object-oriented design languages.

Models of the first class describe the possible states of the system. These models describe the different kinds of objects that can exist in a system, and the possible ways in which objects can be linked to each other. These are known as *static models*. This terminology derives from the fact that they describe properties of the system which could be discovered by looking at snapshots of the system's state. Static models contain no information about how a system changes over time.

Object diagrams are a type of static model, but the most important form of static model is the *class diagram*. As the name suggests, class diagrams define the groups, or classes, that the objects in a system can fall into. They also define a variety of structural relationships between these classes. A class diagram for the diagram editor will be developed in this chapter, derived from the interaction diagrams in Chapter 3.

Models of the second class, the *dynamic models*, describe the message passing behaviour that can be observed in a system, and the changes that will occur in the system as a result of particular interactions. Concrete instances of such behaviour can be described in interaction diagrams, of which UML defines two forms, collaboration diagrams and sequence diagrams.

Interaction diagrams only give details of individual sequences of messages. In the same way that class diagrams summarize all the possible object diagrams that could be drawn to describe a system, some model is needed to summarize all the possible interactions that could take place. All object-oriented design methodologies use some form of state transition diagram to show this information. In UML a particular form of these diagrams known as *statecharts* is used. Statecharts for the diagram editor will also be developed in this chapter.

The design view, therefore, uses abstract forms of diagram to define the overall structure and behaviour of a system. The most important diagrams used in this view are class diagrams and statecharts. As well as summarizing the functionality specified in the use case view, the diagrams produced in the design view specify the structure of the system and act as blueprints for further development.

4.2 CLASSES AND ASSOCIATIONS

Class diagrams bear much the same relationship to object diagrams as classes do to objects. In object-oriented languages, objects exist at run-time, contain data and interact with other objects. Classes exist at compile-time, are defined in the source code of the system, and provide a description or a specification of a collection of objects which have the same properties. Object diagrams describe a configuration of objects that might exist at a given moment while a system is running, whereas class diagrams describe, in concise and abstract form, all the possible configurations of a system.

Classes

As the name suggests, class diagrams show the classes that the objects in the system are instances of. Many decisions about classes have already been made while realizing the use cases for the diagram editor, and are reflected in object diagrams like the one in Figure 4.1. This diagram shows three objects, and specifies the class that each object belongs to. In addition, the links between the objects show some of the ways that objects of these classes can be linked together at run-time.

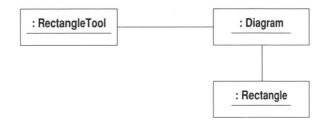

Figure 4.1 Instances of classes

Classes are denoted by rectangles labelled with the name of the class, as shown in Figure 4.2. Objects and classes are deliberately shown using the same graphical element, namely a rectangle. This is intended to suggest that the two concepts are similar, or related in some way. To distinguish classes from their instances, UML adopts the convention that the labels in icons representing instances are underlined.

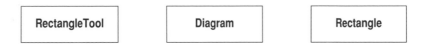

Figure 4.2 Classes

Associations

Class diagrams also show relationships between classes. A link between two objects is modelled by an *association* between the corresponding classes. The link can be thought of as being an instance of the association. Associations are drawn, like links, as lines joining the related classes. Given the links that are shown between the objects in Figure 4.1, we can deduce that associations must exist between the corresponding classes as shown in Figure 4.3.

Conversely, the existence of an association between two classes implies that instances of the classes can potentially be linked, and the absence of an association means that objects can not be linked. For example, in Figure 4.4 a link is shown connecting a rectangle tool with a rectangle, but Figure 4.3 shows no association that this link could be an instance of. The diagram therefore does not represent a possible state of the system. In this way, class diagrams provide a specification of the possible run-time states of a system.

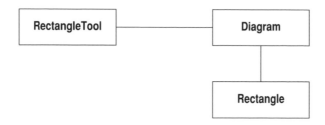

Figure 4.3 Associations

Figure 4.4 An illegal state

Multiplicity

As well as knowing what objects can be linked together, it is also important to know how many links an object can participate in at any one time. For example, Figure 4.5 shows a diagram linked to two rectangles, one of which is at the same time linked to a second diagram object.

All the links in this diagram are instances of the association between the diagram and rectangle classes shown in Figure 4.3. However, whereas it is legitimate for a diagram to contain more than one rectangle, it is not legitimate for a rectangle to be linked to more than one diagram.

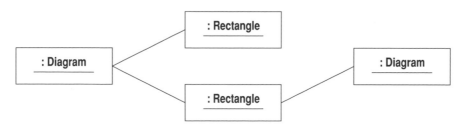

Figure 4.5 A diagram containing two rectangles

Restrictions on the number of links that can exist at a given time are known as *multiplicity constraints*. These constraints are specified as properties of associations. The following constraints apply to the associations shown in Figure 4.3.

1. A rectangle tool must be linked to exactly one diagram.
2. A diagram may or may not have a rectangle tool linked to it. (The current tool may be of a different kind, or there may even be no tool currently active.)
3. A diagram can contain, or be linked to, zero or more rectangles.
4. Every rectangle must belong to exactly one diagram.

UML uses the symbols shown in Table 4.1 to represent the commonest multiplicity constraints. These symbols are written at the ends of associations as shown in Figure 4.6, in which the constraints listed above are formalized.

Table 4.1 Common multiplicity constraints in UML

Symbol	Meaning
1	exactly one
0..1	zero or one ("optional")
* (or 0..*)	zero or more ("many")
1..*	one or more

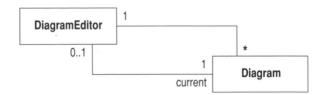

Figure 4.6 Associations with multiplicity constraints

Multiple associations between classes

Figure 3.4 showed a situation where diagram and diagram editor objects were linked by links of two different types. Different types of link should be modelled by different associations, even if they connect the same pair of classes. Figure 4.7 shows the associations corresponding to the links shown in Figure 3.4.

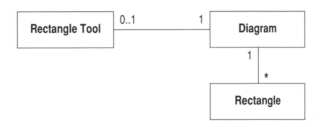

Figure 4.7 A pair of associations

Multiple associations between a pair of classes can be distinguished by labelling, and also by the fact that they may have different properties. For example, the two associations in Figure 4.7 have different multiplicity constraints: a diagram must be linked to the diagram editor by an instance of the upper association, but if it is not the current diagram it will not be linked by an instance of the lower association. These two possibilities were illustrated in Figure 3.4.

4.3 GENERALIZATION

The examples above have, for simplicity, only shown instances of the rectangle class. Different kinds of element exist in the diagram editor, however, and in general a diagram will contain an arbitrary mixture of elements of all possible kinds. Different kinds of tool can also exist. Figure 4.8 shows a different state of the diagram editor which exhibits some of these possibilities.

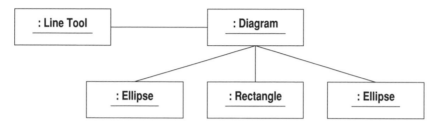

Figure 4.8 A different state of the diagram editor

One way to specify the fact that a diagram may contain any number of elements from different classes would be to define a separate association for each different kind of element, as illustrated in Figure 4.9. This diagram contains three distinct associations, and the links between the diagram and element objects in Figure 4.8 must therefore be understood to be instances of distinct associations, depending on the kind of element being linked.

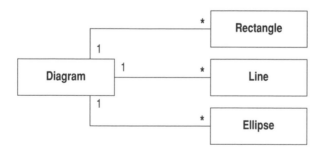

Figure 4.9 Associations to different kinds of element

There are several disadvantages with the approach taken in Figure 4.9, however. Firstly, it creates redundancy: each association has exactly the same multiplicity constraints, for example, and it would be preferable not to have to state them repeatedly. This is related to a second problem, which is that Figure 4.9 represents what can be thought of as a single relationship, namely that of a diagram containing an element, as three distinct associations. From a logical point of view, this seems to misrepresent the situation. Finally, if the diagram editor was extended to handle a new kind of element, it would also be necessary to introduce a new association in order to permit elements of the new type to appear on diagrams.

These points can be summarized by observing that a better model would represent what appears logically to be the single relationship of an element appearing on a diagram by a single association. To do this, we need a way of defining an association whose instances can link objects of more than one element class.

This is achieved indirectly, by defining a new class which represents elements of any possible kind, and then specifying that this is a *generalization* of the classes representing more specialized types of element. This new class and the generalization relationships connecting it to the more specific subclasses are shown in Figure 4.10.

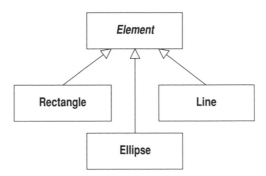

Figure 4.10 A generalization of elements

A generalization relationship between classes is shown using the same notation as generalizations between use cases and actors, an arrow with an open arrowhead. The general class, 'Element' in this case, is often known as the *superclass* in the relationship, and the more specialized classes as *subclasses*.

Often there will be a number of subclasses in a generalization relationship, each representing a different variant of the general concept represented by the superclass. In this case, it is common to combine the arrows that represent the generalization relationships into a single arrow with a 'forked' tail. To see the effect of this, compare Figure 4.10 with the way the generalization is depicted in Figure 4.11. The difference between these two ways of presenting generalization relationships is purely stylistic.

The name of the element class in Figure 4.10 is written in a sloping typeface. This indicates that it is an *abstract* class. By definition, no instances of an abstract class can be created. Abstract classes are defined in order to represent the common properties of their subclasses, and in this case the common property of interest is the fact that all kinds of elements can be stored on diagrams. We can make use of the abstract element class to represent this property by a single association in place of the three associations used earlier, as shown in Figure 4.11.

The meaning of the association in Figure 4.11 is that instances of the diagram class can be linked at run-time to instances of the element class. However, as 'Element' is an abstract class, it has no instances. What the association in fact means is that instances of the diagram class can be linked to instances of arbitrary subclasses of 'Element', as was the case in Figure 4.8.

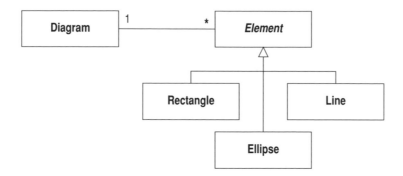

Figure 4.11 A general association

This is permissible because a generalization relationship specifies circumstances in which instances of one class can be *substituted* for instances of another. More precisely, if in a given context it is asserted that an instance of a superclass is expected, a generalization relationship implies that it will always be permissible to replace this by an instance of one the subclasses. In this case, substitutability means that where an instance of the element class might be expected, at the other end of a link from a diagram instance, we can replace it by an instance of any of the subclasses of 'Element'.

Notice that unlike associations, generalization relationships between classes do not introduce a distinct kind of relationship between objects. Instead, they permit the links specified by associations to be used in a more flexible and general way.

4.4 CREATION TOOLS

Just as a diagram can contain elements of different sorts, it can be linked to different kinds of tools at different times. For example, the three kinds of creation tool can be represented by subclasses of an abstract creation tool class parallel to the element subclasses, as shown in Figure 4.12.

One important fact that is not shown in Figure 4.12 is the fact that rectangle tools create rectangles, line tools create lines and so on. This is clearly implicit in the names chosen for the various classes, but this gives only an informal representation of the relationship. It is tempting, but incorrect, to model the relationship as an association between the classes. An association between the rectangle tool and rectangle classes, for example, would imply that instances of these classes could be linked at run-time but, as stated above in connection with Figure 4.4, this is not permitted.

A useful rule of thumb is that associations and links should be used to model connections between objects that are permanent, in the sense that they should be preserved between activations of the program, perhaps by being stored on disk. The connection between a creation tool and the element it creates is strictly temporary, however: once the element has been created and added to the diagram, the tool preserves no record of the new object's identity.

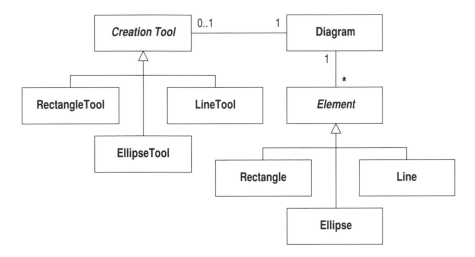

Figure 4.12 The creation tool and element hierarchies

The standard way in UML to model relationships other than associations and generalization is to use a *dependency*. Dependencies are shown graphically as dashed arrows. As dependencies can be used for many purposes, they are usually labelled with a *stereotype* which indicates the nature of the relationship being modelled. UML defines the predefined stereotype 'instantiate' which is used to indicate that instances of one class create instances of another. Using this notation, the fact that rectangle tools create rectangles, for example, can be expressed as shown in Figure 4.13.

Figure 4.13 A creation dependency

4.5 SELECTION TOOLS

The object diagram in Figure 4.14 shows the situation after a single element has been selected. It reflects the design decision that selected elements should be linked to the selection tool as they will be manipulated over an extended period of time. This contrasts with the connection between creation tools and elements, which is very short-lived and not modelled by a link.

Figure 4.14 shows that selection tools can participate in two kinds of link. Firstly, the tool is linked to the diagram that the user is currently manipulating. This link performs exactly the same function as the link between creation tools and diagrams, namely to connect the current diagram and tool. Rather than introducing a separate association to model it, therefore, it is preferable to introduce an abstract tool class to model this common property of creation and selection tools, as shown in Figure 4.15.

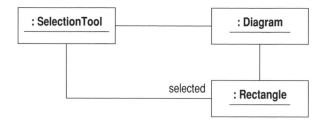

Figure 4.14 A selected element

The second link, connecting the selection tool to the currently selected element, is modelled by a further association in Figure 4.15. When a selection tool is first made active, no elements are selected. As the user works on the diagram with the tool, however, any number of elements could be selected, limited only by the total number of elements on the diagram. One multiplicity constraint for this association is therefore that a selection tool can be linked to zero or more currently selected elements.

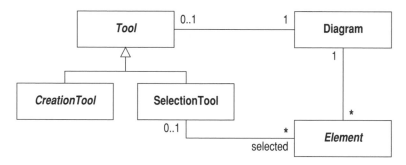

Figure 4.15 Selection tools and their relationships

The multiplicity constraint on the other end of the association, which asserts that an element can be linked to zero or one selection tool, is slightly less obvious. Another way of expressing it is that an element may or may not be linked to a selection tool, as shown graphically in Figure 3.16. If the current tool is a selection tool and the element is one of the selected elements a link will exist, and otherwise it will not. Under no circumstances can an element be selected by more than one tool at a given time.

Notice that Figure 4.15 does not show the subclasses of creation tool and element. In general, information can be omitted from diagrams in UML if it is not necessary to help understand the diagram or the point being made by the diagram.

Figure 3.18 shows a different type of link that can connect selection tool and element instances. If an element is currently being resized, a link is maintained to record the identity of that particular element among all the selected elements. This link should be specified by an additional association, as shown in Figure 4.16.

This association is specified to be optional at both ends. In other words, at most one element can be resized at any one time, and all the elements that are not being resized will not be linked to the selection tool by links of this type.

Figure 4.16 Relationships between selection tools and elements

4.6 FEATURES OF CLASSES

As explained in Chapter 2, objects store attribute values, and have a number of operations which can be invoked by other objects through the message passing mechanism. These attributes and operations are known collectively as the *features* of the class and can be represented graphically in the class notation.

Attributes

Attributes can be defined in a separate section of a class icon. They define the name and type of the data values that can be stored in the instances of the class. Attributes in the diagram editor include those shown in Figure 4.17.

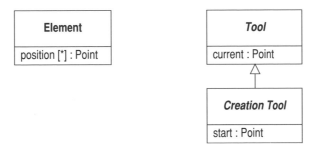

Figure 4.17 Attributes in the diagram editor

Elements are responsible for storing details of their position. This is shown in Figure 4.17 as an attribute called 'position'. The type of this attribute is specified to be 'Point', a data type either defined for this project or provided by the target language.

Different kinds of element may store their positions using different numbers of data elements. Lines, for example, may only store two positions, whereas polygons will require at least three. This uncertainty is modelled in Figure 4.17 by associating a multiplicity with the attribute: in this case it is specified that zero or more data values can be stored in the position attribute.

As we have assumed that press and release messages do not carry with them information about the mouse coordinates where the event took place, tools will have to remember the current position of the mouse whenever a move message is received and use this when handling press and release messages. This can be modelled by including an attribute in the tool class to store the current position of the mouse.

This attribute will be inherited by all the descendant classes of the tool class. Inheritance is a mechanism associated with generalization whereby features defined in a superclass are also available for use in subclasses without being redefined there. In this case all the objects that belong to subclasses of the tool class will have access to the current mouse position, even though the position attribute is not explicitly defined in the class of which they are an instance.

In addition to recording the current position, creation tools require an additional attribute to record the position at which the user presses the mouse when creating a new element. This is shown as an additional attribute in the creation tool class in Figure 4.17. This attribute will in turn be inherited by all the subclasses of the creation tool class. Selection tools have no need for this attribute, so there is no need to define it in the top-level tool class.

Operations

Each message sent to an object in the interactions that realize the use cases in the system should correspond to an operation provided by the object's class. Operations are shown in class icons in a separate compartment, as shown in Figure 4.18. These operations correspond exactly to the messages that are sent to instances of these classes in the use case realizations given in Chapter 3. They specify the type of any parameters of the messages and also the type of any value returned by the message, following a colon.

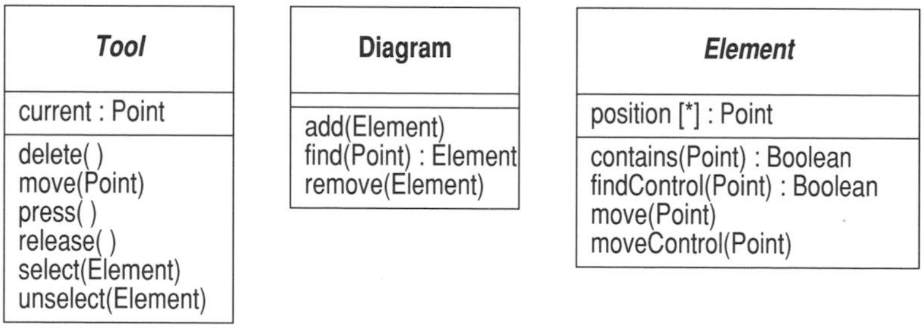

Tool	Diagram	Element
current : Point		position [*] : Point
delete( ) move(Point) press( ) release( ) select(Element) unselect(Element)	add(Element) find(Point) : Element remove(Element)	contains(Point) : Boolean findControl(Point) : Boolean move(Point) moveControl(Point)

Figure 4.18 Operations in the diagram editor

The 'select', 'unselect' and 'delete' operations are defined in the tool class even though the corresponding messages are only sent to selection tools. This is done to ensure that all tools share a common interface and the diagram editor does not have to establish the type of an arbitrary tool at run-time. The implementation consequences of this decision are considered in Chapter 5.

4.7 COMPLETE CLASS DIAGRAM

All the small class diagrams given in this chapter are in effect fragments of a larger, complete class diagram which describes the whole program. This complete class diagram gives a complete specification of the static properties of the diagram editor.

It is often the case that complete class diagrams for systems are too large to be conveniently drawn. In this case, however, the model is small enough to be manageable, and is shown in Figure 4.19. Even here, however, the common convention of omitting class features from the diagram is followed, so this diagram needs to be studied in conjunction with Figures 4.17 and 4.18 to obtain a complete specification of the classes in the system.

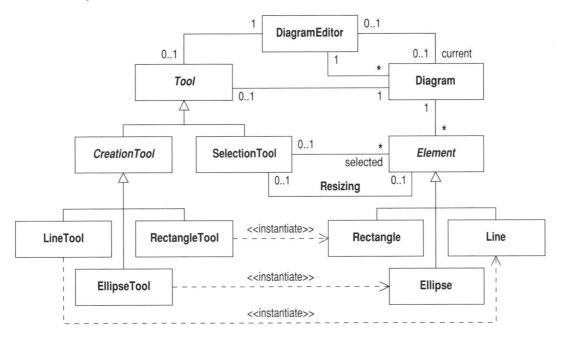

Figure 4.19 Complete class diagram for the diagram editor

4.8 DYNAMIC MODELLING OF THE DIAGRAM EDITOR

The class diagram in Figure 4.19 specifies the data held by the diagram editor, and the way in which data items are related to each other. To complete the design, it is also necessary to consider the dynamic properties of the editor, and in particular the way in which the objects in the system respond to the messages they receive when the system is running.

For example, creation tools can receive three messages: 'press' and 'release' messages indicate that the mouse button has been pressed or released, and 'move' messages indicate that the mouse has been moved, and give the coordinates of its new position. It is not necessary to specify everything about these messages in the system design: for example, the internal details about how a tool object responds to such a message can safely be left until the class is actually implemented. Nevertheless, there are two aspects of the way messages are handled which are usually considered as part of the design.

Sequences of messages

The order in which messages are sent to an object depends on the object's environment, in this case the decisions made by the user of the diagram editor. Objects are not in general capable of dictating what messages are sent to them or when they are sent. In principle, then, we need to specify how an object might respond to any possible sequence of messages.

Sequence diagrams like the ones drawn in Chapter 3 illustrate in detail how an object responds to a particular sequence of messages. In sequence diagrams, however, the sequences of messages shown are examples only, and it is left to the reader to generalize them appropriately. For example, in Figure 3.7 it is understood that multiple move messages could occur in an interaction, depending on how often or how quickly the user moves the mouse, but that the press and release messages occur once only in this interaction.

Furthermore, some sequences are assumed to be impossible, such as any sequence that contained two consecutive press messages without an intervening release, but these are not explicitly ruled out by a set of sequence diagrams. A suitable design notation for dynamic modelling should state explicitly and unambiguously exactly what sequences of messages an object expects to receive throughout its lifetime.

History-dependent behaviour

Some messages have the property of eliciting a different response from an object at different times. For example, when a creation tool receives a move message, a faint outline of the element being created will sometimes be drawn and sometimes not, depending on whether the user has the mouse button pressed down at the time that the message is received.

It might appear that in order to provide this variation in behaviour, the tool would have to check whether the mouse button was being held down on every occasion that it received a move message. In fact it is unlikely to do this, for a number of reasons. Firstly, it would be rather inefficient, and secondly, if the user was employing keyboard shortcuts such as cursor keys rather than using the mouse, the button might not in fact be pressed down.

The diagram editor application is not really interested in the state of the mouse. The press message really means something like, 'this is the start point of the new element; the user is now trying to locate the stop point'. The tool's response to a move message depends on whether the user is currently trying to locate the start or the stop point, and this will depend on whether it has received a press message without a corresponding release. Somehow the tool must remember its *history*, or in other words what messages have already been received, as this determines how it will respond to future messages.

Specifying behaviour

There are two aspects of an object's behaviour which are external to the object and therefore need to be specified as part of a system's design.

1. What sequences of messages the object expects to received.
2. How the object responds to messages, and in particular how this response depends on its history, namely the messages that it has already received.

These properties can be specified by defining a *state machine* for a class. These are shown in *statechart diagrams*, often called *statecharts* for short, and define the behaviour of all the objects belonging to that class.

Informally, a state machine assumes that an object can be in one of a number of different *states* at different times. Objects may change state in response to receiving a message, and so an object's state at a given time is a function of its history, in that it is dependent on the messages that have been received. Furthermore, an object's response to a message may vary, depending on the state it is in when it receives the message. Thus a state machine summarizes both aspects of an object's behaviour mentioned above.

4.9 A STATECHART FOR CREATION TOOLS

One function of statecharts is to show what sequences of messages an object is expecting to receive. Figure 4.20 shows a simple statechart modelling the basic sequence of messages received by a creation tool in the interaction shown in Figure 3.7.

Figure 4.20 A single sequence of messages

Figure 4.20 illustrates the main features of statecharts. A *state*, loosely speaking, corresponds to a period of time when an object is waiting to receive a message. States are shown as rectangles with rounded corners. *Events* correspond to the messages an object can receive. A *transition* is an arrow connecting two states and should be labelled with the name of an event.

At any given time, an object is in one of its possible states. When it receives a message corresponding to an event on a transition leading from its current state, that transition *fires* and the object ends up in the state at the other end of the transition. In Figure 4.20 for example, receiving the sequence of messages shown in Figure 3.7 will cause the creation tool object to move from the leftmost state to the rightmost one.

Unlike sequence diagrams, however, statecharts are capable of representing more than one sequence of messages. When the mouse button is pressed down, for example, the user can move the mouse many times before releasing the button to create a new element. It doesn't matter precisely how many move messages are received; nothing different will happen until a release message is sent. Similarly, the mouse can be moved many times before the button is pressed for the first time.

Figure 4.20 does not allow for these possibilities, however, as it specifies only a simple sequence of messages which permits no iteration. It can easily be amended, however, by adding extra transitions to the appropriate states.

Figure 4.21 shows the amended state diagram. After the user has moved the mouse and the second state has been reached, two possible transitions are available. Further move messages will cause the looping transition to fire, leaving the tool in the same state. Only when a press message is received will the tool move to the next state.

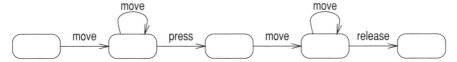

Figure 4.21 A statechart with iterated messages

In Figure 4.21 the mouse must be moved at least once before it is pressed or released. It is probably better to specify that in both cases the mouse need not be moved at all, although if no mouse moves at all were performed, the resulting element would be reduced to a single point on the diagram. This can be modelled by removing the move transitions that lead to the states with the looping transitions, as shown in Figure 4.22.

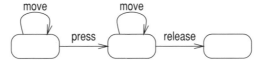

Figure 4.22 Messages iterated zero or more times

When the mouse button is released, the transaction is finished and the user can move the mouse to a new position and then create a new element. This can be modelled by showing that the effect of the release message is to return the tool to its first state. The mouse can then be moved, if necessary, and the button pressed to create a further new element. This ability to create multiple elements is shown in Figure 4.23.

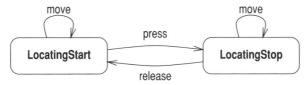

Figure 4.23 Creating more than one element

Figure 4.23 shows that there are essentially two distinct states that a creation tool can be in. One corresponds to the period when the user is trying to locate the start point of a new element, and the other to the period where the stop point is being located. The states in Figure 4.23 have been given labels suggestive of these properties of the states.

The user moves the tool from one state to another by pressing and releasing the mouse button, as shown by the events on the transitions between the states. This means that the 'locating stop' state corresponds to the period where the mouse button is pressed. For reasons discussed in Section 4.8, however, it is better to characterize states by their logical function in an interaction than by accidental differences in the physical state of a peripheral device.

Creation and termination

Figure 4.23 does not indicate how the tool arrives in the locating start state for the first time. In fact, when a tool is created it will be initialized so that this is its initial state. This is modelled on a statechart by showing a special initial state, depicted as a black dot. A transition from an initial state corresponds to the construction of an object, often by means of a constructor call, and terminates at the state the object enters immediately after its creation. The initial state does not, therefore, really represent a state of the tool as the tool has not at that point been created, and therefore cannot detect events. For this reason the initial state is known as a *pseudostate*.

Another special state is used to model the state of an object after it has been destroyed. This *final state* is represented by a bullseye icon. Figure 4.24 shows the statechart for the creation tool with initial and final states added. This diagram makes the assumption that when a tool is to be destroyed and replaced by another, it receives a 'quit' message from the diagram editor.

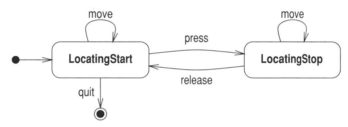

Figure 4.24 Initial and final states

Figure 4.24 models the entire life cycle of a creation tool, by showing the sequences of messages that it can receive and how the state it is in at any given time is a function of the messages it has received up until that point. Any path through the statechart starting at the initial state and finishing at the final state represents a possible life history of a creation tool. Conversely, any given sequence of messages can be tested to see if it represents a possible life history of a tool by seeing if it corresponds to an unbroken path through the statechart.

Actions

Figure 4.24 does not show how an object's behaviour depends on its current state. In this case, the move events on the two states have different effects, in that when a move message is received in the 'locating stop' state a faint image of the new element is drawn on the diagram.

This difference can be shown by adding *actions* to the statechart. Actions are written after the event on a transition, prefixed by a diagonal slash, as shown in Figure 4.25. This diagram specifies that the faint image is only displayed and updated when the user is searching for the stop point of the new element, exactly as required by the specification. An action has also been added to specify the point at which the new element is added to the diagram.

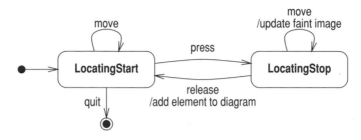

Figure 4.25 Complete creation tool statechart

4.10 A STATECHART FOR SELECTION TOOLS

In exactly the same way as for creation tools, a statechart can be developed showing how a selection tool responds to messages when locating, moving and resizing elements. The statechart in Figure 4.26 specifies the sequences of messages involved in selecting and moving any number of elements. While in the locating state, the user moves the mouse over an element. Then the mouse button is pressed, the moving state is entered, and subsequent move events cause the selected element to be moved. Releasing the mouse button returns the tool to the locating state.

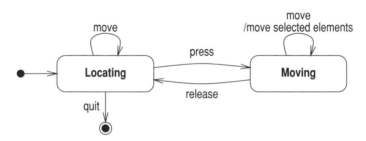

Figure 4.26 Selecting and moving elements

Although this diagram has the same form as that for creation tools, this is merely a reflection of the fact that both exhibit different behaviour depending on whether or not the mouse button is held down. The actions attached to the transitions differ in the two statecharts, as do the meanings of the states, as indicated by the different names chosen for them in Figure 4.26.

Non-determinism

Figure 4.26 does not specify everything about the behaviour of a selection tool. When a press event is received by a selection tool, it may or may not result in an element being selected, depending on where the mouse cursor is at the moment of the press, and the subsequent behaviour of the tool will depend on whether an element was successfully selected or not.

If an element was selected, it and any other selected elements will be moved in response to subsequent move messages. If the attempted selection was unsuccessful, no elements will be moved until a release message has been received. An extra state in addition to the 'moving' state is required to model the fact that the tool's response to move messages can vary from time to time; this new state represents that an error has occurred in an attempt to select an element. Both states can be reached by a transition labelled with a *press* event from the 'locating' state, as shown in Figure 4.27.

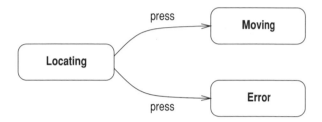

Figure 4.27 An example of non-determinism

Figure 4.27 illustrates the notion of *non-determinism*. We cannot tell from the statechart which state the tool will end up in if it receives a press message while in the 'locating' state. There are two possibilities, but no way of distinguishing between them is given.

Guard conditions

In cases where genuine non-determinism exists in the system being modelled, a statechart like Figure 4.27 is quite appropriate. Most systems, however, are *deterministic*, in that receiving a given event in a given state will always lead to the same outcome. In the case of the selection tool, it all depends on where the cursor is at the point when the press message is generated: if the cursor is over an element, the selecting state will be reached, and otherwise the error state will be reached.

These facts can be shown on the statechart by adding *guard conditions* to the relevant transitions. Figure 4.28 shows how guard conditions can be specified to resolve the ambiguity in Figure 4.27.

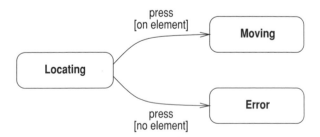

Figure 4.28 Removing non-determinism with guard conditions

A guard condition is written in square brackets after the event label on a transition. A transition with a guard condition can only fire if the corresponding event is detected and its condition is true. In Figure 4.28 only one of the guards can be true at any time, so the non-determinism in Figure 4.27 has been removed.

Completing the statechart

The selection tool actually exhibits a third possible behaviour when a press message is received: if the cursor is over a control point of a selected element, subsequent move messages result in that element being resized. This is different behaviour from that evoked by move messages in the moving and error states, and so a further state is required to model it.

A complete statechart for the selection tool is shown in Figure 4.29. This includes a new 'resizing' state, with an appropriate guard condition on the transition leading to it. It also specifies the actions that take place when a *move* message is received in the moving and resizing states.

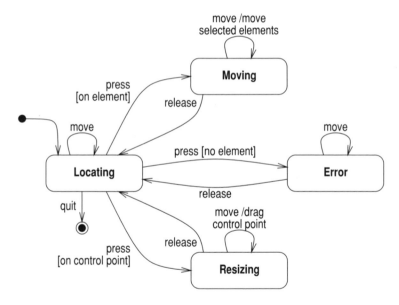

Figure 4.29 Complete statechart for selection tools

4.11 STATECHARTS FOR OTHER CLASSES

It is not necessary to draw a statechart for every class in a system. Normally, statecharts are only drawn for classes with 'interesting' behaviour. For example, a possible statechart for diagrams is shown in Figure 4.30, but although it looks plausible, it does not actually provide any interesting information about the diagram editor.

Firstly, both states have transitions labelled 'add' and 'remove' leading from them, so messages can be received in any order and the diagram imposes no constraints on the life cycles of diagram objects. Secondly, each message evokes exactly the same behaviour in each state, so no interesting state dependent behaviour is being specified.

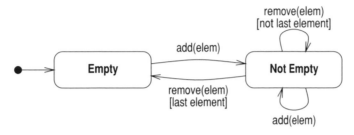

Figure 4.30 A possible statechart for diagrams

4.12 SUMMARY

- The information contained in a set of interaction diagrams about the objects in a system and their interconnections can be summarized in design models, primarily class diagrams and statecharts, which provide a specification of the system.
- Class diagrams show classes and the relationships between them. The properties of classes are defined by their features, both attributes and operations.
- Associations specify the links that can exist between instances of the associated classes. Multiplicity constraints specify how many objects can be linked together.
- Generalization relationships indicate that one class is a specialization of another. Subclasses inherit features from superclasses, and their instances can be substituted for superclass instances.
- Statecharts should be drawn for classes whose instances exhibit state-dependent behaviour. Statecharts specify which sequences of events are expected, and the effect on an object of detecting a particular sequence.
- A statechart shows the possible states of an object, the transitions between those states and the events which trigger transitions.
- Guard conditions can be used to remove non-determinism in statecharts,

4.13 EXERCISES

4.1 Draw an object diagram showing a situation where there are two diagrams, the current tool is a selection tool, and an element is selected which belongs to the diagram which is not the current diagram. Is this object diagram a legitimate instance of the class diagram shown in Figure 4.19? If not, write down in clear English the additional constraint that would be required in order to rule out this situation.

4.2 Draw an object diagram showing the state of the diagram editor where a diagram contains two elements, a line and a rectangle, and the current tool is a selection tool. The only selected element is the line, and the rectangle is being resized. Is this object diagram a legitimate instance of the class diagram shown in Figure 4.19? If not, write down in clear English the additional constraint that would be required in order to rule out this situation.

4.3 Draw a complete class diagram for the diagram editor based on Figure 4.19, but including the attributes and operations of classes and omitting the subclasses of creation tools and elements. Which diagram would be more useful for users of the editor? Which diagram would be more useful to people implementing of the system?

4.4 Exercise 3.12 asked for the creation of text elements to be specified. Make any changes necessary to Figure 4.19 to incorporate text elements and the tool which creates them. If necessary, produce a statechart specifying the behaviour of this tool.

4.5 Extend Figure 4.19 to show group items, as specified in Exercise 3.14.

4.6 Extend the class diagram in Figure 4.19 to show the new classes and associations required by the clipboard feature specified in Exercise 3.15.

4.7 Which of the following sequences of events are specified explicitly by the statechart in Figure 4.25? Assume in each case that the sequence begins immediately after the initialization of the creation tool, when it is in the locating start state.
  (*a*) move; press; release; move
  (*b*) press; move; move; move
  (*c*) press; release; release
  (*d*) move; press; move; move; press; release

4.8 Do all tools accept exactly the same sequences of messages? In other words is there any sequence of events that is permitted by the statechart for creation tools in Figure 4.25, but ruled out by the statechart for selection tools in Figure 4.29, or vice versa?

4.9 Are the statecharts in Figure 4.25 and Figure 4.29 *complete*, in the sense that they specify what should happen for every sequence of messages that the user could generate with the mouse?

4.10 Suppose element creation was a 'one-shot' activity: after a new element has been created, the tool is deleted and before another element is created a new tool has to be initialized. Change the statechart for creation tools to model this new behaviour.

4.11 If press and release messages can be generated by pressing certain keys as well as by use of the mouse it might be possible for a creation tool to receive a press message while it is in the locating stop state.
  (*a*) Assuming that this is to be treated as an error which aborts the creation of the new element, write one or more scenarios describing exactly what happens in this situation.

(*b*) Revise Figure 4.29 to reflect the behaviour specified in your scenarios. Test your updated statechart by seeing what behaviour it would exhibit if the following sequences of messages were received.

   (i) press; press; release; release.

  (ii) release; press; release.

 (iii) press; move; press; release; press; move.

4.12 How should Figure 4.29 be altered to take deletion of elements into account?

4.13 Exercise 3.6 described alternative functionality when the mouse button is pressed over an element which is already selected. Consider what changes would be required to the statechart in Figure 4.29 to model this.

5

DIAGRAM EDITOR: IMPLEMENTATION VIEW

This chapter describes a possible implementation of the diagram editor whose design was discussed in Chapters 3 and 4. Chapter 1 explained how the semantics of the object model ensure that there are close links between designs and their implementations, and some straightforward and systematic techniques for translating UML design notations into code in an object-oriented language are illustrated in this chapter.

The diagram editor is representative of a large class of interactive, single-user applications which have a graphical user interface and detect user interactions by means of input devices such as a mouse and a keyboard. A large amount of low-level code is involved in any such application, to handle the detailed interactions between the application code and the input and output devices.

As this code is common to a wide range of applications, *frameworks* have evolved which provide standard implementations of the core input and output functionality. Rather than writing complete applications from scratch, application programmers nowadays often have only to integrate into a generic framework the code which implements the functionality specific to the application.

Section 5.1 discusses the general notion of a framework, and in Section 5.2 the details of integrating the diagram editor into the Java applet framework are presented. There is nothing in the design to limit the implementation to any particular run-time environment, however, and to demonstrate this Section 5.7 discusses the implementation of the diagram editor in a different framework, Microsoft's document/view architecture.

5.1 APPLICATION FRAMEWORKS

A framework for application development provides the code necessary to create generic 'semi-complete' applications in a particular target environment. Typically a framework for interactive graphical applications will support the following functionality.

1. It will manage the interactions between the application and its environment. In a windowing environment, the framework might support the creation and subsequent management of the windows used by the application. In the case of applets, the framework might provide the functionality necessary for a browser to start and stop applets running on a web page.
2. It will provide means to detect user input and present it to the application in the form of a number of standard and well-defined messages. This input might be generated directly by physical devices such as the mouse and the keyboard, or it might be mediated by user-interface widgets such as menu items and buttons.
3. It will provide a library of graphics functions which enable output to be produced and displayed in the windows controlled by the application.

The term 'framework' is used metaphorically, but is meant to suggest two things. Firstly, the framework code can be thought of as surrounding the application-specific code, in much the same way as a frame surrounds a picture. Secondly, the framework provides a complete but skeletal application which can be used as a framework on which a complete and specialized application can be built.

One visualization of the role of a framework in shielding application programmers from low-level concerns is shown in Figure 5.1. This informal diagram illustrates the way in which the framework shields an application programmer from the details of low-level application programming interfaces (APIs) used to handle input and output. It also indicates how, by providing a standard interface to this low-level functionality, a framework can be reused in many different applications.

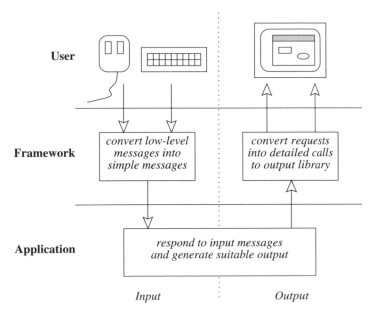

Figure 5.1 The role of a framework

Hotspots

This general description of the role of frameworks does not explain how a programmer can integrate application code with that provided by the framework. Object-oriented frameworks often achieve this by means of *hotspots*. A hotspot is a class in the framework that applications are meant to specialize, as shown in Figure 5.2. The dashed line in this diagram is an informal addition which indicates the boundary between the framework classes and code specific to a particular application.

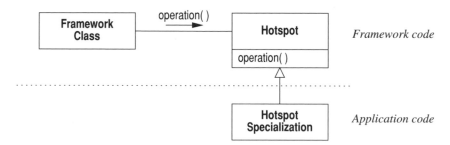

Figure 5.2 A hotspot class

Suppose that the hotspot class provides basic functionality to display a window and its contents. This functionality must be provided in all applications, and there are a number of standard situations where it is executed. For example, if the user opens another window which obscures an application window and then closes or moves that window, the contents of the application window may need to be redrawn to restore the correct display. The framework will detect these events and at appropriate times will send a message to the window class, the hotspot, instructing it to refresh its display.

In general a hotspot class defines a number of operations which are called by the framework at certain standard times. This situation is illustrated in Figure 5.2 by a message being sent from some other framework class to the hotspot. The basic task of the application programmer is to define specializations of hotspot classes and to override operations to implement functionality specific to a particular application.

An operation in a hotspot class may be abstract. Implementations of such operations must be provided by the application programmer before a complete application can be produced. In most cases, however, a sensible default implementation can be written for an operation, even if it is a trivial one which does nothing. In this case, a complete, if trivial, application can be generated from the framework and all the application programmer has to do is to override operations of interest.

Exactly which operations need to be overridden depends on the implementations provided by the framework. Figure 5.3 shows the hotspot receiving a message indicating that the user has moved the mouse. In this case there is no default functionality that the framework can sensibly provide, so the hotspot class provides a null implementation of the operation. The application programmer overrides this operation in the specialized class, and the mechanism of dynamic binding ensures that when the framework class sends a message the application-specific code is executed.

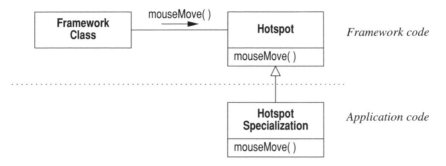

Figure 5.3 Overriding a framework operation

In other cases, it may be possible for a framework to provide a substantial default implementation of an operation. Figure 5.4 shows a situation where the framework is requesting that a window and its contents are redisplayed. In this case, the framework can supply some general-purpose code to redisplay the window background, its borders and scroll bars, and so on. This code is provided in the 'redisplay' method in Figure 5.4. The code which displays application-specific content in the window must, on the other hand, be provided by the programmer.

If the programmer provided this code by overriding the redisplay method, the generic code provided by the framework would be lost. In principle, it could be replicated in the overriding function, but this approach would remove many of the benefits to be gained from using a framework. In such cases a different mechanism is used. The hotspot class defines a second method, called 'displayContent' in Figure 5.4, whose purpose is to display application-specific content in the window. This is given a null default implementation, and it is this function that the programmer overrides.

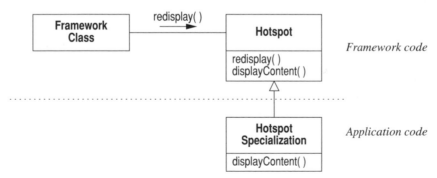

Figure 5.4 Overriding a 'callback' method

The redisplay function calls this additional function at an appropriate place to integrate the application-specific code into the general framework. At run-time, then, when a redisplay message is received, the hotspot redisplay function is first executed; this calls the display content function and by use of dynamic binding the specialized function is executed.

Inversion of control

Use of a framework brings with it a particular style of programming which differs from conventional styles. In the traditional model, the programmer writes a 'main program' which dictates the overall flow of control within an application. The application can be decomposed into a set of classes and functions, some of which may be provided by libraries, but essentially control remains in the hands of the programmer who determines what the user can do when the program is running.

When a framework is used, however, this relationship is reversed, a situation often referred to as *inversion of control*. The flow of control in the program resides in the framework code, and the programmer simply provides a number of functions which are called at certain well-defined places in the process. Control at run-time is in the hands of the user, not the programmer, whose job is to provide code which responds in a suitable way to the user's actions. For this reason, this style of programming is sometimes referred to as *event-driven*.

5.2 THE APPLET FRAMEWORK

The implementation of the diagram editor as a Java applet makes use of two hotspots provided by the Java API, namely the 'Applet' and 'Canvas' classes. The applet class provides the functionality that permits a browser to control an applet, and most importantly to start it running. Every applet must be contain a specialization of the applet class; for the diagram editor applet this will be a new class which can be named simply 'DiagramEditorApplet'.

A canvas is, as the name implies, a surface on which output of various types can be produced. A canvas can be defined to be a component of an applet, and will then automatically be redrawn by the framework whenever necessary, as explained in Section 5.1. As well as enabling output, a canvas can detect user input of various types. In the design, the 'DiagramEditor' class was defined to be the place where user input was routed for handling by the editor application; it is therefore a reasonable choice to declare the diagram editor class to be a specialization of the 'Canvas' hotspot.

The way in which the diagram editor classes are connected to the Java applet framework is shown in Figure 5.5. For simplicity, most of the application classes that do not directly relate to this interface have been omitted from this diagram. The full design of the application was presented in Figure 4.19.

Figure 5.5 and the remainder of the discussion in this chapter also omit some further details of the Java implementation; in particular there is no consideration of the user interface widgets used by the applet to select tools, for example. These are purely Java programming issues, and their omission does not affect the main point being discussed here, that the diagram editor class provides an interface to the applet framework as a result of being declared to be a subclass of Java's 'Canvas' class.

To complete the details of the design of the diagram editor, it is necessary to consider how user input is routed through the framework to the application classes, and how the current diagram is displayed on the screen.

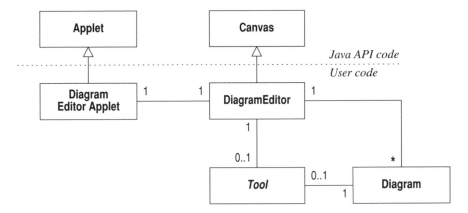

Figure 5.5 The diagram editor as a Java applet

Handling user input

When the user moves the mouse over the surface of the diagram editor canvas, this event is detected by the Java run-time system and translated into a call to the method 'mouseMove', which is defined in the canvas class. This message therefore needs to be overridden in the diagram editor class, as explained in Section 5.1, to specify the way in which this application will respond to mouse moves.

When the diagram editor is running, a mouse move message received by the diagram editor will be translated into a move message suitable for sending to the current tool, as shown in Figure 5.6.

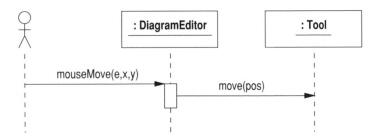

Figure 5.6 Handling user input in the diagram editor

Figure 5.6 should be compared with a sequence diagram such as Figure 3.7, which shows move messages being sent directly from the user to the tool. Figure 5.6 clarifies the situation by adding detail, and shows how messages from the user are sent in the first instance to the diagram editor object and then translated and forwarded on to tools if necessary. Some other messages, such as the 'newDiagram' message in Figure 3.5, are sent to the diagram editor from user interface widgets, and will not be discussed in detail here.

Handling output

The discussion of the design of the diagram editor in Chapters 3 and 4 made no reference to the means by which the current diagram was to be displayed and updated. The rationale for this is that, as discussed in Section 5.1, certain aspects of the display of data are handled by the framework. Normally, it is better to integrate the display of application-specific data into this process, rather than distributing it among the different classes in the design.

All Java user interface components, including canvases, define a method to 'paint' the component, or redisplay its contents on some output device. This method is called by the framework whenever it is detected that the current display might have become corrupted, for example as a result of the user performing various window manipulations on the desktop. As there is no way of telling in advance how much of the display has become corrupted before it is redisplayed, the paint method has in principle to be capable of redisplaying the entire current diagram.

Given this, there is little point in defining display code elsewhere in the application. Such code would simply duplicate what the paint method must in any case provide, and in practice the problems of correctly coordinating display routines that are spread over a number of locations in the program quickly become significant, and lead to annoying errors in the code. One strategy, therefore, is for the application code itself simply to call the paint method after every interaction that may require a change to the display. The interactions required by this strategy are shown in Figure 5.7.

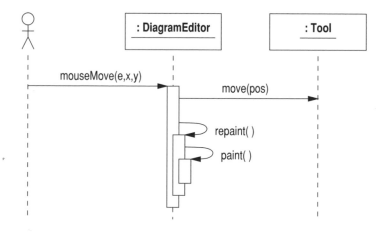

Figure 5.7 Redrawing the current diagram

This diagram is an extension of the interaction shown in Figure 5.6. As before, the user has moved the mouse and the message has been translated and passed on the current tool for further action. As a result of this, however, the state of the current diagram may have changed, and may need redrawing. The diagram editor therefore calls the method 'repaint', shown in Figure 5.7 as a message being sent to the diagram editor itself and giving rise to a corresponding nested activation.

The repaint method is in fact provided by the Java framework, and is not overridden in most applications. It therefore corresponds to the 'redisplay' method shown in Figure 5.4. In this case, however, it is being called by the overridden mouse move method, rather than by another class in the framework. Analogous to the way in which the 'displayContent' method is called in Figure 5.4, the repaint method calls the paint method, which is overridden in the diagram editor class. This is shown as yet another nested activation in Figure 5.7.

In order to get the display updated, therefore, the diagram editor ends up with three nested activations. Two of these, 'mouseMove' and 'paint', correspond to methods that have been overridden in the diagram editor class; the third, 'repaint', is a convenient framework operation which, among other things, calls an overridable function in the hotspot class. This is a concrete example of the second kind of interaction discussed in Section 5.1, and clearly indicates the importance of finding out what methods in a framework should be overridden, and the circumstances in which they are called.

Figure 5.7 does not show what the diagram editor does in response to a 'paint' method, or in other words how the redisplay actually happens. A typical response to this message is shown in Figure 5.8. In Figure 5.7, the client sending the message is the diagram editor itself, but in general other classes in the framework may also call this method. In all cases, the response of the diagram editor is the same.

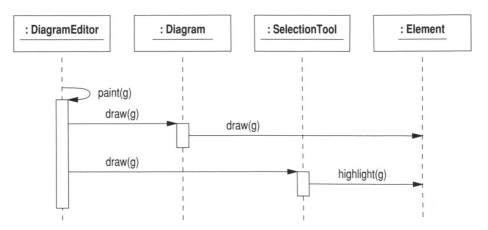

Figure 5.8 Drawing a diagram

Figure 5.8 shows a situation where the current tool is a selection tool, and the diagram contains one element which is selected. In order to redraw the diagram, the diagram editor first tells the diagram to draw itself; in response to this, the diagram in turn tells all the elements it contains to draw themselves. The current tool is then told to draw itself. What effect this has will depend on what type of tool it is; Figure 5.8 shows that a selection tool will instruct any selected elements to highlight themselves, to display the control points. If the current tool was a creation tool, by contrast, a suitable response to the draw message might be to draw the faint rectangle of the element being created, depending on the state of the tool.

The parameter 'g' on the messages in Figure 5.8 is a reference to a *graphics context* in which drawing can take place. This is essentially an abstraction of the output device on which display is taking place. It provides application objects such as elements and tools with access to the Java API for graphical display, without which no actual drawing could take place.

The idea of redrawing the whole diagram every time the user interacts in any way with the editor may seem unacceptably inefficient. In fact, the update happens so quickly in comparison with the rate at which the user interacts with the system that overall performance does not suffer. Because of its simplicity, this brute force approach can be recommended for a wide range of applications.

If there are many elements on the diagram, however, this approach can give rise to a noticeable flicker on the screen, depending on the speed of the machine running the applet. This is caused by the time taken to redraw all the elements. In this case, or in cases where performance is genuinely an issue, there are a number of techniques which can be applied to increase the efficiency of the paint method.

One common technique is to keep track of a *clipping rectangle*, an area which is guaranteed to contain all the bits of the diagram that need to be updated, and to restrict redisplay to this area. An alternative is the technique of *double buffering*, where the updated display is created in memory and then transferred in a block to the screen. As the screen is then updated in a single operation, the flickering effect is no longer apparent. Unfortunately, it is outside the scope of this book to discuss these techniques further here.

5.3 IMPLEMENTATION OF CLASSES

The following sections describe the detailed implementation of the diagram editor in Java, showing how the various UML features in the design are mapped into code. The techniques presented are not the only way of carrying out such a translation, but have the advantage of being clear and straightforward, and emphasizing the close relationship that exists between design notations and programming language constructs.

Classes

Unsurprisingly, classes in a UML class diagram are implemented as classes in object-oriented languages. Figure 5.9 shows a class icon for the tool class, consisting of a name, a set of attributes and a set of operations. This class is naturally implemented as a Java class containing equivalent fields and methods.

When a class is being implemented, the access levels of its members need to be considered. A useful rule of thumb for implementing attributes and operations is to transform attributes into private fields of the implementation class, and operations into public methods of the class. This reflects a widely adopted policy to the implementation of classes which states that a class's data should be private and only accessible through its operational interface.

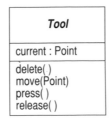

Figure 5.9 The creation tool class

Assigning access levels to the members of a class becomes important when a system is being implemented. Designs do not usually include details of how a class's operations will be implemented, and in particular how they obtain information from objects of other classes, so there is little need to be explicit about the access levels of attributes and operations in classes. These concerns become more important when the system is being implemented. The notation defined by UML for documenting access levels is described in Chapter 11.

Using these guidelines, an outline of a Java class implementing the creation tool class defined in Figure 5.9 is shown below. The class 'Point' from the Java libraries is used as a natural implementation of the point data type that during the design was assumed to be available.

```
public abstract class Tool
{
  private Point current ;

  public void delete() {}
  public abstract void move( Point p ) ;
  public abstract void press() ;
  public abstract void release() ;
}
```

The move, press and release methods are declared to be abstract because every descendant of the tool class has to provide a specialized implementation of them. The delete method, on the other hand, only has significance for selection tools. It is included in the tool superclass so that all tool classes share a common interface, but a null implementation of it is provided so the classes to which it is irrelevant can simply ignore its existence.

Generalization

The generalization relationship between classes can be implemented using inheritance in Java. The two important properties of generalization are the substitutability of a subclass instance where a superclass instance is expected, and the inheritance of class members from superclasses, and both of these properties are preserved by the semantics of inheritance in Java.

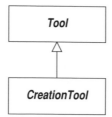

Figure 5.10 Generalization

Figure 5.10 shows a simple example of generalization in the design of the diagram editor, which could be partially implemented in Java as shown below. The attributes are included to emphasize that inheritance works in the same way in both Java and UML, and an example of method overriding is also shown.

```
public abstract class Tool
{
   Point current ;

   public abstract void move( Point p) ;
}

public abstract class CreationTool extends Tool
{
   Point start ;

   public void move( Point p ) { ... }
}
```

Attributes which are inherited, or intended to be inherited, and used by subclasses need to be given a more liberal access level than private. A standard choice in Java, illustrated here, is to use the default access level which makes the fields visible to other classes in the same package as the class declaring the field.

5.4 IMPLEMENTATION OF ASSOCIATIONS

In class diagrams, associations relate classes together. Whereas all object-oriented programming languages provide direct support for the concept of a class, none of the languages in common use provide features which can be directly used to implement associations. When implementing a design, therefore, it is necessary to give some thought to the question of how associations are to be handled.

The role of associations is to define the properties of the links that connect objects when a system is running. A link asserts that one object knows of the existence and location of some other object. In addition, links serve as channels along which messages can be sent to the linked object if necessary.

This suggests that individual links between objects could be implemented using *references*. A reference, being essentially the address of an object, certainly records the object's location and identity, and by means of the reference it is possible to call the linked object's member functions, thus simulating message passing. A simple strategy for implementing an association between two classes is therefore to declare fields in each class to hold references to instances of the associated class.

Associations have certain logical properties, however, which are not explicitly handled by this rather simplistic approach and which need careful consideration in the implementation of associations. These properties are briefly considered in the remainder of this section. A more systematic treatment of various methods for implementing associations is given in Chapter 10.

Bidirectionality

Associations and links simply connect classes and objects, respectively, and place no restriction on the direction in which the connection can be traversed. For example, a link in a collaboration diagram can serve as a communication channel between two objects, and messages can be sent in either direction along this channel, as required by the needs of the design. This property is often expressed by saying that associations and links are *bidirectional*.

References, on the other hand, are not bidirectional. If an object x holds a reference to object y, this gives x access to y and the ability to call the member functions of y, but gives y no knowledge at all of x. To implement a bidirectional link two references are required, one from x to y, and the other from y back to x. To illustrate the difference, Figure 5.11 shows links between three objects contrasted with the references that would be required to implement the links in both directions. References are distinguished from links by means of an arrowhead which shows the direction of access.

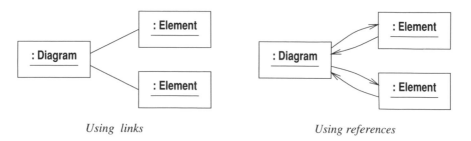

Using links   *Using references*

Figure 5.11 Implementing bidirectional links with references

Although it is certainly possible to implement links as pairs of references in this way, there are a number of good reasons why this is undesirable, and should be avoided if possible. Firstly, in order to support a cyclical structure of references, the relevant class declarations must be mutually referring. This can only be achieved at the cost of increasing the coupling between the two classes, with a detrimental effect on the simplicity and maintainability of the resulting code.

Secondly, the two references implementing a link must be kept mutually consistent throughout the lifetime of the link. They must be created and destroyed together, and must not be altered independently. Programming with references is an error-prone area, however, and by doubling the number of references required the problems are also increased. Even if a safe scheme for maintaining references is defined and consistently adhered to, there may be a significant overhead involved in maintaining both references.

Fortunately it is often not necessary to implement an association in both directions. It might turn out that messages were passed from diagram to element objects, but never in the other direction. In order to support this, it is clearly necessary for a diagram to hold references to its elements, but there seems to be no immediate benefit to be gained from having each element hold a reference to the diagram containing it.

The implementation of associations can therefore be simplified by defining references only in the directions in which the associations are actually used. In practice it turns out that relatively few associations need to be supported in both directions. For example, in the diagram editor it is the case that messages are passed from diagram objects to elements, but never from an element to a diagram. We can therefore decide, for the purposes of simplifying the implementation, not to implement this association in the direction from drawing to tool.

Figure 5.12 shows how this decision can be recorded on a class diagram using the notion of *navigability* defined in Section 2.5. The direction in which the association will be implemented is shown by adding an arrowhead to the association. The association states that each diagram is linked to zero or more elements. This will be implemented by storing references to the elements in each diagram. The multiplicity symbol at the diagram end of the association specified how many diagrams an element can be linked to. This information is now irrelevant, as the reverse direction of the association is no longer being considered, and so this multiplicity symbol is now omitted.

Figure 5.12 Making an association unidirectional

A simple implementation of this unidirectional association could use a predefined container class, such as the vector class provided by the Java libraries, to store the references to elements, as shown below. Also shown is the code for adding an element to a diagram.

```
public class Diagram
{
  private Vector elements = new Vector(16) ;

  public void add( Element e )
  {
    elements.addElement(e) ;
  }
}
```

By choosing to implement the association in one direction only, as in this case, we are making a tradeoff between present ease of implementation and future modifiability. It is now impossible to traverse the association in the direction from diagram to elements. Any future change to the system that makes it desirable for an element to know what diagram it belongs to will now be much harder to implement than it would have otherwise have been, because we will have to add back in the ability to traverse the association in the reverse direction. In this particular case the risk seems to be small, but other cases are less clear cut.

Implementing multiplicity constraints

When an association is implemented with references, it is not always possible to preserve all the information that the class diagram contains about the multiplicity of the association. For example, consider the association shown in Figure 5.13. In order to support the message passing that occurs in the diagram editor it is sufficient that a tool class holds a reference to the diagram it is working on.

Figure 5.13 An association with multiplicity 'one'

However, a property of references in Java is that a reference variable can either hold a null value or a putative address. In effect this means that this implementation in fact always represents an 'optional' multiplicity. The case where the reference is null corresponds to the 'zero' multiplicity, and otherwise a multiplicity of 'one' is implied.

There is no way using simply the data declaration features of Java to state that the multiplicity of an association is exactly one, as the possibility of a null reference cannot be ruled out. Thus when associations are modelled with references the difference between 'optional' and 'exactly one' multiplicities can easily be lost.

The multiplicity constraint can only be preserved by adding code which will at suitable places explicitly check that a null value is not being stored in the variable. For example, the code below throws an exception if an attempt is made to create a tool without associating it with a diagram object.

```
public abstract class Tool
{
  Diagram diagram ;

  Tool(Diagram d) {
    if (d == null) {
      // throw NullDiagramError
    }
    diagram = d ;
  }
}
```

5.5 IMPLEMENTATION OF STATECHARTS

Class diagrams contain static information which can, by and large, be implemented by translating it into structural features of the implementation, such as definitions of classes and their members. Statecharts, on the other hand, provide dynamic information about how an object behaves during its lifetime. This information can also readily be translated into code, but must be reflected more in the implementation of class methods, which need to determine the current state of the object when they are called in order to determine how to react.

As with class diagrams, it is desirable to use a systematic approach to translate the information contained in statecharts into code. This section uses the tool classes from the diagram editor to illustrate one simple technique for doing so.

The creation tool hierarchy

The basic idea underlying the technique is to keep an explicit record of the current state of each tool in a field in the tool class itself. The statechart for the creation tool given in Figure 4.25 defines two distinct states, named 'locating start' and 'locating stop'. These states are defined as constants in the creation tool class, and the 'state' field holds the value corresponding to the current state of the tool.

When a creation tool is created, Figure 4.25 specifies that the initial state is 'locating start'. This property is implemented by having the constructor initialize the state field to this value. The partial class definition below shows this, together with the definition of constant values representing the states of creation tools.

```
public abstract class CreationTool extends Tool
{
  final static int LocatingStart = 0 ;
  final static int LocatingStop  = 1 ;
  int state ;

  CreationTool(Diagram d)
  {
    super(d) ;
    state = LocatingStart ;
  }
  ...
}
```

Messages sent to a creation tool have the potential to elicit different behaviour at different times, depending on the current state of the tool. This can be reflected in the implementation of the class by structuring every method as a switch statement. The switch statement has a case for each possible value of the state variable, and the code for each case specifies what to do if the message is received when the tool is in that particular state.

If this convention is followed, every method in the tool classes will have the form specified by the following template. In some methods many of the cases may be empty; nevertheless, including them all makes the structure of the implementation very clear and easy to modify.

```
public void operation()
{
  switch (state) {
    case LocatingStart:
      // Specific actions for locating start state
      break ;
    case LocatingStop:
      // Specific actions for locating stop state
      break ;
  }
}
```

Much of the specific behaviour implemented in each of the different cases can be derived directly from the actions included on the statechart. For example, if a release message is received when the tool is in the locating stop state, Figure 4.25 shows that an action to create a new element and add it to the diagram is performed. A possible implementation of this action is shown in the locating stop case of the implementation of this method given below.

```
public void release() {
  switch (state) {
    case LocatingStart:
      break ;
    case LocatingStop:
      Element e = newElement(start, current) ;
      diagram.add(e) ;
      state = LocatingStart ;
      break ;
  }
}
```

This example also demonstrates how to implement the fact that some messages cause the state of the tool to change. The methods which implement these messages can achieve this by assigning a new value to the tool's state variable as their last action. Then the next time a message is received by the object, the code corresponding to the new state will be selected and executed.

The creation tool class defines the dynamic behaviour exhibited by all types of creation tools. The creation tool class is abstract, however, and the method shown above is faced with the task of creating a new element of an unknown type. Element creation is therefore delegated to a 'new element' method. This method is defined to be abstract in the creation tool class, and is overridden in subclasses to create an element of the appropriate type.

The concrete subclasses of the creation tool class only need to implement the behaviour that is specific to particular kinds of element, namely how to create and draw elements of the given type. This behaviour is defined in functions 'newElement' and 'drawElement'. The declaration of the rectangle tool class is shown below; those of the line and ellipse tools are very similar.

```
public class RectangleTool extends CreationTool
{
  Element newElement(Point start, Point stop) { ... }
  void    drawElement(Graphics g)             { ... }
}
```

The selection tool class

The strategy underlying the implementation of the statechart for the selection tool class, shown in Figure 4.29, is exactly the same as that used for the creation tool. The only additional features this statechart contains are guard conditions on the transitions leading from the locating state which are labelled with the 'press' message.

These conditions are boolean expressions whose role is to test the current location of the cursor to see if it is positioned over a highlighted control point or an element. These guarded transitions can be easily implemented by means of 'if' statements in the corresponding case of the switch statement to evaluate the guards. Schematically, the implementation of this operation can be represented as follows, although it should be noted that the implementation of the various guard conditions is in practice more complex than shown here.

```
public void press()
{
  switch (state) {
    case Locating:
      if (findControl(current)) {
        state = Resizing ;
      }
      else if (diagram.find(current) != null) {
        state = Moving ;
      }
      else {
        state = Error ;
      }
    case Moving:
      break ;
    case Resizing:
      break ;
    case Error:
      break ;
  }
}
```

5.6 MANAGING TOOLS

The interactions considered in Chapter 3 focused on the realization of individual use cases, and not on transitions between use cases. As use cases represent independent units of functionality, this is not a significant limitation, but in order to complete the implementation of the diagram editor class it is necessary to consider how instances of tools are created and destroyed when the user selects a new tool, creates a new diagram, or moves from one diagram to another.

For example, Figure 3.7 shows a realization of the use case for creating a rectangle, but the required instance of the rectangle tool class is assumed to exist at the start of the interaction shown there. In fact, the user will first have had to select a rectangle tool from the tool bar, if the last use case performed was not also to create a rectangle.

In the general case, then, sequence diagrams such as Figure 3.7 may have prefixed to them a simple interaction which shows the destruction of the previous tool and creation of a new tool. Figure 5.14 gives an example of such an interaction for the case where the user has been moving elements, say, and now wishes to create a new line.

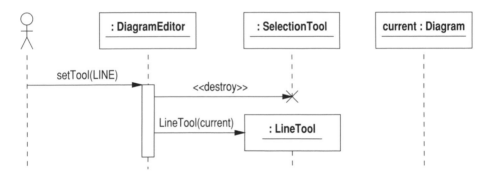

Figure 5.14 Selecting a new tool

In a Java implementation of the interaction shown in Figure 5.14 no explicit destroy message would be sent to the old tool. The new tool would simply be created, and the old tool would in time be dealt with by the garbage collector. It is advisable to show the message explicitly, however, if only to clarify the point at which the old tool can be safely disposed of.

A similar interaction is required in the situation where a new diagram is created. The sequence diagram in Figure 3.5 shows the creation of a new diagram, but makes no reference to the fact that any existing tool will first have to be destroyed, and a new tool created for the new diagram. Similarly, when the user selects the 'next diagram' option to move from one diagram to another, the tool that was active on the first diagram will have to be destroyed and a new tool created for the diagram that is being moved to. Production of sequence diagrams describing these two interactions in detail is left as an exercise.

5.7 THE DOCUMENT/VIEW ARCHITECTURE

Section 5.2 demonstrated how the basic diagram editor design could be integrated with the Java applet framework, and an implementation of the editor as an applet produced. The generic design presented for the diagram editor made no assumptions about the target environment for the program, however, and in principle it would be possible to implement the design in many other environments.

To demonstrate this, this section first gives an overview of a different application framework, the document/view architecture supported by the Microsoft Foundation Class (MFC) library, and then briefly explains how the design of the diagram editor presented in Chapters 3 and 4 could be integrated into this framework and an alternative implementation of the editor produced.

Documents and views

The MFC library provides a wide range of classes to ease the task of developing applications in the Windows environment. It offers support particularly in the following areas:

1. Implementations of some base data types and container classes are provided, such as strings and lists. These classes can be easily reused as basic components in a program, and conform to a traditional library-based model of reuse.
2. A number of classes encapsulate various features of the Windows user interface, such as dialogue boxes, menus and tool bars. In most of these cases, the application programmer takes advantage of the functionality provided by MFC by deriving a specialized subclass of the appropriate class in the library. These subclasses are then normally used as traditional components within an application.
3. The MFC library also defines a standard architecture for Windows applications, which is implemented as an application framework known as the *document/view architecture*. Programmers can base applications on this architecture by deriving application classes from 'hotspots' in the MFC framework. This aspect of MFC therefore fits the model of an application framework as described in Section 5.1.

As the name suggests, the important notions in the document/view architecture are documents and views. Both of these concepts are represented by classes in the MFC framework which act as hotspots. Application development consists largely of the development of appropriately specialized subclasses of these hotspot classes, and overriding the necessary operations they define. A schematic view of the document/view architecture is shown in Figure 5.15.

A document represents the permanent data that is manipulated by an application. Documents can often be thought of as the set of data that it would be natural to store in a disk file between invocations of the program. The name is derived from the example of a text editor or a word processor, where 'documents' would in fact be the various documents that the user was writing.

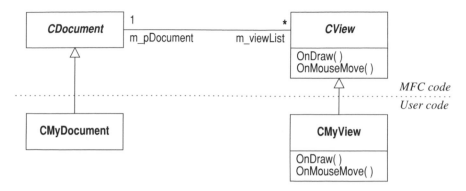

Figure 5.15 The document/view architecture

Each document can be associated with zero or more *views*, as shown by the association in the framework linking the two classes in Figure 5.15. Views have two main responsibilities. Firstly, they are responsible for displaying the data in a document to the user, in some suitable format. Secondly, views control the user's interaction with that data, by detecting input from the user and, if necessary, calling operations defined by the document to update the data stored there.

As well as defining these two hotspot classes, the document/view architecture defines a standard pattern of interaction between documents and views in a running application, as outlined below. As would be expected, this interaction is partly defined by a number of functions defined in the framework which the application programmer can override. A couple of these functions are shown in Figure 5.15 and mentioned below, but it should be emphasized that this discussion does not do justice to the full complexity of the architecture.

1. The user performs some action. This is detected by the framework code, and an appropriate member function of the view class is called. For example, if the user moves the mouse a function called 'OnMouseMove' in the view class is called. If a programmer wishes an application to respond to this event, this function should be overridden in the application's view class.
2. If the user's action causes a modification to the data stored in the document, the view calls the appropriate document member functions to effect the modification.
3. At any time, there may be multiple views displaying the contents of a single document. A change made in one view should be propagated to the other views so that they remain consistent with the current state of the document. The document should therefore at this point tell all its attached views to update themselves.
4. The views redisplay the current state of document, incorporating any modifications caused by the user's last action. This is often done in a function such as 'OnDraw', defined in the framework but normally overridden in specialized view classes.
5. In the course of redisplaying the contents of its document, a view will typically send messages to its linked document object to find out the current state of the document before displaying it.

Implementing the diagram editor

To implement the diagram editor using the document/view architecture, then, the most important task is to identify the classes which will serve as documents and views. The design presented did not explicitly consider the issue of saving diagrams to disk, but it is natural to think that users of the editor would consider themselves to be working with a number of diagrams, each of which might be saved in a separate file. This suggests that the diagram class should be defined as a subclass of the document class provided by the framework.

As explained above, views are responsible for displaying the data in a document, and for responding to user-generated events that are detected by the framework. These are precisely the roles performed by the diagram editor class itself, and it would therefore be appropriate to define this class as a subclass of the view class provided by the framework. These design decisions are documented in Figure 5.16, together with the relationships between tools and diagrams that are preserved from the original design.

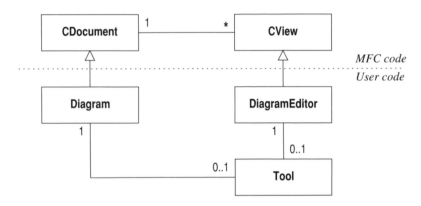

Figure 5.16 The diagram editor and the document/view architecture

Figure 5.16 summarizes the way in which the diagram editor design can be integrated into the framework provided by the document/view architecture. The detailed implementation of the diagram editor in this framework will not be considered further in this book, but it can be carried out following the same strategies that were illustrated in the case of the Java applet implementation, adapted where necessary for use with the C++ language. Further details of this implementation, and the resulting source code, are available from the book's web site.

5.8 SUMMARY

- Much software development now takes place in the context of an application framework. Frameworks provide semi-complete, generic applications and shield programmers from low-level APIs.

- An object-oriented framework will typically define a number of 'hotspot' classes. To develop applications, programmers must specialize these classes and override various operations to provide application-specific functionality.
- The diagram editor can be implemented as a Java applet by specializing the 'Applet' and 'Canvas' classes from the Java APIs.
- Classes in a design map naturally onto classes in an implementation, and generalization to inheritance.
- Programming languages contain no feature with the same properties as associations. Associations can be implemented by means of fields in a class holding references to instances of the association class.

5.9 EXERCISES

5.1 Figures 5.2, 5.3 and 5.4 bend the rules of UML slightly, by including messages on class diagrams. For each of these diagrams, draw a corresponding sequence diagram showing an instance of the framework class and an instance of the hotspot specialization together with the messages that would be sent in each interaction.

5.2 Examine the code of the diagram editor applet, and produce a class diagram showing details of the tool bar and widgets used by the applet. Add these to the class diagram shown in Figure 5.5.

5.3 Produce the sequence diagrams referred to at the end of Section 5.6 which show in detail the interactions that must take place when a new diagram is created, and when the user moves from one diagram to the next.

5.4 Exercises 3.12 and 4.4 discussed the addition of the capability to create text elements to the diagram editor. Based on the design that you produced in answering those questions, add this functionality to the diagram editor applet.

5.5 Implement the 'group item' feature based on the design produced in answering Exercises 4.5 and 3.14.

5.6 Implement the clipboard feature based on the design produced in answering Exercises 4.6 and 3.15.

5.7 Exercises 3.6 and 4.13 described alternative functionality when the mouse button is pressed over an element which is already selected. Modify the implementation of the diagram editor to support this functionality.

5.8 Modify the implementation of the diagram editor so that after an element is created, the selection tool becomes active and the new element is selected. Evaluate the usability of this design.

5.9 Design and implement a modification to the diagram editor program so that the 'delete' button is only enabled if a selection tool is active and at least one element is currently selected.

5.10 It might be convenient if the set of selected elements on a diagram was preserved, even when the diagram was not current. This would mean that when the user moved to the next diagram, the tool active was the one that was active the last time that diagram was visited, instead of a default rectangle tool being activated. Design and implement a modification to the diagram editor so that the tool associated with a diagram is preserved even when the diagram is not current, and is reinstated when the diagram is redisplayed.

Static models of a system describe the structural relationships that hold between the pieces of data manipulated by the system. They describe how data is parcelled out into objects, how those objects are categorized, and what relationships can hold between them. They do not describe the behaviour of the system, nor how the data in a system evolves over time. These aspects are described by various types of dynamic model.

The most important kinds of static model are *object diagrams* and *class diagrams*. An object diagram provides a 'snapshot' of a system, showing the objects that actually exist at a given moment and the links between them. Many different object diagrams can be drawn for a system, each representing the state of the system at a given instant. An object diagram shows the data that is held by a system at a given moment. This data may be represented as individual objects, as attribute values stored inside these objects, or as links between objects.

One aspect of understanding a system is knowing which object diagrams do and which do not represent possible valid states of the system. For example, consider the two object diagrams shown in Figure 6.1, which depict student and module objects in a hypothetical university record system.

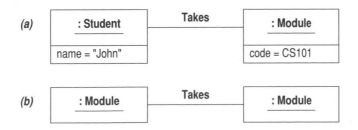

Figure 6.1 Valid and invalid object diagrams

Figure 6.1(*a*) shows a situation where a particular student is taking a module. Assuming that one of the responsibilities of the system is to record which students are taking which modules, this object diagram represents a legitimate state of the system. There will undoubtedly be times when the particular link shown in Figure 6.1(*a*) does not exist. It may even be the case that throughout the whole time that the system is running, this particular configuration of objects never occurs. It does, however, represent a situation that could occur, if the facts about the real world demanded it.

The case is different with Figure 6.1(*b*). It does not make sense for one module to take another, and so in the context of a university record system this diagram is simply meaningless. We cannot ask whether the situation it depicts is true or not, as it fails to depict a meaningful situation at all.

It is not possible, however, to specify a system by explicitly considering all the possible object diagrams and classifying them as legal or illegal, as there are simply too many of them. A more general method is required for specifying the properties that must hold of any object diagram that purports to represent a legal state of the system. UML uses *class diagrams* for this purpose.

A class diagram acts as a kind of specification for a system, and among other things states what kinds of objects can exist, what data they encapsulate, and how objects in the system can be related to each other. A suitable class diagram for the student record system, for example, would make clear that Figure 6.1(*a*) represents a possible state of the system but Figure 6.1(*b*) does not.

This chapter describes the features of UML's class diagrams, and explains how class diagrams are used to specify certain structural properties of software systems. The examples used in this chapter are artificial to the extent that they discuss the static structure of systems without any reference to the processing that this structure is supposed to support. This simplification is of benefit when introducing the details of the notation, but should not be taken as a realistic illustration of how class diagrams are used and developed. As the examples in Chapter 4 indicate, class diagrams are often developed hand in hand with interaction diagrams which help in identifying the classes required in a system.

6.1 PRIMITIVE NOTIONS

Data types

In common with many programming languages, UML defines a number of primitive *data types* and also provides a mechanism whereby new types can be defined. Data types represent simple, unstructured kinds of data such as numeric, character and boolean values. Data types are commonly used to specify the type of an attribute or an operation parameter in a class.

Values of a data type differ from objects in that they have no notion of identity. For example, in an integer data type there is only one value representing the number '2'. This value may be copied and stored in different places if required, but an equality test between two variables holding copies of this value will always return true.

If integers were represented by objects, on the other hand, it would be conceivable that there should be two distinct objects, each storing the numeric value '2'. As these two objects would have distinct identities, this would amount to there being two distinct '2's, a notion which does not make much sense. Put another way, the two objects would be regarded by the system as not being equal, despite the fact that they were meant to represent the same number.

The data types available in UML fall into three categories. Firstly, there are a number of predefined types, including booleans, integers and strings. The UML notation for showing primitive types is shown in Figure 6.2, although it is rarely used.

Figure 6.2 A predefined type

Secondly, there are the so-called language types. These allow type expressions from the target programming language to be used in UML. This is useful in the implementation stages of development, when it is necessary to specify that pointer or array types, for example, are to be used.

Finally, UML provides user-defined types, which are essentially the same as the enumerated types provided in many programming languages. A user-defined type consists of a type name and a number of named data values belonging to the type. No information need be given about the representation of the data values: they are primitive values which should be referred to by name throughout the rest of the design.

The definition of a user-defined type is shown in Figure 6.3. A class icon is used to define the type, labelled with the stereotype 'enumeration' in addition to the type name. The individual data values in the type are listed in a second section in the icon.

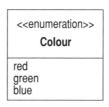

Figure 6.3 Definition of a user-defined type

Multiplicity

There are a number of places in UML where it is necessary to state the number of times a given entity can occur in some context. These are represented by *multiplicities*. A multiplicity is a set of integer values; each member of the set represents one possibility for the number of occurrences of the entity being specified.

Multiplicities are represented in UML using *number ranges*. Each number range consists of a pair of integers separated by dots, such as 0 . . 9. The special symbol * can be used to represent a range which is not bounded above; informally, * can be thought of as 'infinity'. Thus the number range 0 . . * represents all the non-negative integers. A number range where both ends are the same number, such as 1 . . 1, is represented by the single number 1.

If necessary, a multiplicity can be represented by a list consisting of number ranges and individual numbers, preferably arranged in ascending order. For example, suppose that a given entity is optional but that if it is present there must be at least three of them. This multiplicity could be represented as 0 , 3 . . *.

6.2 CLASSES

A basic technique for simplifying the description of an indefinitely large number of objects is to classify similar objects into groups. Objects that share certain properties and behaviour are grouped together, and for each group a *class* is defined. The class does not describe particular properties of individuals, but specifies the common features that are shared by all the objects in the group.

For example, Figure 6.1 shows objects representing students and modules in a hypothetical university record system. In such a system the same pieces of information would be stored about each student, such as a name and an address. By defining a student class we can specify once and for all the information that the system will store about students.

The same goes for operations: the operation of changing an address, for example, is potentially applicable to any student, or in other words, each student object must provide this as one of its operations. By describing the operation as part of the student class, we specify its applicability to all student objects.

In UML a rectangular box is used to represent a class graphically. The name of the class is written in a bold font at the top of the box. The way in which the properties of the objects of the class can be shown is described in the following sections. In many cases, however, it is sufficient simply to include the class name in the icon.

The individual objects whose structure is described by means of a class, are known as the *instances* of the class. Alternatively, we often speak of an object as 'belonging to a class'. Every object is an instance of some class. This is an essential part of the object's definition and, among other things, determines what data will be stored in that object. UML represents objects by using the same kind of icon as the class the instance belongs to, but underlining the class name. In addition, instances may be named. Figure 6.4 shows a 'student' class and two of its instances.

The dashed line is known as a *dependency* and is the notation used by UML to denote a unspecified sort of relationship between two model elements. The label, or *stereotype*, attached to the dependency gives an indication of what particular relationship is being depicted. In Figure 6.4, the 'instanceOf' dependency states that an object is an instance of a particular class.

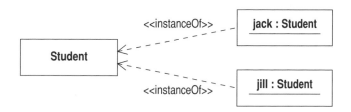

Figure 6.4 A class and its instances

The fact that an object is an instance of a particular class is already expressed by the use of the class name in the label of each object, however, so the notation shown in Figure 6.4 is rarely used. In fact, class and object icons do not in normal circumstances appear together on the same diagrams.

Class multiplicity

The concept of multiplicity can be applied to classes: the multiplicity of a class specifies the number of instances of the class that can exist at any one time. The default multiplicity for a class is 'zero or more', implying that there is no restriction on the number of instances that can be created. This default multiplicity does not need to be shown explicitly on a diagram.

In some cases, however, it is desirable to specify certain limitations on the number of instances that can exist at any given time when the system is running. To enable this, classes can contain a multiplicity annotation, in the top right-hand corner of the class icon. The most common use for this notation is to specify that a class is a *singleton* class which can only have one instance. For example, a student record system might need to record certain information about the university itself, and thus define a class in which to store this information. As the system is entirely internal to a single university, however, it would not make sense to have more than one instance of this class. This constraint is expressed in the class symbol shown in Figure 6.5.

Figure 6.5 A singleton class, showing class multiplicity

6.3 DESCRIBING OBJECTS WITH CLASSES

Every object contains certain pieces of data and a number of operations to process this data. All the objects of a given class contain the same data items, though with differing actual values, and the same operations. This common structure is defined by the class to which the objects belong by defining in the class a number of *attributes*, which describe the data items found in its instances, and a number of *operations*.

Attributes

An attribute is a description of a data field that is maintained by each instance of a class. Attributes must be named. In addition to the name other pieces of information can be supplied such as the type of the data described by the attribute, or a default initial value for the attribute. Attributes are shown in the class icon, separated from the name of the class by a horizontal line, as shown in Figure 6.6. If the attribute type is shown, it is separated from the name by a colon, and initial values follow an equals sign. In the early stages of design it is very common to show nothing more than the name of the attribute.

Figure 6.6 A module class with attributes

Figure 6.6 shows a class representing modules with attributes to model the code number, name and number of credit points of a module. An instance of the class is also shown, illustrating the way in which attribute values are specified in object icons. The first attribute, named 'code', represents the identifier used within the university to refer to the module. No type is specified for this attribute, indicating that no decision has yet been made about how to store this code as a concrete piece of data.

Data types can be used to show the types of attributes. Other classes should not normally be used as attribute types. For example, if a model had classes defined to represent students and modules, it might be tempting to show a module that a student is taking as an attribute within the student class with type 'module'. A better way to model this situation would be to use an association between the student and module classes, as described in Section 6.4.

The attributes shown in Figure 6.6 have *instance scope*, meaning that each instance of the class can store a distinct value for the attribute. Some data describes not individual instances, however, but the collection of all current instances. For example, we might want to record the total number of modules known to the system. One way of doing this is shown in Figure 6.7.

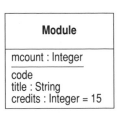

Figure 6.7 An attribute with class scope

Static field

An underlined attribute, such as 'mcount' in Figure 6.7 is said to have *class scope*. This means that there is a single copy of the attribute which is accessible to all instances of the class. Attributes with class scope correspond to static, or class, variables in programming languages.

Attributes can also have an explicitly defined multiplicity. The default multiplicity for an attribute is 'exactly one', implying that each instance of the class can store exactly one data value for each attribute. In some cases, this default is not appropriate, however. Suppose that the module class was extended with an attribute to record the date of an examination to be held at the end of the module. As some modules may not have such an examination, this attribute is optional in the sense that some instances of the class need not store a data value for it. This can be shown by adding a multiplicity specification after the attribute name, as shown in Figure 6.8.

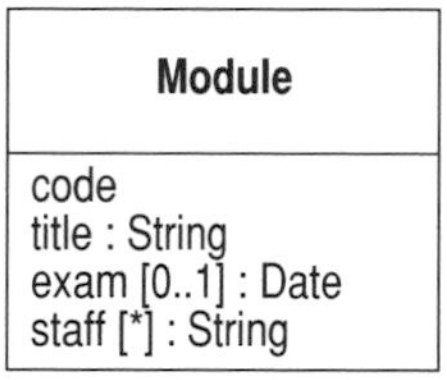

```
┌─────────────────────────┐
│         Module          │
├─────────────────────────┤
│ code                    │
│ title : String          │
│ exam [0..1] : Date      │
│ staff [*] : String      │
└─────────────────────────┘
```

Figure 6.8 Attribute multiplicity

Figure 6.8 also shows an attribute *staff* with a multiplicity of 'many', which is intended to store the names of the staff members involved in the delivery of the module. An attribute with a multiplicity greater than one is in many ways equivalent to an array, and this could also be specified directly by using an appropriate language type.

Operations

As well as attributes, operations can be shown in class icons. These operations are those that are provided by every instance of the class; the module class, for example, might provide operations to set and retrieve the module title and to enrol a student on the module. Operations are shown at the bottom of the class box, after the attributes, and separated from them by a horizontal line. Figure 6.9 shows the module class extended with the definition of a few possible operations.

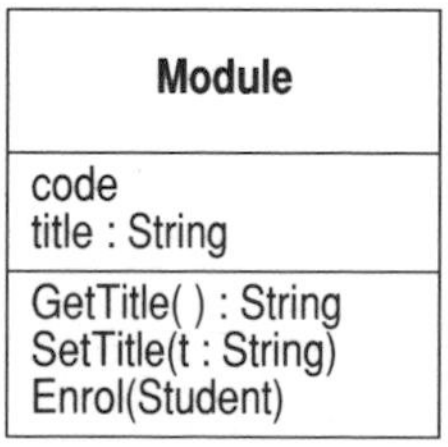

```
┌─────────────────────────┐
│         Module          │
├─────────────────────────┤
│ code                    │
│ title : String          │
├─────────────────────────┤
│ GetTitle( ) : String    │
│ SetTitle(t : String)    │
│ Enrol(Student)          │
└─────────────────────────┘
```

Figure 6.9 A module class with attributes and operations

Operations are named, and in addition can have arguments and return results, like functions in programming languages. The parameter and return types of operations can be either names of basic types, as used for specifying attribute types, or names of classes. As with attributes all the information apart from the operation's name is optional. As little or as much information can be provided as is appropriate at the stage that the development process has reached.

It is very common for operations to be omitted in class diagrams. The reason for this is that it is difficult to decide what operations a class should provide when the class is considered in isolation. The necessary operations are discovered by considering how the system's global behaviour is implemented by the network of objects making up the system. This analysis is performed when constructing the dynamic models of the system, and only towards the end of the design process would it be possible to compile a complete definition of the operations of a class.

The operations in Figure 6.9 have instance scope. This means that they apply to individual instances of the class, and can only be called once an instance has been created. Operations with class scope can also be defined, as shown in Figure 6.10. These apply to the class as a whole, rather than to instances.

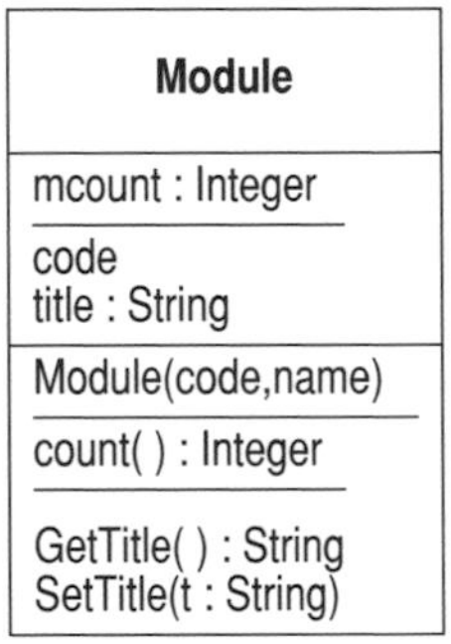

Module
mcount : Integer
code title : String
Module(code,name)
count( ) : Integer
GetTitle( ) : String SetTitle(t : String)

Figure 6.10 An operation with class scope

The most common example of an operation with class scope is the constructor of a class which is responsible for generating new instances of the class. A constructor is shown in Figure 6.10, following the convention that the constructor has the same name as the class. Also shown is an operation 'count' which returns the number of modules that currently exist. With the exception of constructors, operations with class scope can only access attributes which also have class scope, such as 'mcount' in this case.

Object identity

In Chapter 2, the notion of *object identity* was introduced as an essential part of the object model. An object's identity is an implicit part of the object which can be used to distinguish it from all other objects in the system. Every object existing when a system is running therefore must have a unique identity.

It is important to understand that the identity of an object is an internal property of the object model, and quite distinct from any of the attributes of the object. It is quite possible for two different objects to have the same values for all of their attributes, as shown in Figure 6.11. In this case the objects can still be told apart by means of their different identities.

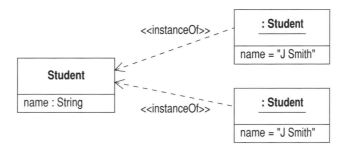

Figure 6.11 Identical but distinct objects

There are cases, however, where objects do have a unique identifying attribute. Students, for example, might have unique identification numbers that are allocated when they enrol for a course. The identification number is a real world piece of data, printed on a student's ID card. It is therefore quite appropriate for it to be included in the model as an attribute of the student class, as shown in Figure 6.12.

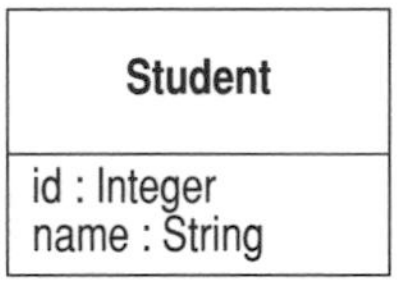

Figure 6.12 A class with an identifying attribute

In common with all class diagrams, Figure 6.12 does not explicitly show the identity possessed by all instances of the class. The identity should not be confused with an identifying attribute, such as the identification number, which happens to have a different value for each instance of the class. The identity of an object is an internal feature of the object model, not part of the data being modelled.

6.4 ASSOCIATIONS

The previous section explained how the different kinds of objects found in a system can be defined by classes. The other major structural feature of object diagrams is the existence of links between objects. In the same way that similar objects are grouped together and described by a single class, related links are described by a single construct, known as an *association*.

As explained in Chapter 2, a link between two objects models some sort of connection between the linked objects, such as a student taking a module. Normally, the idea expressed by a link can be described as a general relationship between the classes involved. In this case, the relationship is that it is possible for students to take modules. It is this more abstract relationship which is modelled by an association.

An association therefore connects two classes and describes a relationship between the classes. Associations are represented in UML as lines joining the related classes as shown in Figure 6.13, which shows an association modelling the fact that companies employ people.

Figure 6.13 An association modelling employment

The association is labelled with a name, 'WorksFor', which is shown near the middle of the association. Association names are often chosen so that, when taken in conjunction with the names of the related classes, something approaching a sensible English sentence describing the association results. In this case, the association represents the fact that people work for companies.

The arrowhead next to the association name indicates the direction in which this sentence should be read. It is necessary in this case because the 'opposite' association, that companies work for people, is a sensible, but quite distinct, relationship and it is necessary to distinguish the two.

Each end of the association is also labelled with a *role name*. Role names describe the class adjacent to them viewed in the context of a particular association. In this case, if a person works for a company, the person is known as the employee and the company as the employer. It is not obligatory in UML to include all, or indeed any of, these labels on an association. It is left to the designer's judgement to provide enough labelling to make the meaning of the association clear.

Associations specify links

The existence of an association between two classes indicates that instances of the classes can be linked at run-time. Figure 6.14 shows an example of a link that is specified by the association in Figure 6.13. As this diagram shows, association names and role names can be attached to links, but this is optional. It is usually sufficient to include labels which make it clear which association the link is an instance of.

Figure 6.14 An instance of the employment relationship

Self-associations

Although associations are typically binary, connecting two classes together, other forms are possible. UML allows associations to connect more that two classes, though in practice these are rarely used. In principle, any situation can be modelled using only binary associations, and binary associations are more easily implemented in conventional programming languages than those involving larger numbers of classes.

Binary associations often connect two distinct classes, but in practice there are also many situations where objects can be linked to other objects of the same class. These situations are modelled by using a *self-association*, a binary association both of whose ends are attached to the same class.

Figure 6.15 shows an example of a self-association and some possible links derived from it. The objects represent airports and the links represent the existence of a connecting flight between the linked airports.

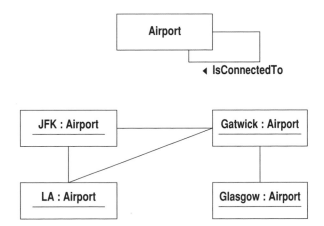

Figure 6.15 A self-association on a class

Multiplicity of associations

Each end of an association can be given a multiplicity. This multiplicity specifies how many objects an instance of the class at the other end of the association can be linked to. For example, Figure 6.16 shows the 'WorksFor' association with added multiplicity annotations. It now specifies that a person can work for exactly one company and also that a company can have zero or more employees.

Figure 6.16 An association with multiplicity annotations

As this example suggests, multiplicity annotations can be read in conjunction with role names, or the names of associated classes, to give a fuller description of the relationship being modelled by the association. The precise meaning of multiplicity annotations, however, is to do with the number of links that can exist at a given time.

For example, the association in Figure 6.16 specifies that any given instance of the Person class must be linked to exactly one instance of the Company class. It follows that the situation shown in Figure 6.17 is illegal on two counts: firstly, because the object representing John is simultaneously linked to two company objects, and secondly because the object representing Jane is not linked to any company object.

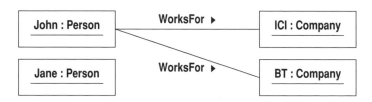

Figure 6.17 Violations of the multiplicity specification

Figure 6.16 also asserts that a company object must be linked to zero or more person objects. In fact, this places no restriction at all on the number of links a company object can have. If no multiplicity is specified, this is the default case.

Labelling associations

In general, multiplicity information should be shown on associations, but association names and role names are optional. The designer can choose the level of detail necessary to make the diagram easily comprehensible.

One situation where some textual labelling is required is where there is more than one association between the same pair of classes. In this case, labels are required to clarify the associations, and to ensure that the correct multiplicity is understood for each association. Figure 6.18 shows an additional association between the person and company classes, showing that people can be customers as well as employees of companies. Notice how the designer has here made the decision that one role name is sufficient labelling to make the meaning of each association clear.

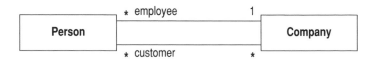

Figure 6.18 Distinguishing between pairs of associations

Role names are also very helpful in distinguishing between the two ends of a self-association, as shown in Figure 6.19.

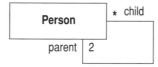

Figure 6.19 Distinguishing the ends of a self-association

Reifying associations

Consider the association 'WorksFor' shown in Figure 6.16, and suppose that a person is employed twice by the same company, in two different roles. An object diagram showing this possibility is given in Figure 6.20: perhaps John is employed as a lecturer during the day, for example, but has to work as a part-time bar attendant in the evenings to make ends meet.

Figure 6.20 Being employed by the same company twice

It is not clear at first sight whether the situation depicted in this object diagram is actually permitted by the given association. The multiplicity of the association states that John can only work for one company, but on one interpretation of the object diagram this property is preserved. John may have two contracts, but they are with the same company, so technically he only works for one company. On the other hand, John possesses two 'works for' links: this seems to allow for the possibility of working for more than one company, even though in this particular case both links shown are to the same object. On the first view, the object diagram in Figure 6.20 would be permissible, but on the second it would represent an erroneous state.

In general, an association can be interpreted in two different ways and the validity of the object diagram in Figure 6.20 depends on which interpretation is taken. The first interpretation regards a link as recording the fact that two objects are related. On this view, it is a matter of fact whether or not John is employed by a company: the existence of a link between the two objects asserts that John is employed, and the absence of a link implies that he is not. The existence of two links between a given pair of objects must on this view be taken as asserting the same fact twice. This is clearly redundant, and on this view the object diagram in Figure 6.20 would be considered to be illegal.

The alternative interpretation thinks of links as being entities in their own right. Each link between a pair of objects then asserts the existence of a separate entity, which in this case might be thought of as a contract. Thus two different links between the same pair of objects can be thought of as two distinct contracts. On this interpretation, the object diagram in Figure 6.20 would be a legitimate instance of the corresponding class diagram.

The difference between these approaches really comes down to the question of whether links have identity in the way that objects do. If they did, two different links between the same pair of objects would be distinguishable by the fact that they had different identities. If links have no identity, however, they can only be identified by looking at the objects linked. In this case it would be impossible to distinguish between two distinct links which connected the same pair of objects.

In common with other object-oriented design methodologies, UML assumes that links do not have identity. A link is simply a pair of objects, and it is impossible for the same pair of objects to be linked twice by the same association. In UML, therefore, the object diagram shown in Figure 6.20 is not a correct instance of the class diagram given in Figure 6.16.

There are situations, however, where the existence of multiple links between the same pair of objects seems to make sense. A standard way to model these situations is to replace the association with an intermediate class and two associations which link the new class to each of the original classes. In the example shown in Figure 6.20 the multiple links can be most naturally thought of as contracts of employment, and a revised class diagram which admits multiple contracts with the same company is shown in Figure 6.21.

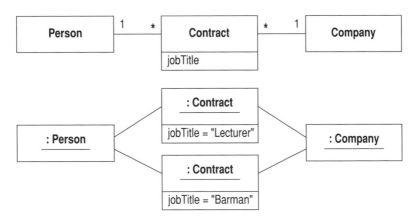

Figure 6.21 Resolving multiple links with an intermediate class

The class diagram of Figure 6.21 has not quite preserved the intended meaning of Figure 6.16, however. In the new model a person can hold multiple contracts, but there is nothing to prevent those contracts being with two distinct companies. This situation was not permitted in Figure 6.16, which only allowed a person to work for a single company. The restriction could be conveyed by adding a constraint to Figure 6.21, as explained in Chapter 9.

This technique of introducing a new linking class is often used in database design to get rid of many-to-many relationships. For each many-to-many relationship a new link class is introduced and the many-to-many relationship replaced by two one-to-many relationships, as in the transition from Figure 6.16 to Figure 6.21.

This is not standard practice in object-oriented modelling, where many-to-many associations are commonly used. The choice of which approach to use should be determined by the properties of the system being modelled, the aim being to produce as accurate a description as possible of the allowable states of affairs in the system.

6.5 THE NEED FOR GENERALIZATION

It is very common for an application to contain a number of classes that are closely related. The classes might either share a number of properties and relationships, or it might seem natural to think of them as representing different varieties of the same thing. For example, consider a bank which offers its customers a variety of accounts including current accounts, deposit accounts and an online account. One important aspect of the bank's operations is the fact that a customer can hold a number of accounts, which might be of different types. A class diagram modelling this is given in Figure 6.22.

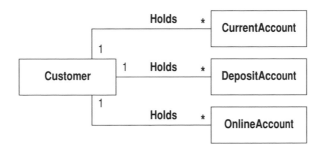

Figure 6.22 A class diagram modelling bank accounts

There are a couple of significant problems with this model, however. Firstly, there are too many associations in the model. From a customer's point of view, holding an account is a simple relationship which is not significantly affected by the fact that different kinds of account can be held. The model in Figure 6.22, however, models this with three distinct associations, thus destroying the conceptual simplicity of the model. Worse still, if a new type of account were added, a new association would also have to be added to the model to allow customers to hold accounts of the new type.

Secondly, the different kinds of account are modelled as completely separate classes. Nonetheless, they will probably have a large amount of common structure, as they are likely to define many similar attributes and operations. It would be highly desirable if our modelling notation could provide a way of explicitly showing this common structure.

These problems can be overcome by making use of the notion of *generalization*. This concept is provided by all object-oriented design notations, and is intimately related to the programming language concept of inheritance. Use of generalization will permit the model shown in Figure 6.22 to be redrawn in such a way as to meet both the objections discussed above.

6.6 GENERALIZATION AND SPECIALIZATION

Intuitively, what is going on in the bank account example is that we start with a general notion of what an account is and what is involved in holding an account. In addition to this, we can imagine a range of different kinds of accounts like the ones listed above which, despite their differences, all behave in very similar ways. The notion of generalization draws directly on this latter intuition: generalization is a relationship between classes in which one class is identified as a 'general' class and a number of others as special cases of it.

Figure 6.23 illustrates the way that generalization is shown in class diagrams. The commonality that exists between the different kinds of account is represented by introducing a new class into the diagram in addition to the original three account classes shown in Figure 6.23. This new class, called 'Account' in Figure 6.23 models the common features shared by the three specialized types of account.

The generalization relationship is represented by an arrow pointing from the specialized classes to the general class. The generalization relationships in Figure 6.23 could be shown as three separate arrows with exactly the same meaning. The layout used in Figure 6.23, where they are merged into a single arrow with more than one 'tail', is used to suggest that the specialized classes are alternatives to one another.

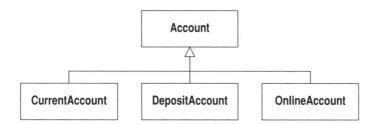

Figure 6.23 Bank account classes using generalization

In a generalization relation, the more general class is often referred to as the *superclass*, and the specialized classes as its *subclasses*. The relationship between superclass and subclass is, as above, usually referred to as generalization. This implies a perspective where one is moving from subclass to superclass, trying to create a more general class to represent some common features of a set of classes. Moving in the other direction, it is sometimes more natural to think of creating a set of subclasses reflecting special cases of a class. This process is known as *specialization*, and the relationship between classes as a specialization relationship. There is no technical difference between generalization and specialization, however: it is simply a question of the perspective the relationship is viewed from.

A generalization relationship is a pure relationship between classes, and does not specify any sort of link or relationship between instances of those classes. It therefore makes no sense to attach multiplicity symbols to a generalization relationship.

Generalization hierarchies

If required, specialization can be carried out to more than one level. Figure 6.24 shows an example of this where two distinct types of current account have been introduced: a personal account for individual customers and a business account for companies.

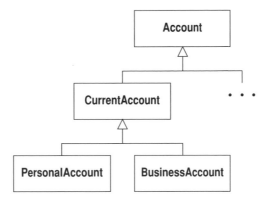

Figure 6.24 A generalization hierarchy

In Figure 6.24 the current account class is a subclass of 'Account', but a superclass of 'PersonalAccount'. The terms 'subclass' and 'superclass' are therefore relative, describing the role a class plays within a particular generalization relationship, rather than any intrinsic property of the class itself. The three dots in the diagram are called an *ellipsis*, and they indicate that there may be other subclasses in addition to those shown, in this case the other subclasses of 'Account' that were shown in Figure 6.23.

Such a hierarchy can be developed to as many levels as required. The *ancestors* of a class in the hierarchy are all the classes found by traversing the the hierarchy towards the top. Its *descendants* are those found by going downward in the hierarchy from the class. 'Up' and 'down' here mean 'towards more general classes' and 'towards more specialized classes' respectively. Although hierarchies are often drawn so that general classes come above their subclasses, there is nothing in the notation that demands this. The superclass is always the one pointed to by the triangle on the line linking the classes.

The meaning of generalization

A common account of the meaning of generalization is that it represents a classification relationship between classes, and in particular the relationship expressed by the phrase 'is a kind of'. So the fact that we can correctly say, for example, that a current account is a kind of account indicates that the classes are appropriately linked by a generalization relationship as shown in Figure 6.23.

This definition gives a very informal explanation of generalization, however, and is open to considerable misinterpretation. A more precise explanation is given by the notion of *substitutability*. For example, consider the association shown in Figure 6.25, which states that a customer can hold zero or more bank accounts.

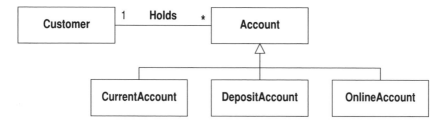

Figure 6.25 Holding various kinds of account

According to the explanation given in Section 6.4, the association in Figure 6.25 implies that instances of the customer and account classes can be linked at run-time. In fact, we would like this single association to permit links between instances of the customer class and any of the account classes. Some examples of the sort of flexibility required are shown in Figure 6.26.

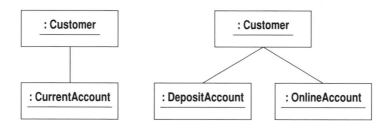

Figure 6.26 Different ways of holding accounts

Precisely this degree of flexibility is provided by the use of generalization in Figure 6.25. If one end of an association is attached to a class which is a superclass in a generalization relationship, instances of that association can link not only to instances of that class, but also to instances of any of its descendant classes, as shown in the object diagrams in Figure 6.26.

This is a specific example of the principle of substitutability, which states that an instance of a subclass can be substituted wherever an instance of a superclass is specified or expected. In the case above, the association specifies that customer objects should be linked to instances of the superclass 'Account', but by substitutability, these instances can be replaced at run-time by instances of any of the subclasses of the class 'Account', as shown in Figure 6.26.

This phenomenon is one form of *polymorphism*. Polymorphism means 'many forms' or 'many shapes', and is a pervasive feature of object-oriented programming languages. In this case, the many forms referred to are the many subclasses of the account class that a customer can in fact be linked to. The slightly surprising thing about it is that whereas the class diagram describes an association with a unique class, instances of the customer class can be linked to instances a range of other classes.

Abstract classes

Superclasses are often introduced into a model to define the shared features of a number of related classes. Their role is to permit overall simplification of a model, through use of the principle of substitutability, rather than to define an entirely new concept. As a result, it is not uncommon for there to be no need to create instances of the root class of a hierarchy, as all the objects required can be more precisely described as instances of one of the subclasses.

The account hierarchy provides an example of this. It is likely that in a banking system, every account must be either a current account, or a deposit account, or one of the other specialized types of account. This means that there are no instances of the root account class, or more precisely, that no instances of the 'Account' class should be created when the system is running.

A class, such as 'Account', which has no instances of its own is called an *abstract class*. Abstract classes are denoted in UML by writing the class name in a sloping typeface, as shown in Figure 6.27.

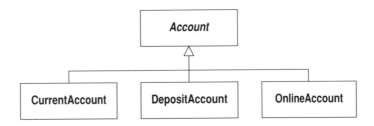

Figure 6.27 The account hierarchy with an abstract root class

It should not be thought that abstract classes, because they have no instances, are redundant and can be removed from class diagrams. The role of an abstract class, or of a root class in a hierarchy generally, is to define the common features of all its descendants. This can contribute significantly to the production of clear and well-structured class diagrams. Also, root classes define a common interface to all classes in a hierarchy, and use of this common interface can greatly simplify the programming of client modules. Abstract classes can provide these benefits just as well as concrete classes with instances.

6.7 INHERITANCE OF ATTRIBUTES AND OPERATIONS

An alternative way of expressing the principle of substitutability is by imposing the requirement that an instance of a subclass has all the properties specified by its superclass. If this is the case, it will not be possible to distinguish between superclass and subclass instances by using only properties specified in the superclass, and hence in any context which uses only these properties it will be quite safe to substitute subclass instances for superclass instances.

In the previous section, the property of interest was the ability to participate in links specified by a given association. Other properties of classes include the possession of various attributes and operations, and *inheritance* is the term normally used for the mechanism whereby these features are made available in subclass instances. This provides the means whereby the common structure shared by a number of classes can be defined in one place and yet made available in a number of different classes.

More precisely, all the attributes and operations defined in the ancestors of a class are also features of the class itself. They are said to have been *inherited* from the ancestor classes, and the process by which this is done is known as *inheritance*. To illustrate inheritance, Figure 6.28 shows part of the account hierarchy with attributes and operations added.

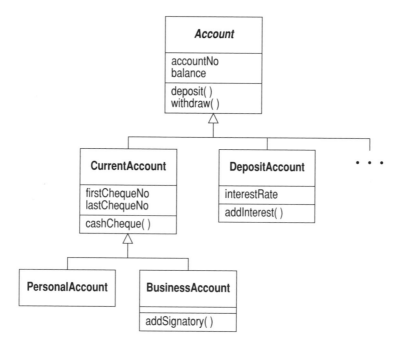

Figure 6.28 Account hierarchy with inheritance

This diagram states that all accounts have account number and balance attributes, and operations to deposit and withdraw amounts of money. These are the features that are assumed to be common to all the account classes in the hierarchy. They are defined in the root class 'Account', but are implicitly present in every other class in the hierarchy.

Inheritance, therefore, means that features shared by more than one class do not have to be written out in full in each class, but can be moved up the hierarchy to the appropriate superclass. In general, this has the effect of avoiding repetition and making hierarchies clearer and easier to read.

Adding features in subclasses

Subclasses are often distinguished from their superclass by the fact that they need to define additional features supporting their own particular specialized behaviour. For example, suppose that current accounts provide a cheque book facility. To implement this, instances of the current account class keep a record of the range of cheque numbers that have been issued for a given account. In addition, an operation is provided to draw a cheque against the account.

Business accounts are a further specialization of current accounts, distinguished by the fact that they are held by companies rather than by individuals. For a business account, it is therefore necessary to record the signatories of the account, namely the people who are permitted to sign cheques, and an operation is provided to add a new signatory to an account.

Additional attributes and operations supporting these requirements are shown in Figure 6.28. The full list of features defined for any class can be obtained by combining the inherited features with those defined in the class itself. For example, the attributes of the business account class are 'accountNo', 'balance', 'firstChequeNo', and 'lastChequeNo', and the operations supported by the class are 'deposit', 'withdraw', 'cashCheque' and 'addSignatory'.

Overriding operations in subclasses

The examples above have shown how, in the context of an inheritance hierarchy, a class can be defined by specifying the new attributes and operations that it requires in addition to those inherited from its ancestors. It sometimes happens, however, that instead of simply adding a new operation, a class requires a modified version of an operation that it has inherited.

For example, suppose that whenever a deposit or a withdrawal is made from an online account an email message is sent to the account holder to confirm the details of the transaction. To implement this, the online account class will have to redefine the deposit and withdraw operations to include this new functionality. Figure 6.29 shows the overriding of these two operations, together with the attribute storing the customer's email address.

When a class provides a redefinition of an inherited feature, it is said to *override* the inherited feature. Overriding is indicated by simply writing the name of the overridden feature in the subclass that redefines it, as shown in the online account class in Figure 6.29. Notice that it is not necessary to do this simply to indicate that a feature is inherited from a superclass.

The fact that a class overrides an inherited operation shows that the class will ultimately provide a different implementation of the operation from its superclass. Normally this implementation can gain access to the operation that is being overridden, but UML does not specify the way in which this happens.

Attributes can in principle also be overridden, but in practice the need for this is rare. Because of the demand for type consistency, the only thing that could be changed in an overridden attribute is the initial value provided.

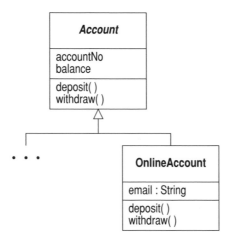

Figure 6.29 Partial account hierarchy, overriding the withdraw operation

Abstract operations

Some abstract classes include operations for which an implementation cannot be given at that point in the hierarchy. For example, a classic example of generalization is shown in Figure 6.30. This hierarchy represents various shapes that might be defined in a graphics system.

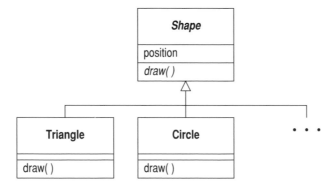

Figure 6.30 Hierarchy of shapes, with abstract class and operation

The root class 'Shape' will define properties common to all shapes, such as a position, and also the operations that all shapes must provide, such as an operation to draw the shape. 'Shape' is an abstract class, however, as it is impossible to have a shape which is not either a triangle, a circle, or one of the other kinds of shape provided by the system. Furthermore, it is impossible to give an implementation of a general draw operation for shapes. Each subclass needs to define this operation for itself, by invoking the appropriate graphics primitives. Nevertheless, the draw operation should be part of the shape class, to indicate that it is provided by all descendants of 'Shape'. To indicate that it is unimplementable, it is written in a sloping font, as shown in Figure 6.30.

Such an operation is known as an *abstract operation*, and any class containing an abstract operation must be an abstract class. An abstract operation must be overridden in descendant classes by a non-abstract operation, as shown in Figure 6.30. Any class which does not either contain or inherit an operation which overrides an inherited abstract operation is itself an abstract class.

6.8 ASSOCIATION GENERALIZATION

Suppose it was the case that a customer could hold at most one account of each type offered by the bank. The class diagram in Figure 6.25 does not accurately model this situation, as it allows any number of accounts of any kind to be held simultaneously. One attempt to model the situation more accurately is shown in Figure 6.31. Unfortunately, this diagram asserts that a customer can hold at most one account. Polymorphism guarantees that this account could in fact be an instance of any of the account subclasses, but there is no way that more that one account could be held at any one time.

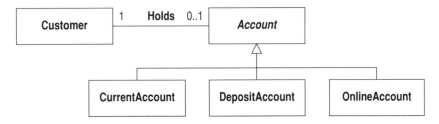

Figure 6.31 An erroneous way of modelling 'at most one account of each kind'

One way of expressing the required constraint would be to supplement Figure 6.25 with informal textual annotations stating the desired restriction. Textual annotations on class diagrams are frequently used to express shades of meaning that cannot be captured by the graphical notation. These annotations are known as *constraints*, and are discussed in more detail in Chapter 9.

An alternative approach might be to attempt to override the association in the case of subclasses, in much the same way as attributes and operations of superclasses can be overridden in subclasses. Figure 6.32 shows an attempt to do this.

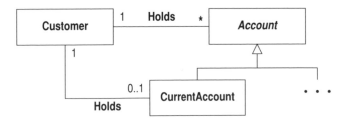

Figure 6.32 Trying to override an association

The meaning of this diagram is rather obscure, however, and the effect is certainly not what is required for the scenario sketched above. What has been defined is a completely new association linking customers to current accounts, in addition to the original, inherited association which links customers to accounts of any sort. This would enable customers optionally to hold a current account in addition to any other accounts they might hold by way of the original association. The situation further is confused by the fact that both associations have the same name. In this case, presumably, the additional association is quite pointless.

One way of describing the problem is to notice that, just as current accounts are a special case of accounts, so the property of holding a current account is a special case of holding an account generally. This leads naturally to the thought that the 'Holds' association connecting customers to high interest accounts in Figure 6.32 is a specialization of the upper one. This relationship can be indicated by linking the two associations with a generalization arrow, as shown in Figure 6.33.

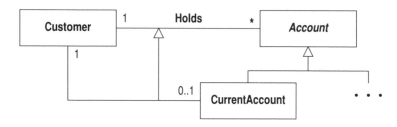

Figure 6.33 Association generalization

Figure 6.33 can be understood as follows: customers can hold many accounts, as before, and those accounts can be of any kind. Any links between a customer and a current account, however, should be understood as being described by the specialized association which in this case limits the number of current accounts that can be linked to a customer to be at most one.

Parallel hierarchies

A second situation in which association generalization is useful is where an association connects the root classes in two parallel class hierarchies, but where there are also constraints on which subclasses can be associated together. In some situations, these constraints can be represented by additional associations connecting the relevant subclasses, which are defined as specializations of the general association.

For example, the diagram in Figure 6.34 shows a simplified account hierarchy, together with a customer hierarchy which describes a distinction between individual and institutional customers. The diagram shows that only individuals can hold current accounts and that business accounts can only be held by institutional customers. Without the use of association generalization, the model in Figure 6.34 would allow any type of customer to hold any type of account.

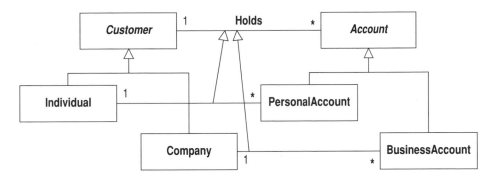

Figure 6.34 An overly permissive model of account holding

The situations in which association generalization is applicable are common, and it is important to understand why the constraints it expresses cannot be captured using simple associations. In many cases, however, it may be clearer to express these constraints textually rather than using the notation of association generalization which, as Figure 6.34 shows, is visually rather complex.

6.9 AGGREGATION

Associations can be used to model any sort of relationship between objects, and the name of the association gives information about precisely what relationship is being modelled. In common with many design notations, however, UML singles out one particular relationship for special treatment, namely the 'part of' relationship that holds between objects when one is a part of another, or inversely, when an object consists of a collection of other objects.

Figure 6.35 shows a typical example of aggregation, in which an electronic mail message is specified as containing a header, a body and an unspecified number of attachments. As all three of these items can be considered to be parts of the message, the associations linking the classes are further specified to be aggregations. Aggregation is symbolized by adding a diamond symbol to the association end next to the class representing the object which 'contains' the objects at the other end.

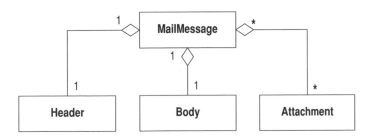

Figure 6.35 An example of aggregation

As Figure 6.35 shows, multiplicity annotations can be used on aggregation relationships in exactly the same way as on normal associations. As well as indicating the different number of headers, body and attachments in a single message, the multiplicities specified in Figure 6.35 also show that, unlike headers and bodies, an attachment can be a part of more than one message simultaneously.

The meaning of aggregation

In cases like this, the use of aggregation achieves little more than suggesting informally that objects of one kind form part of objects of another kind, in some sense. It imposes no constraints on a model in addition to those already implied by the use of an association, and if there is any doubt about the applicability of aggregation, a good rule is simply to leave it out.

One case where aggregation does have a useful role to play is if the objects in a system are arranged, at run-time, in a hierarchical manner. An example of this was given in the stock control system discussed in Chapter 2. In that system, a general notion of a component was defined: a component could either be a single part, or an assembly consisting of a number of subcomponents. The class diagram in Figure 2.10 defined the relationships between these classes. However, object structures such as the ones shown in Figure 6.36 are perfectly legal instances of the model of Figure 2.10.

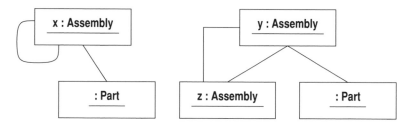

Figure 6.36 Cyclical object structures

The problem with the object structures shown in Figure 6.36 is that they show an assembly that is a part of itself, directly or indirectly. This is not a meaningful notion when applied to physical objects such as parts and assemblies, and also means that any operation which traverses the part hierarchy will loop. These problems can be removed by the use of aggregation, as shown in Figure 6.37.

Two properties of aggregation mean that the object structures in Figure 6.36 are not legal instances of the class diagram in Figure 6.37. The first property is *antisymmetry*, which simply means that a link which is an instance of an aggregation cannot be used to link an object to itself. This rules out the first situation shown in Figure 6.36 where the assembly named *x* is linked to itself.

The second property is called *transitivity*: in informal terms this is explained by the observation that if A is a part of B, and B is a part of C, then A is also a part of C. More formally, if object A is linked to B and B to C by links which are instances of the same aggregation, then A should also be thought of as linked to C.

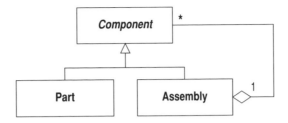

Figure 6.37 Specifying acyclic structures

The properties of aggregation work together in the following way to rule out the second possibility shown in Figure 6.36. As y is linked to z, and z to y (by a different link), the property of transitivity implies that y should be thought of as being linked to itself. However, this is the situation that antisymmetry deems to be illegal, showing that the situation depicted is not a legal state of the system.

Aggregation therefore has a useful role to play in specifying that legal states of a system should not include cyclical object structures. However, these properties of aggregation do not necessarily have anything to do with the intuitive idea of a relationship between wholes and parts. For example, consider the associations shown in Figure 6.38. The ancestor association can correctly be shown as an aggregation, as it has the property of transitivity: one's ancestors' ancestors are also one's own ancestors. By making it an aggregation rather than a plain association, we can assert that nobody can be one of their own ancestors. However, it is implausible to suggest that in any sense people are parts of their ancestors.

Figure 6.38 The applicability of aggregation

Although we would like to impose the same kind of restriction on the 'father' association, as nobody can be their own father, we are prevented from doing so by the transitivity property of aggregations. One's father's father is one's grandfather, not one's father as would be required if the relationship was to be transitive. This suggests that the semantics of the 'parent' relationship cannot be accurately modelled using the simple notation of UML.

Finally, it should be noted the properties of antisymmetry and transitivity described above only apply in cases where the aggregation enables objects to be linked to instances of their own class. This will happen when the aggregation is a self-association as in the case of the ancestor relation, or where a generalization enables recursive object structures to be created, as in the case of assemblies. For straightforward cases of intuitive whole–part relationships, such as those illustrated in Figure 6.35, aggregation specifies nothing more than a straightforward association would.

6.10 COMPOSITE OBJECTS

Composition is a strong form of association in which the 'part' objects are dependent on the 'whole' objects. This dependency manifests itself in two ways. Firstly, a 'part' object can only belong to one composite at a time, and secondly, when a composite object is destroyed, all its dependent parts must be destroyed at the same time.

In the example of the email message given in Figure 6.35, it might be reasonable to model the relationships between a message and its header and body as composition relationships, as it is likely that neither a header nor a body exist once a message has been deleted, and while they exist they belong to a single message. As shown in Figure 6.39, the notation for composition is similar to that for aggregation, except that the diamond at the 'whole' end of the relationship is solid.

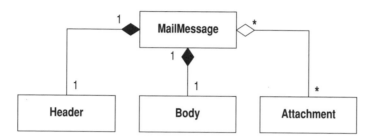

Figure 6.39 The use of composition

The relationship between a message and its attachments is unlikely to be correctly modelled using composition, however. Firstly, the diagram asserts that an attachment can belong to more than one message at the same time, and secondly, it is likely that attachments can be saved, and therefore they will have a lifetime that exceeds that of the message that they are attached to.

This basic notion of composition is not strong enough to enforce certain natural properties of composite objects, however. For example, consider the class diagram in Figure 6.40, which gives a simple model of certain aspects of a computer. It states that a computer is a composition of a processor and a number of ports, and that the ports must be connected to the processor.

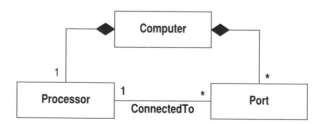

Figure 6.40 The structure of a computer

Figure 6.41 illustrates one situation permitted by this model, where a port which is part of one computer is connected to a processor which is part of a different computer. On a natural view of the physical relationships being modelled here, this situation is simply meaningless. Clearly, the parts of a computer make up that computer by virtue of being attached to each other and the use of composition was meant to model this fact.

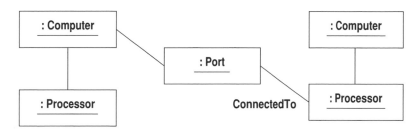

Figure 6.41 An impossible situation

To model this, we need a way of stating that the association between ports and processors is also encapsulated with the composite objects representing computers. This can be depicted by drawing the classes and associations that form part of the composite inside the class icon for the computer, as shown in Figure 6.42.

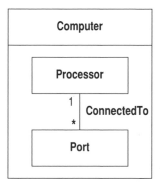

Figure 6.42 The computer as a composite object

The meaning of this diagram is that associations inside a composite object can only link objects which are part of the same composite. There are implied associations linking the composite class and the classes within it, so the diagram of Figure 6.42 is basically a stronger form of Figure 6.40, with added semantics sufficient to rule out the kind of object diagram shown in Figure 6.41.

There are of course cases where it is desirable to link parts of different composites. For example, consider a number of computers linked together into a network. The physical linkage might be accomplished by connecting pairs of ports, and this could be modelled by means of an association on the port class in the class diagram.

If this association was drawn entirely within the 'computer' composite object box, however, this would have the implication that ports could only be connected if they belonged to the same computer, as explained above. If we are trying to model a network, however, this is clearly not what we want, as the whole point of the model is to show links between different computers.

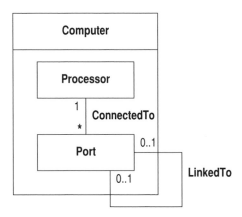

Figure 6.43 Connecting computers together

To show this possibility, the association for linking ports has to be drawn in such a way that it passes outside the composite object box, as shown in Figure 6.43. This means that the ports linked by the relationship can belong to different composite objects, as required.

6.11 ASSOCIATION CLASSES

Attributes describe properties of the instances of a class. A student class might have an attribute 'name', for example, and then every student object would contain a data value giving the name of the student. Sometimes, however, it is necessary to record information that is more naturally associated with the link between two objects than with either of the objects considered individually.

For example, consider the association between students and the modules they take shown in Figure 6.44 and assume that the system needs to record all the marks gained by students on all the modules that they are taking. The class diagram notation introduced so far does not enable us to model this situation very easily.

Figure 6.44 A simple model for recording exam results

For example, it is not sufficient to add a 'mark' attribute to the student class, as students in general take many modules and therefore it will be necessary to record more than one mark for each student. An attribute which allowed a set of marks to be stored would get round this problem, but would not preserve the information about which mark was gained for which module.

It would be undesirable to try to resolve the problem by having student objects identify the modules by explicitly storing some kind of module identifier. This would duplicate some of the information modelled by the existing association, and would introduce potentially significant problems of consistency checking, because of the duplication of the module code information within the model.

Because each module can be taken by many students, the same problems arise if we consider storing the marks that students receive for a module in the module object itself. It therefore appears that not all the data in a system can easily be modelled as attributes of classes. What is required is some way of associating data with the link between two objects rather than with either of the individual objects. Intuitively this makes sense in the current case: an exam mark is not something that a student has in isolation, but is rather something that follows from the fact that the student took a particular module or, in other words, was linked to it.

Association classes provide a means of associating data values with links. An association class is a single model element in UML, which merges the properties of both associations and classes. In particular, an association class can, like an association, link two classes and yet at the same time have attributes, like a class, to store data belonging specifically to the link.

Figure 6.45 shows an association class enabling the mark a student receives for a module to be stored. This replaces the association 'Takes' defined in Figure 6.44. The name of an association class can be written either next to the association, or in the class part of the notation, which is connected to the association by a dashed line. The choice of whether to label the association class with a verb, in the style of an association, or with a noun, in the style of a class, is left to the discretion of the designer, but will often depend on whether the label is written in the class icon, or near the association.

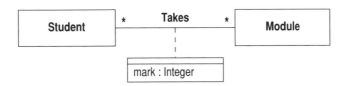

Figure 6.45 An association class

The meaning of an association class is that appropriate attribute values will be associated with every link corresponding to the association part of the construct, one value for each attribute defined in the class part of the construct. Association classes very often have a many-to-many multiplicity, as with the example in Figure 6.45. They can equally well be used in other circumstances, however. Consider the class diagrams in Figure 6.46 which show two different ways to model employees' salaries.

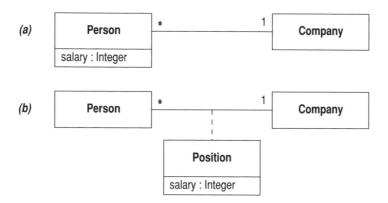

Figure 6.46 Two ways of modelling salary

A company employs many people, each of whom has a particular salary. Because the diagram states that each person only works for one company, there is only one salary to store per person. It could be argued that in this case the objections raised in the case of students' marks do not apply, and so salary could be modelled as an attribute of the person class, as shown in Figure 6.46(a). Strictly speaking, this is true. There are, however, good reasons for preferring an alternative model using an association class, as shown in Figure 6.46(b).

Firstly, it can be argued that Figure 6.46(b) is simply a more accurate reflection of the real world situation being modelled. People only have salaries because they hold a certain position within a company, and the salary a person receives is normally defined by the position they hold. A salary is not an intrinsic property of a person, and should not be modelled as an attribute of the person class but rather as an attribute of the link between instances of these classes.

There are more practical issues as well. If the system evolved in such a way that the multiplicity of the association changed, the model of Figure 6.46(a) could cause significant maintenance problems. Suppose that the system was extended to store information about the dependents of the company's employees. These people are not themselves employees, and so an 'optional' multiplicity would have to be introduced at the company end of the association. The salary attribute would now be meaningless for those people who were not employees.

Alternatively, the multiplicity of the association might be changed to many-to-many, perhaps if all the individual companies within a large conglomerate were included, and employees were permitted to work for more than one company. In this case, it would be necessary to use an association class, for the same reasons that applied in the student mark example. The costs of modifying the system to implement such a change could be very large, however.

Using association classes even when they are not strictly necessary can therefore introduce a measure of flexibility into a model, and potentially increase the maintainability of the resulting system.

Associations and association classes

Association classes share the properties of both associations and classes.
that, as well as enabling data values to be stored with links, association c
enable an association to participate in further associations, just as classes can

For example, suppose that students have to register explicitly for modules that they wish to take. The information associated with each registration might include the mark the student gains for the module and the semester in which the module is taken. A class, in the sense of a group of students who are taught together, might then be defined as a set of registrations, namely those for all the students registered to take a particular module in a particular semester.

This situation could be modelled by using an association to identify the registrations that correspond to a particular class, as shown in Figure 6.47. Notice that the semester of a registration is recorded structurally, by means of a link to the appropriate instance of the class representing classes.

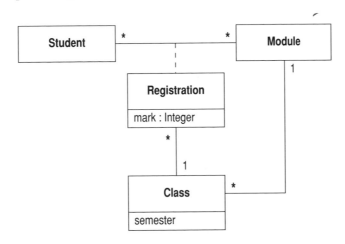

Figure 6.47 An association class participating in an association

Now, suppose that a particular course allows a student to register more than once for the same module. Perhaps if the module is failed, the student is allowed to retake it. The models in Figures 6.45 and 6.47 do not allow for this possibility. Even when an association class is used, as in Figure 6.47, it is only possible for a student to register once for a given module. If we allow for the possibility of retakes, however, we need the ability to link the same student and module objects more than once.

This problem has already been discussed in Section 6.4 in connection with multiple contracts of employment with the same company. The fact that the links are described by an association class does not alter the fact that only one link is permitted between any given pair of objects. As before, we need to replace the direct association class by a pair of associations, the first linking a student to (many) registrations and the second linking each registration to a single module.

6.12 QUALIFIED ASSOCIATIONS

Consider the following example, which is based on certain details of a Unix-like file system. The file system contains a number of files which are known to the system by means of a unique internal identifier which is quite distinct from any file name seen by the user. From the user's point of view, files can be named and placed in directories. A file can appear in more than one directory, and a different name can be given to a file each time it appears in a directory. A file can even appear in a single directory more than once, provided that a different name is used for each occurrence, thus giving users many ways to access the same file. Within a directory each name can only be used once. The same name can be used in many directories, however, and need not identify the same file in each case.

The basic relationship between files and directories can therefore be modelled by a many-to-many association: a directory can hold many files, and a file can appear in many directories. The name by which a file is known is not an attribute of the file object; files do not even have unique names, but instead a name is assigned each time a file appears in a directory. The name of a file is therefore an attribute of the link between a file and a directory, and it is therefore natural to attempt to model the situation using an association class containing the file name, as shown in Figure 6.48.

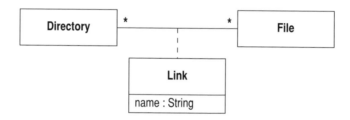

Figure 6.48 A simple model of Unix file names

There are two ways in which this diagram is an inaccurate reflection of the facts of the situation, however. Firstly, it does not express the fact that file names must be distinct within a directory. It would be quite possible according to the model for all the files linked to a particular directory to have the same value for the 'name' attribute.

Secondly, Figure 6.48 does not allow for the possibility of multiple links between the same file and directory. A given file can appear in a directory more than once, under different names. As discussed in Section 6.4, however, the semantics of associations only permit one link between a given pair of objects.

Both problems can be resolved by using a *qualifier*, as shown in Figure 6.49. Qualifiers are used in cases where some piece of information can be used as a key to uniquely identify one out of a set of objects. The relevant properties of a key are that in a given context each key value can appear only once, and must somehow identify a single object which is described by the key. In this example, the file name acts as a key. A context is provided by a directory, within which a key value (file name) can only appear once. Each file name in a directory names a unique file.

Figure 6.49 Modelling file names with a qualifier

An attribute of an association class which has properties which enable it to act as a key is known in UML as a *qualifier*. Qualifiers are written next to the class which defines the context within which values of the qualifiers pick out objects. The qualifier is written in a small box adjoining one of the classes in the association. The association line is connected to the qualifier box rather than the class, as shown in Figure 6.49, and the normal range of multiplicity symbols can be used on the association.

Part of the meaning of Figure 6.49 is the same as that of Figure 6.48, namely that files and directories are connected by a many-to-many relationship of containment, and that a name is given to each occurrence of a file in a directory. The association in Figure 6.49 does not look like a many-to-many relationship, however: the multiplicity at the file end is 'optional', not 'many'. Figure 6.50 gives an informal illustration of how a qualifier might be implemented; note that the notation used here to illustrate the way in which qualifier values might be stored is not part of UML.

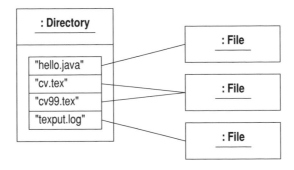

Figure 6.50 Qualifiers at run-time

Intuitively, the meaning of a qualified association is that instances of the class with the qualifier maintain a mapping from qualifier values to instances of the class at the other end of the association. In this case, each directory will maintain a mapping from file names to file objects.

The multiplicity at the far end of a qualified association refers to the number of objects, instances of 'File' in this case, which can be 'linked' to each value of the qualifier. In Figure 6.49 this multiplicity is zero or one, which means every file name in the mapping must be linked to one file object, but that not every possible file name need appear in the mapping. The ones that do not appear are those to which the zero multiplicity applies: as they do not appear in the mapping, no file can be associated with them. If the directory object is considered as a whole, however, it is clear from Figure 6.50 that directories can still contain many files

The use of a qualified association in Figure 6.49 addresses both the problems that were identified in Figure 6.48 above. The fact that file names must be distinct within a directory is guaranteed by the fact that each possible file name can only appear once in a mapping contain within a directory object. There is nothing to prevent more than one file name being linked to the same file object, however, thus dealing with the second problem noted above.

Qualifiers and identifiers

Qualifiers are often used in connection with attributes which serve to identify objects in the real world. For example, Figure 6.51 shows part of a student registration system where students are known to the university, and each student is given a unique identification number.

Figure 6.51 An identifying attribute

This model does not make it clear that the identification number for every student is unique, however. To include this constraint on the diagram, it would be normal to rewrite the attribute as a qualifier on the university class, as shown in Figure 6.52.

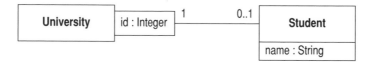

Figure 6.52 Identifiers as qualifiers

Because of object identity, it is never necessary to introduce attributes containing unique identifiers into a data model simply to distinguish different instances of a class. Where they exist in the real world, however, they should be included and can often be modelled using qualifiers.

6.13 MULTIPLE INHERITANCE

All the examples of generalization considered so far have contained classes which inherit from only one superclass. This situation is known as *single inheritance* and is by far the most common use of generalization. It is also possible, however, for a class to have more than one superclass. This phenomenon is universally known as *multiple inheritance*, although in the context of UML at least, the term 'multiple generalization' would be more logical.

The purest form of multiple inheritance involves a class which is a subclass of two completely unrelated superclasses. Suppose that an office automation system provides two major applications. The first enables documents of various kinds to be word processed and printed, and involves a generalization hierarchy with an abstract root class 'Document' representing various forms of document, such as reports, notes and memos. The second application deals with the sending of messages between the users of the system. It deals with a hierarchy with abstract root class 'Message', which again has various subclasses describing the different kinds of message handled.

In general, the objects classified by these two hierarchies are distinct: certain forms of document, such as notes, are not usefully thought of as messages, whereas some messages, such as phone calls and electronic mail messages have no existence as documents. It is possible to imagine cases, however, where a classification as a document or as a message might seem equally appropriate. For example, a memo is a message which also has a physical existence as a document. In Figure 6.53 this property is modelled by making the 'Memo' class a subclass of both 'Document' and 'Message', to indicate this shared nature.

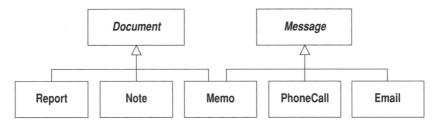

Figure 6.53 Multiple inheritance

In simple cases like this, the semantics of multiple inheritance are basically the same as ordinary generalization. Classes like 'Memo' which have more than one superclass inherit the attributes and operations of all of their superclasses, and can participate in associations connected to any of the superclasses. The only possible source of confusion is in cases where attributes or operations with the same name are inherited from more than one superclass. This situation is known as a *name clash*. In this example, it is plausible that both documents and messages might have an attribute 'date'. UML does not rule out the use of multiple inheritance in cases like these, but does demand that some account is given of how the ambiguity is to be resolved. In this case, the two dates could be renamed as 'date of writing' and 'date of sending'.

Inheriting from a common ancestor

A slightly more complex example of multiple inheritance is shown in Figure 6.54, which depicts another variation of the bank account hierarchy introduced earlier. Here the class of all accounts is divided first between those accounts which provide cheque book facilities and those which pay interest. Concrete account classes are depicted on the next level of the hierarchy

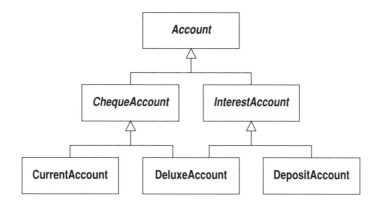

Figure 6.54 Multiple inheritance with a common ancestor

It is quite possible, of course, for some accounts both to pay interest and to provide cheque book facilities. This is the case with the 'deluxe' account class in Figure 6.54, which is shown to be a subclass of both the immediate subclasses of 'Account'. The significant difference between this case and that shown in Figure 6.53 is that both the superclasses of 'Deluxe Account' inherit from the base 'Account' class, whereas in Figure 6.53 the two parent hierarchies of the 'Memo' class were quite distinct.

An interesting point about Figure 6.54 concerns the way in which 'Deluxe Account' inherits the attributes and operations of the base 'Account' class. It might be thought that as both the superclasses of 'Deluxe Account' inherit from 'Account', so 'Deluxe Account' would inherit *two* copies of all the attributes and operations of 'Account'. In this case, this would clearly be undesirable: we do not want to inherit two account number attributes, for example, or two deposit operations. The approach followed by UML prevents such duplication of attributes and operations. In a case of 'repeated inheritance', where there are two or more paths in the inheritance hierarchy from a class to a given superclass, only one copy of the attributes and operations of that superclass are inherited.

Mixins

Another approach to modelling the situation described in Figure 6.54 makes use of a technique known as *mixins*, and in this case avoids the complications of repeated inheritance and overlapping generalization. A mixin is an abstract class which is intended to be used to add a fairly discrete piece of functionality to an existing concrete class. The term 'mixin' is meant to suggest mixing in a new piece of functionality to that already provided by the class.

In this case, we might notice that providing a cheque book facility for an account is a fairly independent piece of functionality that does not affect the remainder of an account's specification. It is necessary to add attributes to record which cheques have been issued for an account, and an operation to cash a cheque, but these operations do not interact significantly with the other operations of the account classes.

A class diagram illustrating this approach is shown in Figure 6.55. The account hierarchy has been somewhat simplified, in that the current account class is now an immediate subclass of the base class. The added functionality for providing a cheque book is inherited independently from a new mixin class 'Cheque Book'.

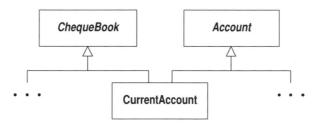

Figure 6.55 An example of a mixin class

This model provides a clear separation between the two aspects of the current account class, and the cheque facility mixin class can clearly be reused with other classes, such as deluxe accounts, that also require cheque books.

Discriminators

There are some situations when a given class can meaningfully be classified along more than one dimension. For example, consider the documents handled by the office automation system described earlier. From the point of view of a company's record keeping systems, documents might be divided into those which need to be archived, and those which do not. The archivable documents might include reports and memos, whereas notes are intended as temporary records and do not need to be archived. Figure 6.56 shows the relevant generalization relationship, and shows that the archive consists only of the permanent documents.

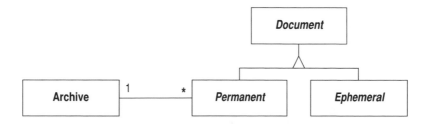

Figure 6.56 Classifying documents for archiving purposes

The company's billing system, on the other hand, might need to distinguish between chargeable documents, such as reports prepared for clients, and non-chargeable documents, such as proposals and internal memos. An account held for a particular client would only record details of chargeable documents prepared for that particular client. A class diagram showing this situation is given in Figure 6.57.

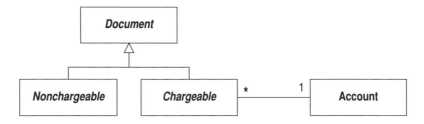

Figure 6.57 Classifying documents for billing purposes

The salient point about Figure 6.56 and Figure 6.57 is that the base document class is being specialized in two independent ways, for two distinct purposes. To distinguish the two, the generalization relationships can be described by means of *discriminators*. A discriminator is a label for a generalization which gives an informal idea of the property being used to distinguish the subclasses, and a name which can be used to refer to the generalization later.

Figure 6.58 combines the generalizations shown in Figures 6.56 and 6.57 into a single diagram, using the discriminators 'lifetime' and 'financial status' to distinguish between them. The generalizations that are labelled with the same discriminator can be thought of as mutually exclusive alternatives. Concrete descendant classes of 'Document' must specialize exactly one class from each of the discriminator families. For example, the memo class is a specialization of 'Ephemeral' from the lifetime discriminator, and 'Nonchargeable' from the financial status discriminator.

6.14 SUMMARY

- Static models describe structural relationships between the data in a system. Object diagrams show the objects at a given instance and of the links between them.
- Class diagrams show the general properties that a system's data must satisfy at all times. Given a class diagram, we can decide whether an object diagram represents a possible state of the system being specified or not.
- Classes describe the different kinds of object in a system. As well as a name, classes have attributes and operations which describe the state and behaviours of the objects which are instances of the class, namely those objects described by it.
- Links between objects are defined by associations on a class diagram. Associations show which classes can be connected by a given kind of link and how many objects a given object can be linked to. This information is given by means of multiplicity annotations. Associations can be labelled and have a role name at each end.
- Generalization defines a relationship between classes where any instance of one class, the subclass, can be substituted for, or treated as if it was, an instance of another class, the superclass. A given class can have any number of mutually exclusive subclasses. This process can be carried out as often as required, giving rise to generalization hierarchies.

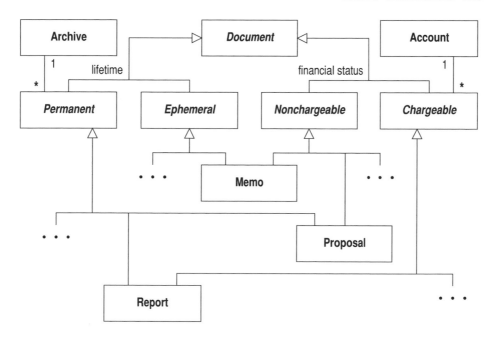

Figure 6.58 Classifying documents using parallel generalization

- The attributes and operations of a superclass are inherited by its subclasses. Sub-classes can define additional attributes and operations to express their specialized properties. If necessary, the definitions of inherited operations can be overridden in a subclass.

- An association to a class can be instantiated by links to instances of any of its subclasses. This leads to polymorphism where a single association can in fact specify links between objects of different classes.

- Abstract classes are classes which are intended to have no instances. They represent a partial concept, and are introduced to help structure a generalization hierarchy.

- The properties of an association on a superclass can be refined for that class's subclasses by using association generalization.

- In some cases, information in a class diagram is better thought of as belonging to a link than to an individual object. This can be modelled by making use of association classes. Association classes share the properties of both associations and classes, and can participate in further associations if required.

- Qualified associations can be used in the situation where a piece of data acts as a key whereby objects of an associated class can be retrieved.

- Aggregation is a specialized form of association intended to capture the semantics of the whole–part relationship. One common use of aggregation was discussed, namely to prohibit loops and cycles in object diagrams.

- Composition represents a strong form of aggregation where the lifetimes of instances of one class are contained within those of another.

- Multiple inheritance describes situations where a class has two or more immediate superclasses. Attributes and operations of all superclasses are inherited normally, but in a name clash occurs as a result of this process, the model is considered to be ill-formed.
- A single class can participate as superclass in two or more generalization relationships simultaneously; this situation is known as parallel generalization. Discriminators can be used to clarify the aspect being used for specialization in each case.

6.15 EXERCISES

6.1 Draw UML class and object icons representing each of the following. Assume that the basic types of your favourite programming language are available to specify attribute types.

(a) A class representing a position, with attributes giving the x and y coordinates of a point. Also show two instances of this class, the origin, with coordinates $(0, 0)$, and the point $(100, -40)$.

(b) A class representing a counter with operations to set or reset the counter to zero, to increment and decrement the value stored by a specified amount, and to return the current value.

(c) A class representing a switch which can be turned on or off.

6.2 Draw the class diagram corresponding to Figure 6.47 which would correctly model the situation where a student could take a given module more than once.

6.3 Define multiplicities for the following associations:

(a) 'Has on loan', linking people to books in a library system.

(b) 'Has read', linking people to books.

(c) 'Is occupying', linking chess pieces to squares on a chess board.

(d) 'Spouse', linking class 'Person' to itself.

(e) 'Parent', linking class 'Person' to itself.

6.4 In Figure Ex6.4, state which of the object diagrams are legitimate instances of the class diagram given. Assume that all links in the object diagrams are instances of the association in the corresponding class diagram. If an object diagram is not a legitimate instance, explain why not.

6.5 Repeat question 1 for the diagrams given in Figure Ex6.5.

6.6 Companies may employ many people, and people may work for many companies. Each company has a managing director, and every employee in a company has a manager, who may manage many subordinate employees. Add suitable labelling to the class diagram in Figure Ex6.6 to make this intended meaning clear.

6.7 In Figure Ex6.7, state which of the object diagrams are valid instances of the class diagram given. If an object diagram is not a valid instance, explain why not.

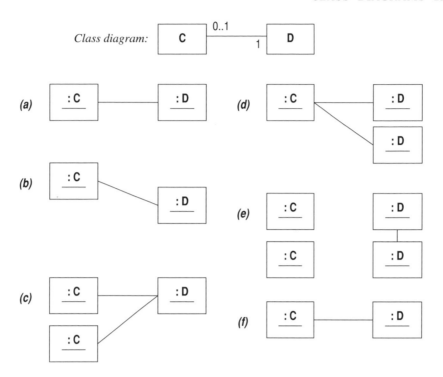

Figure Ex6.4 An 'optional' association and some candidate object diagrams

6.8 Figure Ex6.8 models some aspects of a file system where directories contain subdirectories and files, a file system consists of a set of files below a root directory and users can own directories and files, read files and have a home directory.

(*a*) Draw an object diagram corresponding to this class diagram, showing the file system, a user object corresponding to your account, your home directory, a sub directory called mail, a file called .login in your home directory, and a file called message1 in the mail directory.

(*b*) The specification of the file system could be made more Unix-like if a new class "Node" was introduced. This is a superclass of "File" and "Directory". Redraw the class diagram using this new class to *reduce* the number of associations in the diagram.

(*c*) Does the introduction of the "Node" class have any effect on the object diagram you drew for part (*a*)?

(*d*) Consider whether composition or aggregation could correctly be used in these diagrams.

6.9 A spreadsheet consists of an array of cells. The array is divided into horizontal rows, each labelled with a single character, and vertical columns, each labelled with an integer. Each cell therefore has a unique label, such as 'C17'. Cells can either be empty, or can contain a number, a string or a formula. Draw a class diagram expressing these facts.

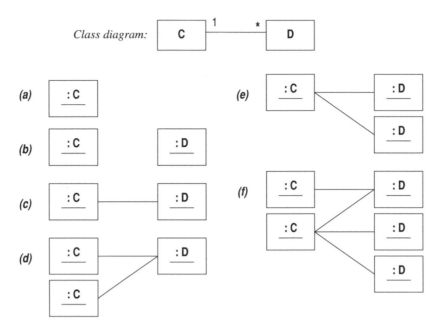

Figure Ex6.5 A 'many' association and some candidate object diagrams

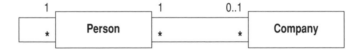

Figure Ex6.6 Associations related to employment

6.10 Draw a class diagram summarizing the following facts about a library. Discuss your design decisions, and any limitations of your model.

> For each book held by the library, the catalogue contains the title, author's name and ISBN number of the book. There may be multiple copies of a book in the library. Each copy of a book has a unique accession number. There are many registered readers belonging to the library, each of whom is issued with a number of tickets. The system records the name and address of each reader, and the number of tickets that they have been issued with. Readers can borrow one book for each ticket that they possess, and the system keeps a record of which books a reader has borrowed, along with the date that the book must be returned by.

6.11 Based on the following description of part of the syntax of a programming language, construct a class diagram showing the structure of programs written in the language.

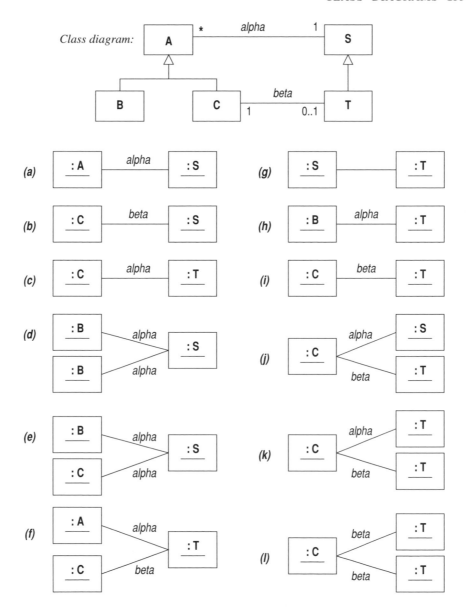

Figure Ex6.7 Generalizations and candidate object diagrams

A *module* consists of a collection of named *features*. A feature can either be a *variable*, a *routine* or a nested module. Routines consist of a *declaration part* and a *statement part*. Features local to the routine can be declared in the declaration part, and the statement part consists of a non-empty sequence of statements. Statements can be *loops*, *conditionals* or *assignments*, and each assignment contains a reference to the variable which is being assigned to.

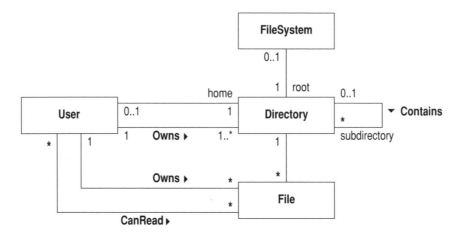

Figure Ex6.8 A class diagram for a file system

6.12 Here is an extract from the documentation of a drawing tool for graphical workstations.

> The objects in the package are divided into *primitive objects* and *compound objects*. The primitive objects are: *arc, ellipse, polyline, polygon, box* and *text.*
>
> A primitive object can be moved, rotated, flipped vertically or horizontally, copied or erased. The *text* primitive may not be flipped.
>
> A compound object is composed of primitive objects. The primitive objects that constitute a compound cannot be individually modified, but they can be manipulated as an entity; a compound can be moved, rotated, flipped vertically or horizontally, copied or erased. A compound that contains any boxes may only be rotated by 90 degrees.

Based on this description, draw a class diagram using generalization to show the relationships between the various different kinds of graphical object in the drawing package. Discuss the limitations of your model, and any significant design decisions that you make.

6.13 Users of a network are authorized to use certain workstations. For each such machine, they are issued with an account and password. Draw a class model describing this situation, and discuss any assumptions that you make.

6.14 The UK banking system consists of a number of banks. Each bank has a number of branches, each identified by a unique sort code. Banks maintain accounts, each with a unique account number; in addition, each account is held at a particular branch of the bank. Some accounts allow cheques to be written; each cheque is identified with a cheque number.

Draw a class diagram to represent this information, paying particular attention to the use of qualified associations. Explain any assumptions or design decisions that you make.

6.15 Imagine a library full of books. Each book contains a bibliography; each bibliography consists of a number of references to other books. Typically, a book will be referred to in many places, and therefore a reference can appear in more than one bibliography.

Draw a class diagram for this situation, and discuss the possible uses of aggregation in the diagram.

6.16 A customer places an order with a supplier. The order is for various numbers of different kinds of parts; the distinction between different kinds of parts can be ignored for the purposes of this exercise. An order consists of a number of order lines; each line specifies a particular part from the suppliers catalogue, and says how many are to be ordered. In response to an order, the supplier makes up a delivery, consisting of all the ordered parts. Describe this situation in a class diagram, and discuss the possible use of aggregation in your diagram.

6.17 Draw a class diagram modelling the system described in the following:

A company has decided to computerize the circulation of documents round its offices, and to do this by installing a network of *electronic desks*. Each desk provides the following services:
- a *blotting pad*, which can hold a document that the user is currently working on. The blotting pad provides basic word-processing facilities;
- a *filing cabinet*, which models a physical filing cabinet. It is divided into drawers, and each drawer is divided into folders. Documents can be stored either in drawers or in folders within drawers;
- a *mail service*, which allows the user to communicate with other users on the network. Each desk is provided with three *trays*, corresponding to the IN, OUT and PENDING trays in traditional offices. The network will automatically put new mail in a user's IN tray, and periodically take documents from the OUT tray and mail them to their recipients.

Documents can be moved between the mail trays and the blotting pad, and between the blotting pad and the filing cabinet. There is no provision to move documents directly between the trays and the filing cabinet. Only one document can be on the blotting pad at any given time.

6.18 Many programming languages define a notion of *scope*. Every identifier is declared within some scope, and it is an error to declare two or more identifiers with the same name in the same scope. Scopes can be nested, however, and an identifier can be defined in an inner scope with a name that has been used in an outer scope. Draw two class diagrams modelling these facts about scopes and identifiers, one using qualifiers and one not. Compare the two resulting diagrams and decide which is the more accurate representation of the situation being described.

6.19 Draw a class diagram summarizing the aspects of the window manager described below:

> When you are running the system, your work takes place on the *desktop*, the screen space occupied by the window manager. At any time you will be running a number of applications; each application will be displayed on the desktop either as an icon or in an application window. The control application starts when the window manager is started up; terminating this application terminates the current session.
>
> As you work with applications, two kinds of windows appear on your desktop: application windows, and windows contained within the application windows, often known as *document windows*. All windows contain a title bar, maximize and minimize buttons, a control-menu box, and optionally horizontal and vertical scroll bars. In addition, application windows contain a menu bar; operations chosen from the menu bar can affect either the application window or any of the document windows contained within it.

Based on your class diagram, write a navigation expression which denotes all the windows, both application and document, which are currently visible on the desktop.

6.20 Construct an object model for the Electronic Noticeboard (EN) system described in the following:

> The EN is a system designed to facilitate communication between a group of users of a computer system. It enables notices to be posted that all users can read, and permits discussions to take place between the users.
>
> When a user logs on to the EN, they are presented with a user workspace that contains two main areas, the *noticeboard* and the *discussion groups*. The user has to choose which area they want to access; it is possible to move freely between the areas at any later stage.
>
> The noticeboard contains a list of notices, and a user can choose between reading any of the existing notices, or adding a new notice to the noticeboard. A notice must have an expiry date; after that date it will be archived and will no longer appear on the standard noticeboard. By default, all notices appear to all users until their expiry dates; a user can choose to remove specified notices from their private view of the noticeboard, however, although this is not recommended.
>
> The system also maintains discussion groups each dealing with a particular topic. Each discussion consists of a number of contributions. Users can choose which, if any, of the discussions they wish to read. By default, only unread contributions in a particular discussion will be presented to the user. A discussion is started when a user posts an initial contribution. Other users can respond to this by posting *followup contributions*, which in turn can generate further followups. If a followup is deemed to have moved sufficiently far away from the original topic of discussion, it can be identified as the initial contribution of a new discussion group; it will then be accessible through both the old and new groups.

All notices and contributions are archived, together with their date and in the case of contributions, a record of the contributions, if any, that they are following up.

A user starting a new discussion can specify that only a subset of the registered users of the EN can access the group. It is possible to allow users to have read-only, read-write or no access to a group. By contrast, all notices are readable by all users. A user can only read an archived contribution if they had read access to the group it was originally posted to.

6.21 Produce an object model based on the information contained in the following description of the `info` system provided with the Emacs text editor. Where appropriate, give justifications for the design decisions you make.

The `info` system in Emacs provides a simple hypertext reading facility enabling on-line documentation to be browsed from within the editor. The `info` system consists of a number of *files*, each roughly corresponding to a single document. Each file is divided into a number of *nodes*, each node containing a small amount of text describing a particular topic. One node in the system is identified as the *directory* node: it contains information about the files available in the `info` system, and is presented to the user when the system is started.

Nodes are connected together by *links*: each link connects two nodes, and operations are provided enabling the user to move from one node to another via a link: in this way it is possible to browse through the complete document. There are three important kinds of links, called *up*, *next* and *previous* links: the names imply that the nodes in a document will be structured in a hierarchical manner, but this is not enforced by the system. In addition to links, a node can contain a *menu*. A menu consists of a number of entries, each of which connects to another node in the system.

When the system is running, a record is kept in a *history list* of all the nodes that have been visited, thus enabling users to retrace their path through the document.

7

INTERACTION DIAGRAMS

Class diagrams are used to specify the static structure of a system, namely the objects that can exist at run-time, the data each object contains, and the links that can exist between them. Object diagrams can be used to illustrate potential states of the system but because of the size and complexity of most systems they are typically used only for illustrative purposes.

When a system is running, various interactions take place, in the form of messages being passed between objects. Interactions arise from the execution of use cases, or the call of an operation in a class. The messages that are sent determine the system's behaviour, but they are not shown on static diagrams such as class diagrams. This chapter examines some of the notation that UML provides for specifying the dynamic properties of a system.

To specify an interaction, it must be stated which messages will be sent, in which order, and under which circumstances. When an operation or use case is executed, the particular sequence of messages that is generated may be different on different occasions but will always be constrained by the specification of the operation.

This chapter examines the two types of diagram that UML provides for specifying interactions, namely *collaboration diagrams* and *sequence diagrams*. Broadly speaking, these two types of diagram provide alternative ways of expressing the same information, and they are collectively referred to as *interaction diagrams*.

7.1 COLLABORATIONS

Interactions are often illustrated by adding messages to an object diagram. For example, consider an operation in a banking system to transfer funds from one account to another. Each time this operation is invoked, a certain amount of money is withdrawn from one account and deposited in another.

An object diagram could be used to illustrate such a transaction: it would show two objects of a suitable account class, together with any other objects that were involved in the transaction, and also the messages which effected the transfer of money from one account to the other. Examples of this approach to documenting interactions are given in connection with the stock control program in Chapter 2, for example in Figure 2.9.

However, such object diagrams are really only illustrations of particular interactions and do not provide a general specification of an operation. There are at least three reasons why this use of object diagrams is unsatisfactory as a general method for specifying interactions.

Firstly, an object diagram showing a transfer of funds will show two account objects which send and receive the messages appropriate in that particular case. In general, however, a specification should state that any account object can participate in a transfer, either as the account from which money is taken or that in which it is deposited, and that the messages it sends and receives will vary from case to case.

Secondly, an object diagram shows a fixed number of objects, and the links between them. On the different occasions that an operation is called, however, both the number of objects involved and the pattern of links between them may vary, and the interaction that is generated will vary accordingly. For example, an alternative form of the transfer operation might allow money to be withdrawn from one account and shared out between a number of other accounts. A specification of an operation should state in a general way what will happen in these different cases, rather than showing a few examples and leaving it up to the reader to infer what will happen in other cases.

Thirdly, some operations may exhibit different functionality on separate occasions; perhaps if no transfer is made when the account from which money is withdrawn would become overdrawn as a result. In general, this implies that the course of an interaction may be affected by properties of the data stored in objects. Different possibilities could be shown on separate object diagrams, but it would be preferable to have a notation that can show alternative possibilities on a single diagram rather than having to draw a set of illustrative examples.

In order to achieve the required generality, interaction diagrams in UML are based on the general notion of a *collaboration*, rather than on object diagrams. A collaboration is a general description of the ways in which objects can be linked together in order to support the behaviour to be specified. Collaborations are related to class diagrams, as both of them specify ways in which objects can be linked together. However, whereas class diagrams specify all the possible object structures in a system, collaborations specify only those which are relevant to a particular type of interaction.

An object diagram can be thought of as a particularly simple form of collaboration that shows only a fixed number of objects linked together in a particular way, and as explained above, object diagrams are commonly used in simple cases to illustrate interactions. In general, however, collaborations provide a way of describing all the various related object structures which are capable of supporting a given operation or use case. To show this potential variety, collaborations are defined not simply in terms of classes, but rather in terms of the *roles* that instances of those classes can play in various interactions.

7.2 CLASSIFIER ROLES

Collaborations consist of *roles*. A role describes a particular way in which an object can participate in an interaction. For example, each transfer of funds involves two instances of an account class, but they participate in the transaction in different ways. One object has money withdrawn from it, and the other has money deposited in it.

This can be specified by defining two roles for this transaction, which might be called the 'winner' and 'loser' roles. A general description of the transaction can then be given by saying that money is taken from a loser and transferred to a winner. Whenever a fund transfer takes place, an object is assigned to each role, one being the winner and one being the loser. In different transactions, however, a particular account object might sometimes be a loser and sometimes a winner.

A *classifier role* therefore describes a role that objects can play in interactions. The notation for a classifier role is shown in Figure 7.1: the name of the role and its *base class* are shown in a rectangular icon, separated by a colon. Objects that are to play a particular role in an interaction must be instances of the role's base class or one of its descendant classes.

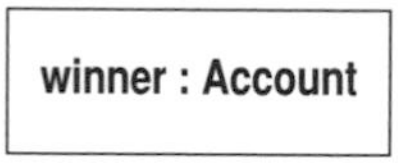

winner : Account

Figure 7.1 A classifier role

This notation is clearly related to that used for both objects and classes. Unlike a class, however, a classifier role has a name; even if the name is omitted, the colon should be included to distinguish a role from a class. The name and class of a role are not underlined, however: this signifies that a classifier role is not an instance, but a more general notion which can itself have objects as instances.

In a given interaction, an object playing a particular role will not normally make use of all the features provided by the base class of the role. For example, an account object playing the role of 'winner' will receive messages depositing money in the account, but not withdrawing it. In principle, it would be possible to specify a role without naming a base class, but simply listing the features that objects playing that role must support. UML does not allow this flexibility, however: the only way of specifying the properties of a classifier role is by naming a base class. This means that roles often correspond to coherent subsets of a class's functionality that are not made explicit on a class diagram.

The distinction between objects and classifier roles is sometimes not clearly made in the literature on UML. In particular, diagrams often show objects participating in interactions rather than roles. In these cases, the objects shown are intended to be 'prototypical' objects. It is understood that other objects could be substituted for such a prototypical object in various circumstances, in much the same way as different objects can play a given role in various transactions. In practice, this causes little confusion, but in order to differentiate the two concepts, roles and objects will be clearly distinguished in this book.

7.3 ASSOCIATION ROLES

A collaboration consists of a number of classifier roles connected by *association roles*. Objects playing the roles at the end of an association role are linked in the collaboration, and hence can communicate by sending messages.

Figure 7.2 shows a collaboration which supports the interaction illustrated in Figure 2.6 for finding the cost of a part in the stock control program of Chapter 2. It consists of three classifier roles, linked by two association roles. No base class is specified for the client role, because an object playing this role does not have to have any particular properties.

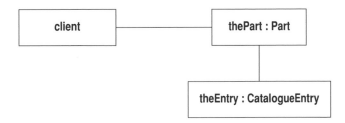

Figure 7.2 A collaboration

An association role connecting two classifier roles indicates that objects playing those roles can be linked to each other, and hence exchange messages, in interactions based on the collaboration. One way in which objects can be linked is if there exists an association defined between their classes, and in this case the association is said to be the *base association* of the association role. The association between the part and catalogue entry classes shown in Figure 2.10 is therefore the base association for the association role between the corresponding classifier roles in Figure 7.2.

The other association role in Figure 7.2 does not have a base association, however. As the client role has no base class, it is not possible to pick a specific association to be the base association. The association role simply indicates that the client must be linked to, and hence able to send messages to, the part. This suggests that an association between classes is not the only way that objects can come to be linked, and hence able to communicate with each other.

7.4 TRANSIENT LINKS

An association between two classes implies that instances of the classes can be linked and messages sent between them. An association implies a fairly permanent connection between objects, however, often implemented as a data member or field within a class. There are other situations in which objects are able to communicate, and in these circumstances they are also described as being linked. These links are often short lived, and are known as *transient links*, to distinguish them from links that are instances of associations.

UML distinguishes the following four types of transient link. These correspond to the different ways in which one object can gain access to another in such as way as to be able to send messages to it.

1. One object can be passed to another as a parameter of a message. In programming languages, this is often implemented by passing a reference to the object. In this case the object receiving the message knows the identity of the parameter object, and can in the operation body send messages to that object. Such a link is transient because it is only available while the operation is executing.
2. Implementations of operations can declare local variables of another class, create temporary objects of that class and then send messages to these objects during the execution of the operation. Again, a link corresponding to a local variable only lasts for the duration of an operation call.
3. If any global variables exist and are visible, an object can send messages to an object stored in such a variable.
4. An object can always send messages to itself, even though no explicit 'link to self' is defined. In programming languages, this capability is provided by defining a pseudo-variable called 'this' or 'self'.

Transient links are important in collaborations because during the execution of an operation messages are often sent to parameter objects, local variables and to the object executing the operation itself. Association roles can be labelled with one of the following stereotypes to indicate the type of link that they support: 'parameter', 'local', 'global', 'self' and 'association'. The first four correspond to the four types of transient link listed above. The 'association' stereotype indicates that a link is an instance of an association rather than a transient link. It is the default case, and can be omitted.

For example, suppose that in the stock control program an assembly is sent a message asking it how many parts of a particular type it contains. A client object sending this message might pass the catalogue entry object representing the part type of interest as a parameter of the message, and in the course of handling the request, the assembly object would retrieve the part number from this catalogue entry object.

Figure 7.3 shows this interaction on a suitable collaboration. The parameter 'part' is used as the name of the corresponding classifier role, and the association role connecting this to the assembly object is labelled with the appropriate stereotype to indicate that this link exists because of the parameter that was passed.

7.5 INTERACTION DIAGRAMS

Two kinds of diagram are defined in UML for showing interactions, sequence diagrams and collaboration diagrams. Collaboration diagrams show classifier and association roles, and superimpose messages on association roles, as shown in Figure 7.3. Sequence diagrams show classifier roles only, but make the sequencing of messages very clear. Depending on the nature of the interactions being illustrated, one or other form of diagram may be preferable.

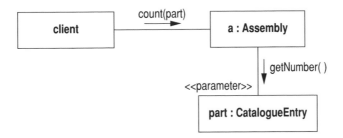

Figure 7.3 A collaboration with a transient link

As well as showing sequences of messages, both types of interaction diagram can explicitly show the creation and deletion of objects, iterated and conditional message passing, and objects sending messages to themselves. The major difference between the two forms of diagram is the way they show the order in which messages are sent.

Sequence diagrams

A sequence diagram showing the interaction in Figure 7.3 is given in Figure 7.4. The classifier roles involved in the interaction are displayed at the top of the diagram. Association roles are not shown. The vertical dimension in a sequence diagram represents time, and the messages in an interaction are drawn from top to bottom of the diagram, in the order that they are sent.

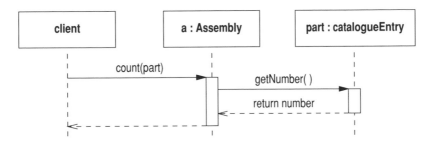

Figure 7.4 A simple sequence diagram

Each role has a dashed line, known as its *lifeline*, extending below it. The lifeline indicates the period of time during which objects playing that role actually exist. In Figure 7.4 all objects exist throughout the entire interaction, but examples where objects are created and deleted during an interaction will be examined later.

Messages are shown as arrows pointing from the lifeline of the role sending the message to the lifeline of the receiver. When a message is sent, control passes from the sender of the message to the receiver. The period of time during which an object is processing a message is known as an *activation*, and is shown on a lifeline as a narrow rectangle whose top is connected to a message.

When an object finishes processing a message, control returns to the sender of the message. This marks the end of the activation corresponding to that message, and is marked by a dashed arrow going from the bottom of the activation rectangle back to the lifeline of the role that sent the message giving rise to the activation. Activations and return messages are optional on a sequence diagram, but using them systematically often makes it much easier to discern the structure of an interaction.

In the course of processing a message, an object may send messages to other objects. These messages are depicted as arrows from the activation corresponding to the first message to the lifeline of the receiver, where they give rise to a second activation. Assuming that a conventional procedural flow of control is being modelled, the period of time occupied by this second activation will be 'nested' within the period of time occupied by the first activation, as shown in Figure 7.4.

Arguments passed with a message are shown in conventional functional style. Data values returned to the sender of a message are shown on the return messages at the end of an activation.

Collaboration diagrams

A collaboration diagram corresponding to the sequence diagram in Figure 7.4 is shown in Figure 7.5. With the exception of the notation used to show return values and the sequencing of messages, it is identical to the diagram shown in Figure 7.3.

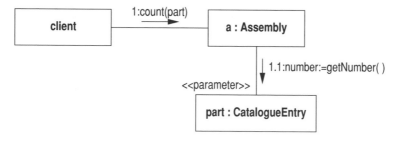

Figure 7.5 A simple collaboration diagram

Unlike sequence diagrams, collaboration diagrams show association as well as classifier roles. As a result, message sequencing cannot be shown graphically and messages are numbered to indicate the order in which they are sent. Messages can be numbered sequentially, but more commonly a hierarchical numbering scheme is used. Figure 7.5 shows a very simple example of this, where the messages are not numbered 1 and 2, as might have been expected, but 1 and 1.1.

The rationale for adopting this hierarchical scheme is to enable the numbering of messages to reflect explicitly the structure of nested activations that is made explicit on the sequence diagram in Figure 7.4. The correspondence between the two notations is shown schematically in Figure 7.6. This diagram shows the messages on an abstract sequence diagram labelled with the numbers they would have on an equivalent collaboration diagram.

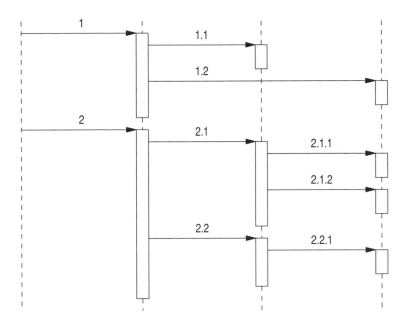

Figure 7.6 The hierarchical numbering of messages

Numbers are assigned to messages in Figure 7.6 in the following way. Within each activation, messages are numbered sequentially starting from 1. This includes messages sent from the leftmost lifeline in the diagram. Each activation can be identified with the number of the message that gave rise to it. For example, the activation that starts when message number 2.1 is received should be thought of as being activation number 2.1.

A unique label can then be generated for each message by adding the number of the message to the end of the number of the activation sending the message, with a dot to separate the numbers and to reflect that another level of nesting of control flow has been initiated. For example, the two messages sent by activation 2.1 are labelled as 2.1.1 and 2.1.2 respectively.

With practice, information about activations can be read off collaboration diagrams fairly readily by interpreting the message numbers in this way. Most people find the graphic representation given by sequence diagrams easier to read, however, and this is a major factor in the popularity of this form of diagram.

Collaboration diagrams do not include return arrows at the end of activations, as these would complicate the diagram to an unacceptable extent. Data that is returned from a message is prefixed to message name, and separated from it by an assignment symbol ':='.

The major advantage that collaboration diagrams have over sequence diagrams is that they clearly specify the mechanism used to support each message, by suitably labelled association roles as shown in Figure 7.5. As sequence diagrams do not show association roles, it is important to check that messages are not sent where there is no suitable link between objects to support the message.

7.6 OBJECT CREATION

Suppose that the stock control program from Chapter 2 is to be extended with the capability to store details about orders. For the purposes of this example, an order will be defined to consist simply of a number of order lines, each of which specifies a certain number of parts of a particular type. Figure 7.7 shows a class diagram summarizing the necessary facts about orders.

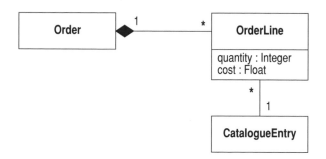

Figure 7.7 Orders in the stock control system

The relationship between orders and order lines is one of composition, because we assume that when an order is destroyed all lines on that order are also destroyed. This is a characteristic application of the semantics of composition, as explained in Section 6.9. The cost attribute of the order line class records the total cost of parts ordered on that line; it should be computed when an order line is created, by multiplying the cost recorded in the catalogue entry object by the number of parts ordered.

Let us assume that to create an order line, a client object must send a message to an order specifying the part and the quantity to be ordered. A new order line object will then be created and added to the order. A sequence diagram illustrating this interaction is shown in Figure 7.8.

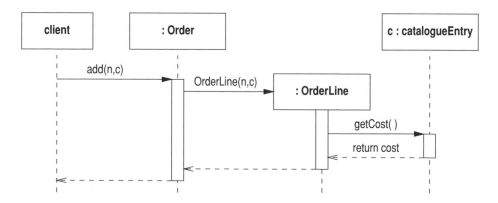

Figure 7.8 Object creation on a sequence diagram

The new order line object is created in response to a message labelled 'add' sent from the client to the order. The parameters of this message supply the number of parts to be added and the catalogue entry object corresponding to the required parts.

In response to this message, an order object creates a new order line object, and the constructor call creating this object is shown as the next message in the interaction. On a sequence diagram, the classifier role representing a new object is drawn at a position corresponding to the time at which the new object is created, and the message that creates the new object is shown terminating at the role symbol, not on a lifeline as with normal messages. Sequence diagrams thus show very graphically when new objects are created in the course of an interaction.

The activation immediately below the order line icon in Figure 7.8 corresponds to the execution of the object's constructor. The diagram shows that during the construction of order lines the cost of the relevant parts is retrieved from the catalogue entry object that was passed as a parameter. This value will be used in the initialization of the order line's 'cost' attribute. At the end of this activation, control returns to the order, and the order line's lifeline continues as normal.

In the course of this interaction two new links are created, one linking the order line to the order that contains it and one linking the order line to its catalogue entry object. These links correspond to the associations shown on Figure 7.7. They cannot be shown in Figure 7.8 as association roles are not depicted on sequence diagrams. Figure 7.9 shows the same interaction on a collaboration diagram, including the two new links.

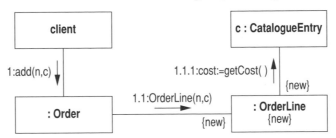

Figure 7.9 Object creation on a collaboration diagram

Collaboration diagrams cannot explicitly show the time at which a new object is created. In order to distinguish elements that are created during the course of an interaction from those which existed at the start, classifier and association roles corresponding to new objects and links are annotated with the property 'new'.

7.7 OBJECT DESTRUCTION

The converse of the creation of new objects is object deletion. Suppose that order lines are removed from orders when a client sends a 'remove' message to the order. A sequence diagram showing object deletion is illustrated in Figure 7.10. Messages which cause the destruction of objects are labelled with the stereotype 'destroy'. The lifeline of the object destroyed terminates in a large cross.

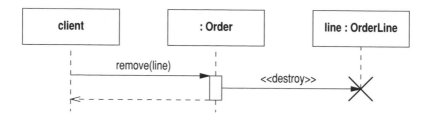

Figure 7.10 Object deletion on a sequence diagram

As with object creation, collaboration diagrams cannot explicitly show the time at which an object is destroyed. Instead, the object and any links that are destroyed are labelled with the property 'destroyed', as shown in Figure 7.11. If an object is created and destroyed in the course of a single interaction it can be labelled on a collaboration diagram with the property 'transient'.

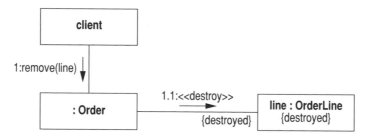

Figure 7.11 Object deletion on a collaboration diagram

7.8 ITERATED MESSAGES

In many cases, the number of objects playing a particular role can vary from one interaction to another. For example, consider an interaction describing how to find the cost of an assembly in the stock control program. The fact that assemblies can have any number of components cannot be represented on an object diagram such as Figure 2.9 which, for illustrative purposes, only shows a fixed number of components.

The number of objects that can play a given role in an interaction can be specified by adding multiplicity annotations to the appropriate classifier roles. Figure 7.12 shows a collaboration which uses this notation to show that an assembly involved in an interaction can contain zero or more components.

Figure 7.12 Classifier roles and multiplicity

This use of multiplicity should be contrasted with the use of multiplicity on class icons. On a class diagram, we are interested in knowing how many instances of a class could exist in the system. In most cases, the answer will be 'any number', and so the default multiplicity of a class icon is 'zero or more'. For classifier roles, however, we are interested in the number of instances of the base class that will participate in a single interaction. More often than not, there will only be one instance per interaction, and this is the default multiplicity for roles.

In order to find out the cost of an assembly, a message must be sent to each of the components, no matter how many there are. To emphasize the fact that a single symbol could correspond to multiple messages, notation is added to message labels to indicate an iterated message send. This notation is shown on Figures 7.13 and 7.14 for the cases of sequence and collaboration diagrams, respectively.

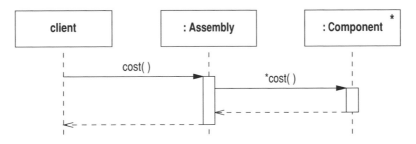

Figure 7.13 Iterated message passing on a sequence diagram

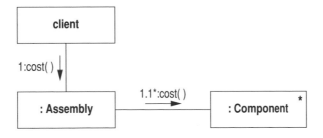

Figure 7.14 Iterated message passing on a collaboration diagram

7.9 MULTIOBJECTS

An alternative way of showing multiplicity information associated with a classifier role is to use a *multiobject*. Rather than representing a role which can be played by many objects, a multiobject represents a collection of objects of the base type of the multiobject. The effect of this is for many purposes equivalent to specifying a role with a multiplicity of zero or more. The notation for a multiobject is shown in Figure 7.15.

Figure 7.15 Showing multiplicity with a multiobject

The distinction between a multiobject and a role with multiplicity is rather subtle. It has to do with the fact that an object that can hold zero or more links to other objects usually does so in virtue of being linked to a suitable data structure, such as a list or a vector. Figure 7.16 shows a pedantically complete collaboration which depicts all the objects that might actually exist in the situation shown in Figure 7.15.

Figure 7.16 Multiplicity with an intermediate data structure

As well as being time-consuming to write, and unnecessarily complicated to read, a diagram like Figure 7.16 represents a premature commitment to a particular data structure class. At an early stage of design, it may not be appropriate to specify what data structure will be used to hold a collection of links. Figure 7.15, then, can be viewed as an abbreviation of Figure 7.16 which removes this premature commitment.

Technically, then, a multiobject represents a single object, namely a collection of objects of some other sort. It follows that a multiobject is a suitable target for messages which perform some operation on a set, such as finding a particular element within the set. For example, suppose in the example of Figure 7.15 that it was necessary to locate the order line corresponding to a particular type of part. We will assume that there is at most one order line per order for a given type of part. An interaction to accomplish this is shown in Figure 7.17.

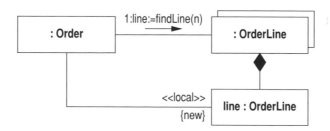

Figure 7.17 Finding a specific order line

Figure 7.17 shows an order object sending a message to a collection of order lines, asking for the line which corresponds to the catalogue entry with part number 'n'. As the multiobject represents only a single object, the collection of lines rather than the lines themselves, this message should not be marked as an iterated message.

Figure 7.17 also shows the order line that is returned by the 'findLine' message as a separate symbol, distinct from the multiobject and labelled to indicate that it is the same object that was returned by the 'findLine' message. To indicate that it is not a new object, but merely one of the order lines represented by the multiobject, it is linked to the multiobject with a composition link, thus indicating that it is part of the set of order lines represented by the multiobject. The order object creates a new link to this line in a local variable.

If an object wants to send a message to all the objects represented by a multiobject, it cannot in principle do so directly. As the multiobject represents the single object containing the other objects, a single message should be sent to it. Some form of iteration will have to take place to get the message to all the objects represented.

However, it would complicate diagrams unnecessarily to show interactions in such detail, and so the convention is adopted that an iterated message to a multiobject, such as the one shown in Figure 7.18, is understood as being an abbreviation for the more complicated processing that would be involved in iterating through all the objects in a multiobject and sending a message to each one individually.

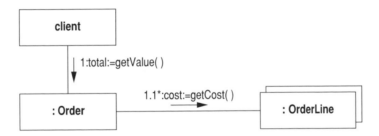

Figure 7.18 Finding the total cost of an order

7.10 CONDITIONAL MESSAGES

The notation discussed so far in this chapter does not enable any variations in the course of an interaction to be shown. Both collaboration and sequence diagrams provide means for showing *conditional* message passing or, in other words, messages which are only sent under certain circumstances. Together with the notation for iterated message passing, this in principle allows interaction diagrams to show the design of an algorithm in full detail, though in most cases this flexibility is not used because of the complexity of the ensuing diagrams.

To illustrate the simple notation for conditional messages, consider the following scenario. Suppose that stock levels for parts are held in catalogue entry objects, and that when a message is received to add a new order line to an order, the order object should first check that sufficient parts of the requested type are in stock before creating the new order line object and adding it to the order. This interaction can be illustrated by the sequence diagram in Figure 7.19, an extension of that shown in Figure 7.8.

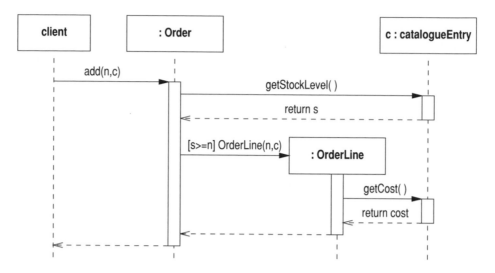

Figure 7.19 Conditional messages on sequence diagrams

To illustrate the fact that the message creating the order line object will only be sent under certain circumstances, a *condition* is attached to it. This consists of a boolean expression written in square brackets. If the condition evaluates to true at the point in the activation when the message is reached, the message will be sent. Otherwise, control will jump to the point following the return message corresponding to the message bearing the condition.

Exactly the same notation can be attached to messages in collaboration diagrams, as Figure 7.20 shows. As with the sequence diagram above, this is an extension of the interaction shown in Figure 7.9.

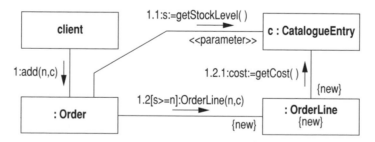

Figure 7.20 Conditional messages on collaboration diagrams

Figures 7.19 and 7.20 illustrate the situation where a particular message may or may not be sent, depending on the state of the system at the time of despatch. A more general form of conditionality allows alternative courses of action to be followed in different circumstances; perhaps if the stock level is sufficiently high the interaction proceeds as shown in Figures 7.19 and 7.20 but if not, a message is sent to the catalogue entry object asking it to restock the given type of part.

This kind of interaction can be shown explicitly on sequence diagrams but not on collaboration diagrams. The notation is illustrated in Figure 7.21, largely for the sake of completeness. In most cases the visual complexity of this notation will interfere with the ability of the diagram to communicate the details of the interaction to readers, and alternative forms of documenting the design of the algorithm would be used.

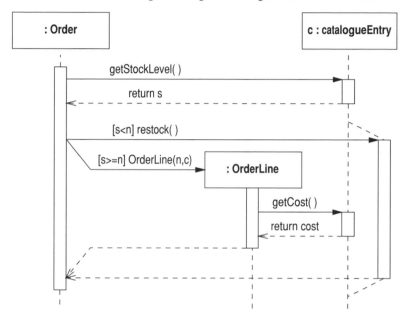

Figure 7.21 Alternative messages on a sequence diagram

Unlike Figure 7.19, the sequence diagram in Figure 7.21 shows an alternative message at the point where the new order line object is created. The new message is guarded by the opposite condition to the first, namely that the stock level is too low to permit the order to be made. One of the two messages will be activated as the interaction proceeds, and to avoid total visual confusion, one of them is angled away from the other. This does not mean that it is sent later, however, or that it takes an appreciable amount of time to send.

Each time the flow of control reaches this point in the interaction, one or other of the branches will be activated. Later in the interaction there is a point where the two branches rejoin; after this point the interaction continues in a normal sequential manner. The join of control following the fork is shown by the meeting of the two return messages that correspond to the branching messages.

The catalogue entry object will receive different messages depending on which branch is executed. It would not be correct to show all these messages arriving at one lifeline, as this would imply that all messages were received in a single interaction. Instead, the lifeline of the catalogue entry object branches, reflecting the fork of control in the order object. Messages from one alternative are sent to one branch of the lifeline, and those from the other to the other branch.

As well as a fork of control, the diagram now contains a branching lifeline, as the history of a catalogue entry object in the course of the transaction now contains alternative possibilities. Reading from top to bottom of the sequence diagram in Figure 7.21 only one branch of the lifeline will be followed in any one interaction. One unsatisfactory feature of this notation is that the condition that causes this branching is not associated with the lifeline itself. This can rapidly lead to obscurity in diagrams that are more complex that Figure 7.21.

7.11 MESSAGES TO SELF

Occasionally it can be useful to show explicitly the messages that an object sends to itself. Often such messages can be thought of as internal details of the object's implementation, but sometimes showing them can clarify the description of an algorithm. This is particularly true if further messages are sent to other objects as a result of the message that the object sends to itself. In this case, showing all the messages is necessary to understand the details of the nesting of activations within the interaction.

As with messages to other objects, a message that an object sends to itself gives rise to a new activation, but in this case the new activation takes place in an object that already has a live activation. On a sequence diagram, the recursive nature of this new activation is shown by superimposing the new activation on top of the original one, as shown in Figure 7.22.

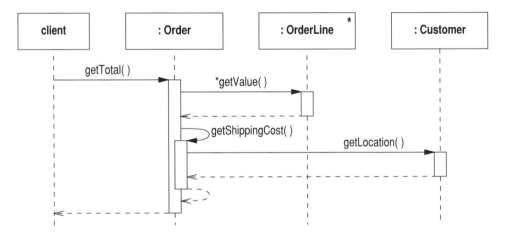

Figure 7.22 A recursive activation

The interaction in Figure 7.22 shows how the total cost of an order is calculated. First, the cost of each order line is obtained, and then the order object sends itself a message to calculate the shipping costs of the order. In programming terms, this would correspond to the decision to implement this functionality as a separate method within the order class, as it may need to be called from more than one place.

In response to this message, a further message is sent to the customer object linked to the order, to find out the address of the customer from which, presumably, the cost of delivering the order can be calculated. This message is sent from the nested activation, making the flow of control from message to message completely explicit. At the end of the nested activation a return message is shown looping back to the activation that was responsible for sending the message.

Recursive activations are not shown so explicitly on collaboration diagrams but, as with normal activations, each recursive activation gives rise to an extra level of hierarchy in the numbering of subsequent messages, and in this way the dependency of one message on another is kept clear. Figure 7.23 shows the same interaction as Figure 7.22, but on a collaboration diagram. Notice that a transient link labelled with the 'self' stereotype is used as a vehicle for a message sent by an object to itself.

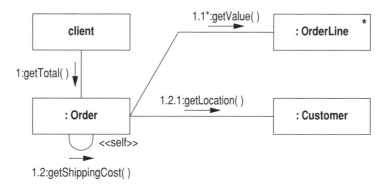

Figure 7.23 A message to self on a collaboration diagram

In Figures 7.22 and 7.23 nested activations have been shown arising from an object sending a message to itself. There is no reason in principle why a nested activation should not arise from a message sent from a different object, in the situation where object A sends a message to object B, and in the course of responding to that message object B sends a message back to object A.

7.12 SUMMARY

- Interactions are often shown by including messages on object diagrams. This technique is not suitable for specifying the details of complex interactions.
- Interaction diagrams are based on collaborations. Collaborations specify the different roles that objects can play in interactions.
- Association roles connect classifier roles in collaborations, and indicate how objects can be linked and hence exchange messages in interactions.
- Association roles can correspond to associations in the class model, but various types of transient link between objects can also be specified, to model the sending of messages to local variables and operation parameters.

- Sequence diagrams depict the classifier roles involved in an interaction. The sequencing of messages is shown very clearly, as arrows between objects' lifelines, with time flowing down the diagram.
- Collaboration diagrams depict association roles as well as classifier roles. As a result, a hierarchical numbering scheme has to be used in order to clarify the sequencing of messages.
- Both types of interaction diagram can show object creation and destruction and, in order to clarify the details of an algorithm, an object sending a message to itself. In this latter case, an additional recursive activation is generated.
- Like class diagrams, collaborations can contain multiplicity annotations which specify the number of objects that can participate in interactions. Multiobjects provide another way of showing collections of objects, in particular.
- Conditions can be used on interaction diagrams, to show both the optional sending of messages and also alternative flows of control.

7.13 EXERCISES

7.1 Draw a schematic collaboration diagram showing the same structure of interactions as the sequence diagram shown in Figure 7.6.

7.2 Redraw the sequence diagrams in Figures 3.4, 3.10 and 3.14 as a collaboration diagrams, making use where appropriate of the full range of notation introduced in this chapter.

7.3 Draw a sequence diagram corresponding to Figure 7.17, and comment on the relative usefulness of the two forms of diagram in this case.

7.4 After reading Chapter 12, redraw Figures 12.18 and 12.24 as sequence diagrams, and comment on the relative strengths and weaknesses of the two forms of diagram in these cases.

7.5 The diagram editor application introduced in Chapter 3 is to be extended with the facility to copy all the currently selected elements. At any point when a selection tool is active, the user can send a *copy* message to the tool. The selection tool will then send *clone* messages to all the currently selected elements. In response to each *clone* message a new element will be created and returned. The selection tool will then add these new elements to the diagram. The new elements will become selected, and the originals unselected.

Assuming that a selection tool is active, with one element selected:

(*a*) Draw an object diagram showing the configuration of objects before the element is copied.

(*b*) Draw a sequence diagram illustrating the interactions generated when the user copies the selected element.

(*c*) Draw an object diagram showing the configuration of objects after the element is copied.

(*d*) Would a sequence diagram or a collaboration diagram depict this particular interaction more clearly? Give reasons in support of your answer.

7.6 Use the notation for showing alternative flows of control to combine Figures 3.10 and 3.12 into a single sequence diagram showing both the basic and alternative courses of events in the select element use case of the diagram editor.

8

STATECHARTS

In an interaction, an individual object may be sent one or more messages, and these messages are received in a particular order. In other interactions, however, the same object may receive quite different messages. The order in which particular messages are sent to the object may also vary from case to case, depending on the details of each interaction. By considering all the possible interactions that an object could participate in, it can be seen that an object should be capable of responding sensibly to a very wide range of sequences of messages throughout its lifetime.

We have seen in Chapter 6 that object diagrams are not used to specify all the possible states of a system: firstly, there are simply to many states to document exhaustively, and secondly, as well as knowing what the possible states are, we need to know which states are impossible, or illegal. For exactly the same reasons, sequence and collaboration diagrams are not used to describe all the possible interactions that an object can participate in.

In both cases, the solution is the same, namely to use a more abstract form of notation that allows the system to be specified, and not just illustrated. In UML, a behavioural specification of an object is given by defining a *state machine* for the object. A state machine specifies an object's responses to the events it might detect during its lifetime. In UML, state machines are normally documented in type of diagram known as *statecharts*.

Interaction diagrams and state machines present two complementary views of the dynamic behaviour of a system. Interaction diagrams show the messages passed around the system over a short period of time, which is typically the duration of a single user-generated transaction. These diagrams must therefore depict a number of objects, namely those that happen to be involved in that particular transaction. A statechart, on the other hand, tracks an individual object throughout its entire lifetime, showing all the possible sequences of messages that the object could receive, together with its response to these messages.

8.1 STATE-DEPENDENT BEHAVIOUR

Many objects exhibit *state-dependent behaviour*. Loosely speaking, this means that the object will respond differently to the same stimulus at different times. For example, consider the behaviour of a simple CD player which consists of a drawer to hold the CD, if any, that is currently being played, and an interface consisting of three buttons labelled 'load', 'play' and 'stop'. The load button causes the drawer to open if it is currently shut, and to shut if it is open. The stop button causes the player to stop playing. If the stop button is pressed when no CD is playing, it has no effect. Finally, the play button causes the CD contained in the drawer to be played. If it is pressed when the drawer is open, the drawer shuts before playing starts.

This CD player exhibits state-dependent behaviour in at least two ways. For example, when the drawer is open, pressing the 'load' button shuts it, and when it is shut, pressing 'load' causes it to open. Furthermore, if a CD is playing, pressing the stop button causes playing to stop, but if no CD is playing, this action has no effect.

In this example we can identify at least three distinct states that the CD player can be in. The different effects of pressing 'load' indicate that we need to distinguish an 'open' and a 'closed' state, and the different effects of pressing 'stop' suggest that there is a third state, which might be labelled 'playing', which is distinct from either of these. It is also noteworthy that the CD player may change state in response to events. For example, pressing the 'load' button repeatedly will cause the CD player to switch between the open and closed states.

Agreeably enough, the three states in this example correspond to observable differences in the physical state of the CD player, but this will not always be the case. The fundamental principle for distinguishing states is that an object in a particular state will respond differently to at least one event from the way in which it responds to that event in other states. States thus identified may or may not correspond to easily detectable external features of the object.

The notion of state used in behavioural modelling should be distinguished from that discussed in Chapter 2, where an object's state was defined to be the aggregate of the values of its attributes at a given time. The behavioural notion of state is wider than this: it is perfectly possible for an object's attributes to differ at two different times, and yet for it to be in the same behavioural state. An example of this is provided by the 'closed' state of the CD player: the presence or absence of a CD in the drawer can be considered to be different attribute values of the CD player, yet in either case we can still consider the player to be in the closed state.

The identification of behavioural states is not a rigorous process. States are distinguished by the fact that the object may respond differently to events when in different states, but what counts as a relevant difference in response is to some extent a question of judgement. The important properties of behavioural states are, firstly, that an object has a number of possible states and it is in exactly one of these states at any given time. Secondly, an object can change state and, in general, the state it is in at a given time will be determined by its history. Finally, depending on its state, an object may exhibit different responses at different times to the same stimulus.

8.2 STATES, EVENTS AND TRANSITIONS

Statechart diagrams, usually simply called *statecharts*, show the possible states of an object, the events it can detect, and its response to those events. In order to construct a statechart for an object, therefore, we must first establish, at least provisionally, what states it can be in and what events it can detect. For the example of the CD player, we have identified the open, closed and playing states which will serve as a basis for developing a statechart.

In software terms, it is common to assume that the events detected by an object are simply the messages sent to it. It is not necessary to be so specific when starting a design, however: all that is required is the more general notion of an object being able to detect an external event. In the case of the CD player, the external events that can be detected are simply the pressing of the three buttons. A state machine for the CD player will therefore involve at least three events, 'load', 'play' and 'stop'.

In general, detecting an event can cause an object to move from one state to another. Such a move is called a *transition*. For example, if the CD player is in the open state, pressing the load button will cause the drawer to shut and the CD player to move into the closed state. The basic information shown on a statechart is the possible states of the entity and the transitions between them, or in other words the way that detecting various events causes the system to move from one state to another.

A statechart describing a basic model of the CD player is shown in Figure 8.1. The states of the system are shown as rounded rectangles, with the name of the state written inside them. State transitions are shown by arrows linking two states. Each such arrow must be labelled with the name of an event. The meaning of such an arrow is that if the system receives the event when it is in the state at the tail of the arrow, it will move into the state at the head of the arrow. It follows that events will normally appear on a state diagram more than once, as it will be possible for the object to detect the same event in many different states.

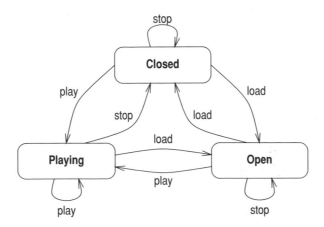

Figure 8.1 A simple state machine for a CD player

In Figure 8.1, every state has three arrows leaving it, one for each event detectable by the CD player. This kind of completeness is not an essential property of state machines but simply reflects the fact that the user of the CD player can press any of the three buttons at any time. If an event does not cause a change of state, the corresponding transition simply loops on a state. An example of this is the transition that shows what happens when the play event is detected and the CD player is already in the playing state. Such transitions are referred to as *self-transitions*.

Events, like messages, can carry data with them, written in parentheses after the message name. None of the events in the CD example need to carry additional data, but examples of this will be seen in the example considered in Section 8.10.

Execution of state machines

A simple state machine, such as the one shown in the statechart in Figure 8.1, can be thought of as 'executing' in the following manner. At any given moment the object is in exactly one of the states shown on the diagram. This is known as the *active state*. Any outgoing transaction from the active state is a candidate for *firing*. For example, if the active state of the CD player is the 'open' state, the transitions that are candidates for firing are the self-transition on that state, the transition labelled 'load' leading to the closed state, and the transition labelled 'play' leading to the playing state.

The events that can cause transitions to fire are known as *triggers*. When an event is detected, an outgoing transition from the active state which is labelled with the name of that event will fire. The state at the other end of the transition that fires then becomes the active state, and the process repeats with the difference that the candidates for firing now are the outgoing transitions from the new active state.

If no outgoing event from the current state is labelled with the name of the event detected, the event is simply ignored. No transition is fired, and the current state remains active. If it is necessary to specify that it is an error for a particular event to be detected while a state is active, an error state can be defined and a transition added leading to the error state and labelled with the name of the prohibited event.

8.3 INITIAL AND FINAL STATES

The diagram in Figure 8.1 describes the functioning of the CD player when it is in use, but it does not say what happens when the machine is switched on and off. We will assume that when the machine is switched off it exhibits no behaviour, and that when it is powered on it always goes straight to the closed state.

We can show this latter behaviour by adding an *initial state* to the state diagram; initial states are shown as small black disks. A transition leading from an initial event shows the state that the object goes into when it is created or initialized. An initial state for the CD player is shown in Figure 8.2 with a transition showing that the player is always in the closed start after being switched on. Notice that no event should be written on a transition from an initial state.

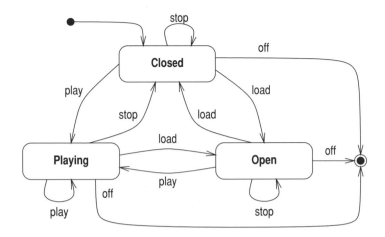

Figure 8.2 Initial and final states

As well as an initial state, a state diagram can show a *final state*. This represents the state reached when an object is destroyed, switched off, or otherwise stops responding to events, and is shown by a small black disk within a larger circle. In general, a final state can be reached from many different states. In the case of the CD player, the event that causes the final state to be reached is the player being switched off. We can model this as a new event called 'off'. The machine can be switched off at any point, so the final state is linked to all the other states by a transition labelled with the 'off' event.

The meaning of the final state depends on the nature of the object being described by the statechart. If a software object, an instance of a class, reaches its final state it will literally be destroyed: its destructor, if it has one, will be called and the memory it occupies will be retrieved.

However, Figure 8.2 clearly should not be interpreted as saying that the CD player is physically destroyed each time it is switched off: such a design would be unlikely to make it to market. What is really being modelled is the behaviour of the software that controls the CD player: when it is switched off the control program is terminated, and the machine will not respond to any events until it has been switched on again.

8.4 GUARD CONDITIONS

The statechart in Figure 8.2 gives an oversimplified description of the behaviour of the CD player. One problem is that the player does not always go into the playing state when the play button is pressed. It will do so if there is a CD in the drawer when the event is detected, but otherwise the drawer will simply shut, if it is not already shut, and the player will go into the closed state. This means that an accurate model should contain two transitions labelled 'play' from the closed and open states, both. Which transition is actually followed on any given occasion will depend on the contents of the drawer at that time.

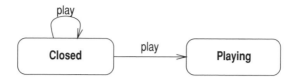

Figure 8.3 Two possible outcomes of pressing 'play'

Figure 8.3 shows the two possible outcomes of pressing the play button when the drawer of the CD player is closed. This is an example of a *non-deterministic* statechart. The diagram shows that two possible transitions can be triggered by a play event, but does not explain when one will fire rather than the other.

There is nothing wrong with non-deterministic diagrams in principle, but if the system being modelled is in fact deterministic, a non-deterministic diagram must be leaving out some information about the system. In the case of the CD player, there is no real non-determinism when the button is pressed, as the subsequent behaviour of the player is determined by the contents of the drawer. A more accurate model should remove the non-determinism present in Figure 8.3 by showing what causes one transition to be followed rather than another.

This information can be shown on the statechart by adding *guard conditions* to the play transitions, stating the circumstances under which the transitions will fire. Guard conditions are part of the specification of a transition, and are written in square brackets after the event name that labels the transition. Guard conditions are often written in informal English, as here, but if desired a more formal notation can be used, such as the OCL language described in Chapter 9.

Figure 8.4 shows the statechart for the CD player extended to include guard conditions which differentiate the full and empty states of the drawer. For simplicity, the initial and final states, which are not relevant to the current discussion, have been omitted from this diagram.

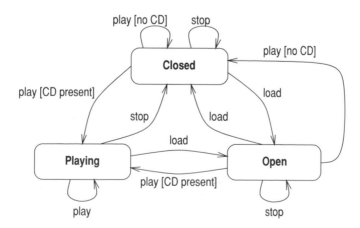

Figure 8.4 Using guard conditions to distinguish transitions

The effect of the guard conditions on the execution of a state machine is as follows. When an event is detected, any guard conditions on transitions which are labelled with the name of that event are evaluated. If a transition has a guard condition, it can only fire if that transition evaluates to true. If all guard conditions evaluate to false and there are no unguarded transitions, the event will be ignored.

If more than one transition has a guard condition that evaluates to true, exactly one of them will fire. In this case, non-determinism has been reintroduced into the state machine; normally guard conditions on a set of outgoing transitions are chosen so that no more than one of them can be true at any given time.

For example, suppose that the CD player is in the open state and the play button is pressed. The first thing that will happen is that the drawer will close; this is necessary so that the machine can detect whether or not a disk is present. It is important to notice that at this point, despite the fact that the drawer is closed, the CD player is not in the closed state. It is still in the open state, evaluating the guard conditions on the play transitions to see which transition should fire. This illustrates a point made earlier, that the states in the CD player's state machine do not necessarily correspond exactly to the physical states of the CD player.

If a CD is present, the transition leading from the open to the playing state will fire. The state machine moves directly from the open to the playing state and does not, even temporarily, pass through the closed state. If it did, it would have to detect a second event to fire a transition to move it to the playing state. Only a single event, however, the pressing of the play button, is necessary to move it from the open to the playing state. The physical fact of the drawer closing can be modelled on the statechart if desired as an *action*, as described in the next section.

8.5 ACTIONS

Statecharts can show what an object does in response to detecting a particular event. This is shown by adding *actions* to the relevant transitions in the diagram. Actions are written after the event name, prefixed by a diagonal slash. Figure 8.5 shows the statechart for the CD player with actions added to show the points at which the drawer is physically opened and closed.

Actions can either be described in English, in pseudo-code, or by using the notation of the target programming language. Transitions often carry both conditions and actions. If this is the case, the condition is written immediately after the event name, followed by the action.

Actions are thought of as short, self-contained pieces of processing which take an insignificant time to complete. The defining characteristic of an action is that it is completed before the transition reaches the new state. This implies that an action cannot be interrupted by any other event that might be detected by the object, but must always run to completion. Actions which are not atomic in this sense, or processing which is carried out while an object is in a given state, can be described by *activities* instead of actions, as described in Section 8.6.

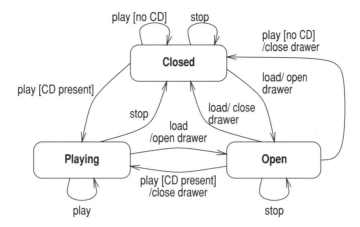

Figure 8.5 Actions for manipulating the drawer of the CD player

Entry and exit actions

Suppose that every time the play button is pressed with a CD in the drawer, the playing head of the CD player positions itself at the start of the current track. This could be shown on the statechart by writing a suitable action on every transition labelled 'play' that leads to the playing state. However, this is rather clumsy and redundant, and the same effect can be achieved more economically by including an *entry action* in the playing state, as shown in Figure 8.6.

Entry actions are performed every time a state becomes active, immediately after actions on transitions leading to the state have completed. For example, if the CD player was in the open state and the play button was pressed, the drawer would close and the transition to the playing state would fire. As a result of this, the playing state would become active, and the entry action in the playing state would immediately be executed.

States can also be provided with *exit actions* which are performed whenever a transition is fired to leave the state. The exit action in Figure 8.6 states that whenever an action is performed that causes playing of a CD to stop, the first thing to happen is that the playing head of the CD player is raised.

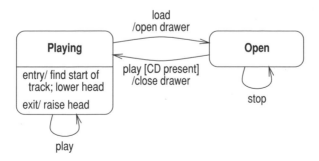

Figure 8.6 Entry and exit actions

Notice that self-transitions count as changes of state. When a self-transition on a state fires, the state temporarily ceases to be active, and is then reactivated. This means that when a self-transition is followed, first the exit and then the entry action of the state are executed, if they exist. In Figure 8.6 this means that the effect of pressing the play button when a CD was being played would be to reposition the playing head at the start of the current track, thereby restarting the track. This behaviour is in fact exhibited by many CD players.

8.6 ACTIVITIES

Obviously, when it is in the playing state, the CD player is doing something, namely playing the current track of the CD. Extended operations that take time to complete can be shown as *activities* within states. Like actions, activities are written inside the state, prefixed with the label 'do' as shown in Figure 8.7.

Figure 8.7 The activity of playing a track

The distinction between actions and activities is that, unlike actions which are thought of as being instantaneous, activities take place over an extended period of time. When a state becomes active, its entry action is performed and then its activity begins, and the activity continues to run throughout the period when the state is active.

Entry actions must be completed before the object can respond to any events. Activities, on the other hand, can be interrupted by any event that causes an outgoing transition from the state containing the activity to fire. For example, the activity of playing the track would be interrupted and terminated if a 'stop' event was detected before the track finished. When a transition leaving a state fires, execution of the activity is interrupted before the exit action is performed.

Completion transitions

As well as being interrupted by events, some activities will come to an end of their own accord. For example, this will happen to the activity in the playing state in Figure 8.7 when the end of the track is reached. In some cases the termination of an activity causes a state transition, and the statechart should specify what state becomes active next.

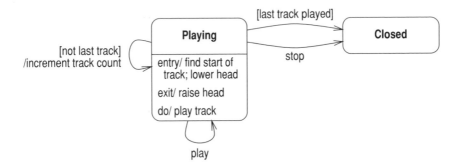

Figure 8.8 Completion transitions

This can be done by means of a *completion transition*. Completion transitions are transitions which have no event labels. They can be triggered when a state's internal activity terminates normally without being interrupted by an external event. Figure 8.8 shows the playing state of the CD player with two completion transitions, one leading from the playing state to the closed state, and one self-transition on the playing state.

While the CD player is playing, the user can press either the play or stop button to interrupt the current track. If neither of these events is detected, the current track will eventually come to an end. In this case, there is no external event to detect, so the only candidate transitions for firing are the completion transitions. What happens next will depend on whether the track that has just finished was the last track on the CD.

The completion transitions have guard conditions to distinguish between these two cases. If the last track has just finished playing, the transition leading to the closed state will fire, and the CD player will stop playing altogether. Otherwise, the self-transition will fire: the track counter will be incremented, the playing state will be re-entered, and the CD player will begin to play the next track on the CD.

Internal transitions

Self-transitions count as changes of state so, as explained above, if either of the self-transitions in Figure 8.8 fires, the activity in the playing state will be terminated and the exit action of the state executed before the state is re-entered, its entry action executed, and its activity restarted.

Sometimes it is necessary to model events which leave an object in the same state, but without triggering a change of state and the execution of entry and exit actions. For example, suppose the CD player has an 'info' button which when pressed causes the time remaining on the current track to be displayed. This should happen without interrupting the ongoing playing of the track.

This can be modelled as an *internal transition* within the playing state. Internal transitions are written inside the state, labelled with the name of the event that causes them, as shown in Figure 8.9. Unlike self-transitions, internal transitions do not cause a change of state and therefore do not trigger entry and exit actions.

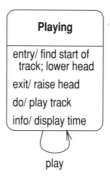

Figure 8.9 A state with an internal transition

8.7 COMPOSITE STATES

Figure 8.5 is rather cluttered and hard to read, and there is a certain amount of redundancy in it, with certain transitions occurring more than once in a virtually identical form. If statecharts are to be usable in practice for complex systems, some method of simplifying diagrams is required. One such technique is provided by allowing a state to contain a number of *substates*. The substates are grouped together in the enclosing state because they share certain properties which can more concisely be represented as properties of a single 'superstate'.

One property that states can share with other states is their behaviour, or in other words, the transitions that they participate in. For example, when the CD player is in the open or closed state, its response to a play event with a CD in the drawer is the same, namely to move to the playing state and to play the CD. Slightly less obviously, the response is the same even if there is no CD present: the player ends up in the closed state. This may or may not involve a change of state, depending on whether the drawer was originally open or closed, but the net effect of the event is the same.

Figure 8.10 shows a statechart for the CD player which uses a superstate to factor out this common behaviour. A new state called 'not playing' has been introduced, and the open and closed states now appear as substates of this new state. The 'not playing' state is known as a *composite state* consisting of the two nested substates.

This new state exists only to group together related states, and does not introduce any new behavioural possibilities for the CD player. Composite states have the following properties. Firstly, if a composite state is active, exactly one of its substates must also be active. So in Figure 8.10, if the CD player is not playing it must also be in either the open or closed state.

Secondly, an event that is detected while an object is in a composite state can trigger outgoing transitions from either the composite state itself or from the currently active substate. For example, suppose that the CD player is in the closed state. If a load event is detected, the transition leading to the open state will fire, and the open state will become active. This is an internal transition of the not playing state, however, and so it remains active, but with a different active substate.

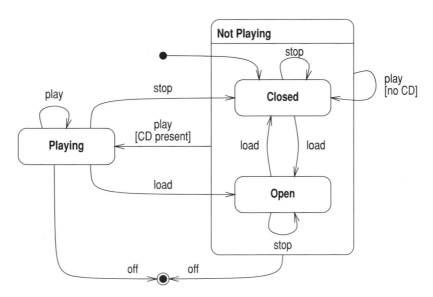

Figure 8.10 The CD player using substates

Suppose on the other hand that a play event is detected. There are no outgoing transitions labelled 'play' leaving the closed state, but there are such transitions leaving the not playing state. As this state is also active, these transitions will be enabled and depending on whether there is a CD in the drawer or not, one or other of them will fire. If a CD is present, the playing state will become active. If not, the closed state will become active, but by means of a self-transition leaving the not playing state.

Substates are perfectly normal states, and transitions to them can freely cross the boundary of the superstate. The stop and load transitions from the playing state in Figure 8.10 illustrate this property. They now cross the boundary of the 'Playing' state, but have not altered in form or meaning from Figure 8.5. Transitions can also connect substates within a single superstate, as the load transitions between the open and closed states demonstrate. Finally, transitions can go from a substate to a state outside the superstate, although Figure 8.10 does not contain an example of this.

Properties of composite states

The nested states within a composite state form a sort of 'sub-statechart' and, in addition to normal states, a composite state can contain initial and final states. An initial state in a composite state shows the default substate that becomes active if a transition to the composite state terminates at the boundary of the composite state. A final state in a composite state indicates that ongoing activity within the state has finished. Arrival at a final state enables completion transitions from the composite state to fire.

Composite states can also have entry and exit actions of their own. These are activated in exactly the same way as with simple states whenever the state becomes, or ceases to be, active.

For example, suppose that pressing a pause button on the CD player causes playing to be interrupted. When the button is pressed again, playing continues from the position where it was paused; in other words, unlike the situation where the play button is pressed, the track is not restarted. The statechart in Figure 8.11 models this behaviour.

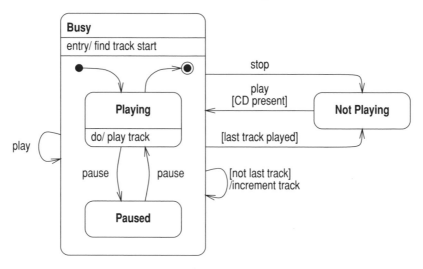

Figure 8.11 Modelling the pause button

This diagram can best be understood by following through some sequences of events in detail. Suppose that the CD player is in the not playing state, and the play button is pressed with a CD in the drawer. The transition labelled 'play' will fire, making the state labelled 'busy' the active state. As a result the entry action of the state is performed and the start of the current track located. This transition does not specify which substate of the busy state becomes active, however, so the internal transition from the initial state to the playing state fires, making the playing state active. As a result, the activity of playing the current track starts.

If the user does nothing to interrupt this, at the end of the track the completion transition from the playing state to the final state within the busy state will fire. This is the normal behaviour when a state's activity terminates. This in turn triggers a completion activity from the composite state. Assuming that there are more tracks to play, the self-transition on the busy state will fire, the track counter will be incremented, and the busy state will be re-entered. As before, this will cause the start of the new track to be located and playing of it to start.

Now suppose that the user presses the pause button before the end of the track. This will interrupt the activity of playing the track and cause the transition to the 'paused' state to fire. When the user presses pause again, the transition leading back to the playing state will fire, and the activity of playing the track will restart. In this case, however, all the transitions have been internal to the busy state, and so the entry action of locating the start of the track will not have been triggered. The playing head will therefore not have been moved and playing will restart from the point of interruption, as required.

8.8 HISTORY STATES

Suppose that the behaviour of the CD player is as described in Figure 8.11, and that the user presses the play button when the CD player is in the paused state. This will fire the self-transition labelled 'play' on the busy state, so the paused state will be exited and the busy state re-entered. The entry action will cause the start of the track to be found and, as the self-transition only leads to the composite state, the transition from the initial state will be followed, leaving the machine in the playing state, playing the CD.

Suppose, however, that the actual behaviour exhibited by the CD player is different, and that pressing the play button when the CD player is paused restarts the track, but leaves the player in the paused state. The user has to press the pause button again before playing will restart. One way of modelling this would be to replace the self-transition on the busy state labelled 'play' by two self-transitions, one on the playing state and one on the paused state.

However, it would be possible to avoid replicating transitions if a transition to a composite state could 'remember' which substate was active last time the composite state was active and automatically return to that substate. If the CD player is playing, it should carry on playing from the start of the track if 'play' is pressed, but if it is paused, it should stay paused until the pause button is pressed again.

This effect can be achieved by the use of a *history state* as shown in Figure 8.12. History states are represented by a capital 'H' within a circle, and can only appear inside composite states. A transition to a history state causes the substate that was most recently active in the composite state to become active again. Now, if 'play' is pressed when the CD player is paused, the self-transition on the busy state will be followed, terminating at the history state. This will cause an implicit transition to the last active substate, which in this case was the paused state, as required.

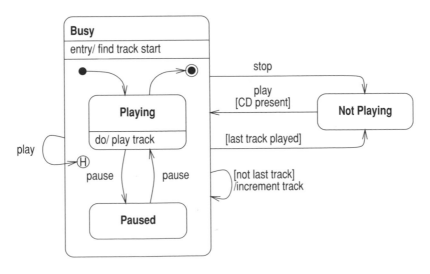

Figure 8.12 A history state

If the stop button was pressed when the CD player was paused, followed by 'play', Figure 8.12 specifies that the player would revert to the playing state. If it was required that it should still be paused, even if playing had been stopped and restarted, this could be modelled by extending the end of the play transition from the boundary of the busy state to the history state.

This raises the question of what would happen if the history state was the first substate of the busy state to be made active: in this case there would, by definition, be no history to remember. In this case we must specify a default state that will be made active. This is done by drawing an unlabelled transition from the history state to the required default, which in this case would be the playing state.

8.9 SUMMARY OF THE CD PLAYER

Figure 8.13 shows a complete statechart describing the behaviour of the CD player, incorporating many of the points that have been discussed in this chapter. This diagram has been derived by combining Figures 8.10 and 8.12. An initial state has been added to the 'not playing' state, and also an additional history state to indicate that pressing the stop button while no CD is being played has no effect, and does not cause the player to change its state.

Further extensions and modifications to this diagram are suggested as exercises at the end of this chapter.

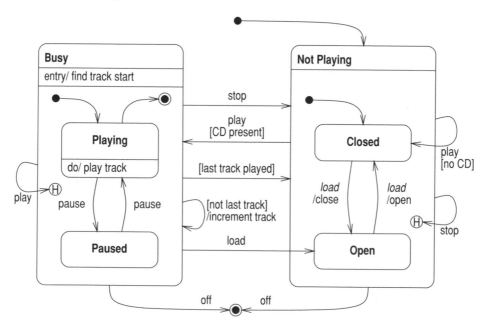

Figure 8.13 Complete statechart for the CD player

8.10 DYNAMIC MODELLING IN PRACTICE

This section illustrates a process which can be useful for constructing a statechart, and in so doing explains how information derived from interaction diagrams can be used to derive statecharts. The example used is the automatic ticket machine described in the following paragraphs.

The ticket machine can accept money and other input from a passenger, and at the end of a successful transaction issues the requested ticket and any necessary change. When no transaction is in progress the machine displays either the message 'Exact money required' or 'Change available'. The message displayed determines whether the next customer must enter exactly the amount of money required to pay for the ticket selected, or whether the machine is able to give change when more money than necessary is entered.

The interface of the machine consists of a number of buttons, each corresponding to a given type of ticket. If the user presses one of these buttons, the machine displays an amount of money to be entered, namely the cost of the ticket. As the user enters money into the machine, the amount displayed is reduced by the amount that the user entered. As soon as an amount of money greater than or equal to the cost of the ticket has been entered, one of two things can happen. If the machine originally displayed the 'Change available' message, the required ticket together with any necessary change will be issued. If the 'Exact money required' message was displayed, a ticket will only be issued if the user entered exactly the amount of money requested. If the user has entered too much money, all the money entered will be returned.

At the beginning of the transaction, the user has the option of entering money before selecting a ticket type. If when a ticket is finally selected, enough money has already been entered to pay for it, a ticket and change will be issued as in the previous case. If the money entered is less than the cost of the selected ticket, the machine will display the remaining cost and will carry on as in the previous case.

In any event, if no input is received from the user in any period of 30 seconds, the transaction will be terminated, and any money that has already been entered will be returned to the customer. A 'cancel' button is also available to enable the user to terminate a transaction explicitly.

State machines and event sequences

A statechart summarizes all the possible sequences of events that an object can receive. It can sometimes be rather difficult to identify all the states that are necessary to model the object's behaviour accurately, however. The technique presented here avoids this difficulty by considering only one sequence of events at a time, and gradually building up a complete description of the required statechart.

Individual sequences of events can be obtained from interaction diagrams. The messages arriving at an individual object, when arranged in the order in which the object receives them, make up such a sequence. On the statechart for that object, it must be possible to trace a path corresponding to each such sequence of events.

When constructing a statechart we can start by taking a single sequence and defining a simple statechart which represents that sequence only. Further sequences of events can then be integrated into this preliminary statechart, and in this way a complete diagram can be built up in a step-by-step manner.

The remainder of this section will illustrate this process for the example of the ticket machine. A number of typical transactions involving the ticket machine will be considered, and a complete statechart will be gradually built up. Formal object interaction diagrams will not be drawn, as there is only one object involved in these transactions, namely the ticket machine itself, and the only messages sent are a sequence of events generated by the user.

Selecting a ticket before paying

Suppose that a user first selects a particular ticket type, and then enters three coins, one after the other. The total value of the three coins amounts to more than the cost of the ticket, so the machine issues the ticket and the required change, and returns to an idle state waiting for the next transaction. A sequence of four events is received by the machine in this case: a 'ticket' event is followed by three 'coin' events. Each of these events has associated data giving the cost of the selected ticket and the value of each coin entered, but we will ignore this detail for the moment.

A very simple statechart can be drawn for any individual sequence of events simply by assuming that every event corresponds to a transition between two states; in effect we place states at the beginning and end of the sequence, and also between each pair of events. In the current case we end up with the statechart shown in Figure 8.14. As this is only a preliminary diagram, no attempt has been made to label the states.

Figure 8.14 Preliminary statechart for the ticket machine

Although this statechart is an accurate model of the single sequence of events considered, it requires some restructuring before it will serve as an adequate foundation for the statechart of the ticket machine. Firstly, Figure 8.14 defines only one transaction, whereas the ticket machine is capable of carrying out repeated transactions, one after the other. To model this, we can unify the first and last states of Figure 8.14. As these states represent the situation where no transaction is in progress, we will label this new state 'Idle'.

Secondly, the number of coins entered in the sample transaction above is essentially arbitrary. Any number of coins could be entered in a transaction: the precise number required depends on the cost of the selected ticket and the value of the coins that are entered. Some kind of loop is required to show the possibility of entering an arbitrary number of coins. This can be achieved by combining the three intermediate states of Figure 8.14 into a single state with a self-transition.

A refined version of the statechart for this initial transaction which incorporates these modifications is shown in Figure 8.15. This consists of only two states, derived from the initial five states of Figure 8.14 as explained above. The machine starts off in the idle state, and when the user selects a ticket the transition leading to the 'paying for ticket' state is followed. When coins are subsequently entered, one of two things can happen. If the total amount of money entered is enough to pay for the selected ticket, the transition back to the idle state is followed. If on the other hand more money is required, the self-transition on the paying state is followed, and further coins must be entered to continue the transaction.

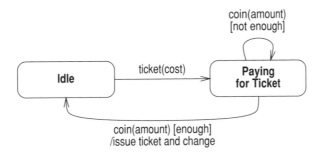

Figure 8.15 A more refined statechart

Figure 8.15 uses several features of the statechart notation introduced earlier to clarify the behaviour of the machine in this transaction. Firstly, parameters are attached to the various messages to transmit the cost of the ticket and the value of each coin to the machine. Secondly, there are two transitions labelled with the 'coin' event leaving the paying state. They are distinguished by means of an informal guard condition which checks whether enough money to pay for the selected ticket has been entered. Finally, the actions performed by the machine if enough money has been entered are also shown on the transition leading back to the idle state. In this example, we are assuming that the machine is able to issue the required change.

Paying before selecting a ticket

We have now dealt with one possible transaction, and constructed a preliminary statechart. The next step is to consider a second transaction and to integrate it as far as possible into the existing statechart, extending the statechart where necessary.

As well as initially selecting a ticket, the specification of the ticket machine also allows the user to enter money before selecting the required ticket. The sequence of events corresponding to this transaction starts with a number of coin events, and when a ticket event is received the ticket and change are issued and the transaction finishes. We can assume that the transaction starts in the idle state already identified in Figure 8.15. There is a problem with the first event, however, as Figure 8.15 contains no transition labelled 'coin' leading from the idle state. We therefore need to extend the statechart with a suitable transition, leading to a new state.

As in the previous case, any number of coins can be entered, and we can model this by means of a self-transition on this new state. Finally, a ticket event will be received, and the machine will issue the ticket and change and return to the idle state. Figure 8.16 shows the statechart with these additions.

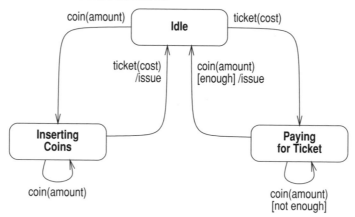

Figure 8.16 Incorporating a second transaction

Integrating the transactions

The two transactions considered so far are mirror images of each other. In the first, the ticket type was selected before any coins were entered, and in the second, after all the coins have been entered. The specification of the ticket machine allows for a third possibility, however, where some coins are entered before the ticket type is selected, but then further coins need to be entered to make up the cost of the ticket. This possibility is not catered for on Figure 8.16: once coins have been entered, selection of a ticket type returns the state machine to the idle state, leaving no possibility of continuing the transaction by entering more coins.

What is required is an additional transition labelled 'ticket' leading from the 'inserting coins' state of Figure 8.16. This transition should be differentiated from the existing one by means of a condition. The necessary condition is the same as the one that distinguishes whether insertion of a coin causes the machine to return to the idle state when the user is paying for a ticket, namely whether enough money has been entered to pay for the selected ticket or not.

This new transition could lead to a new state: to meet the specification of the ticket machine, the new state would have to allow for coins to be entered until the value of the ticket had been reached, whereupon the ticket would be issued and the machine would return to the idle state. This is precisely the behaviour provided by the existing 'paying for ticket' state, however, so the new transition can be defined to arrive at this state, as shown in Figure 8.17. The names of the states have been changed to reflect the relevant difference between them more accurately, which is simply whether or not the user has selected the ticket type.

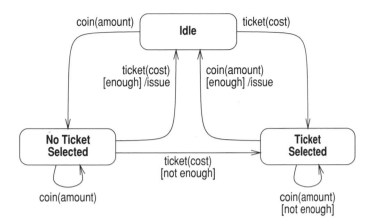

Figure 8.17 Integrating the two transactions

The statechart in Figure 8.17 summarizes all the possible sequences of events that the user can generate in the course of a transaction that terminates in the issue of a ticket, in the sense that any given sequence of events corresponds to a connected path through the statechart. In a transaction, any number of coins can be entered, the ticket type can be selected once, and these events can take place in any order.

Users of the ticket machine will not always behave in such a sensible manner, however. It is easy to imagine a user selecting a ticket type, then having second thoughts and selecting an alternative type before entering any coins. The statechart of Figure 8.17 does not allow for this possibility. Once a ticket type has been selected, the machine enters the 'ticket selected' state, and there are no ticket transitions out of this state. There seems to be a contradiction here between what the user can in fact do and what the statechart specifies.

One way of explaining this kind of phenomenon is to note that although the user can in fact press the ticket selection buttons repeatedly, this does not necessarily mean that 'ticket' events are received by the machine. It might be the case, for example, that the ticket selection buttons were deactivated once the 'ticket selected' state is entered, and only reactivated when the idle state is reached again.

If this were not the case, some explicit account of additional ticket events would need to be given in the statechart. This could be achieved in a number of ways, perhaps by introducing an error state if such events were to be disallowed, or a self-transition on the 'ticket selected' state if they were permitted. In a realistic example, of course, the choice between these options would be governed by the actual behaviour of the ticket machine being modelled.

Figure 8.17 accurately models the basic behaviour of the ticket machine. To complete the model it is necessary to show the alternative ways in which transactions can be terminated, namely by pressing the cancel button or by a timeout, and also the alternative behaviour in the situations where the machine requires that the exact cost of tickets is entered. Before completing the ticket machine statechart, the notation required to model these features will be introduced.

8.11 TIME EVENTS

If no input is received from the user for 30 seconds, the ticket machine will time out: the current transaction will be terminated, and any money entered will be returned to the customer. A time out should be modelled by a transition, as it will change the state of the ticket machine from an intermediate state in a transition back to the initial idle state. However, it is not obvious what event should label such a transition: the whole point, after all, is that such a transition has to fire precisely when no event is detected.

UML defines special *time events* which can be used in these cases. Figure 8.18 shows a transition that will fire 30 seconds after the 'no ticket selected' state is entered. This can be understood by imagining that an implicit activity of each state is to run a timer, which is reset every time the state is entered. An outgoing transition from a state which is labelled with a time event will fire as soon as the timer has been running for the period of time specified in the time event. In Figure 8.18, notice that the timer is reset every time a coin is entered, because a self-transition counts as a change of state and triggers a state's entry actions.

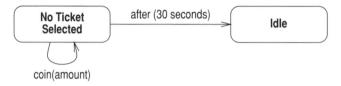

Figure 8.18 A time event

Following the keyword 'after', any period of time can be given as a parameter. An alternative form of time event consists of the keyword 'when' followed by a a specified point in time. This defines a transition which will fire when the specified time is reached.

8.12 ACTIVITY STATES

In Figure 8.17, two separate transitions lead back to the idle state after a transaction has been successfully completed. In each case it is necessary to check whether the machine is able to return any change that is required. If it can, the change and the ticket should be issued, and if not the money entered should be returned.

This behaviour could be represented by a pair of transitions with appropriate guard conditions and actions, but these would have to be repeated on each route back to the idle state. To avoid this repetition, an *activity state* can be used to simplify the structure of the statechart, as shown in Figure 8.19.

An activity state represents a period of time during which an object is performing some internal processing. As such, it is shown on a statechart as a state which contains only an activity. In Figure 8.19, as soon as a customer's input to a transaction is complete, the activity state becomes active, corresponding to the machine working out whether it is capable of returning the change required to complete the transaction.

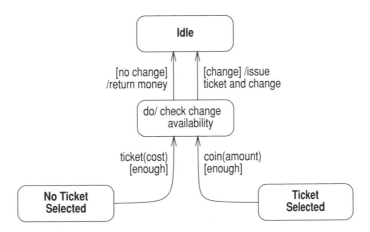

Figure 8.19 An activity state

The internal processes represented by activity states often cannot be interrupted by external events, and in these cases the only transitions leaving an activity state will be completion transactions. In Figure 8.19 there are two such transitions, differentiated by guard conditions that state whether or not change is available. In each case, these transitions also carry an appropriate action.

Activity states should be used sparingly on statecharts, as the purpose of a statechart is usually to show the response of an object to external events and not to model internal processing in detail. On occasion, however, they can be useful, as in Figure 8.19, as devices to simplify the structure of a statechart.

8.13 SUMMARY OF THE TICKET MACHINE

Figure 8.20 shows a complete statechart for the ticket machine. It incorporates the various points made in the preceding sections, and also shows the effect of the user pressing cancel in the middle of a transaction.

To reduce the number of transitions required to specify the interruption of a transaction by either a time out or a cancellation, a composite state has been included in Figure 8.20. It is intended to correspond to the period of time during which a transaction is in progress.

8.14 SUMMARY

- Statecharts provide a specification of the behavioural aspects of objects that can be illustrated on interaction diagrams.
- Statecharts show the events that an object can detect throughout its lifetime, and its responses to those events.

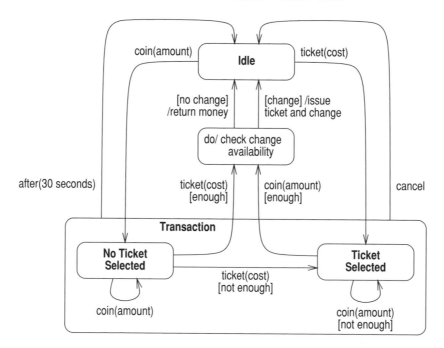

Figure 8.20 Complete statechart for the ticket machine

- In general, objects exhibit state-dependent behaviour. States are distinguished by the fact that the detection of an event can have a different effect, depending on what state the object is in.

- The detection of an event can cause a transition to fire, where an object moves from one state to another.

- Guard conditions can be used to show which one out of a set of transitions actually fires on a particular occasion.

- Actions specify the response of an object to an event. Entry and exit actions on states are equivalent to actions on all incoming and outgoing transitions, respectively.

- States can include activities which take place throughout the time that an object is in that state. Activities can be interrupted by user-generated events. If an activity terminates without interruption, a completion transition out of the state will be followed.

- Composite states can be used to simplify complex statecharts. A transition from a superstate applies equally to all of the nested substates. The effect of a transition to a superstate is specified by means of an initial state within the superstate.

- Statecharts can be developed by considering individual sequences of events, derived from object interaction diagrams, in turn. Firstly, a simple statechart is developed to model one such sequence, and then this is extended where necessary by considering additional sequences.

8.15 EXERCISES

8.1 What state is the CD player specified in Figure 8.13 in after the following sequences of events are detected? Assume that a CD is always present when tested for.

(*a*) initialize, load.

(*b*) initialize, load, play, stop.

(*c*) initialize, load, play, pause, play

(*d*) initialize, play, stop, load.

(*e*) initialize, load, pause, play.

8.2 This question refers to the dynamic model of the CD player given in Figure 8.13. Suppose that the player is turned off when it is in the open state, with no CD in the drawer and the drawer open, and is then immediately powered on again. What state is the CD player in after these operations? What is the physical condition of the drawer of the CD player? What will happen if the user now presses the load button? What buttons would the user have to press in order to close the drawer of the CD player?

8.3 Draw a revised version of Figure 8.12 modelling the requirement that the CD player should remain paused even when 'stop' and then 'play' are pressed.

8.4 Is a default transition required from the history state in the not playing state in Figure 8.13? If not, why not? If so, which substate should it go to?

8.5 The description of the CD player in this chapter has left vague the details of how it records which is the current track. Assume that the CD player has an attribute called the 'track counter' which behaves as follows.

When no CD is in the drawer, the track counter is set to zero. When a CD is detected, the track counter is set to 1; this happens when the drawer is physically closed following the detection of either load or play event. The track counter determines which track start is located, and hence which track is played, whenever the busy state is entered.

Two buttons, labelled 'forward' and 'back', allow the user to adjust the track counter manually. If no CD is in the drawer, these buttons have no effect. Otherwise, pressing 'forward' increments the track counter and pressing 'back' decrements it. Pressing either of these buttons when the CD player is in the busy state causes the playing head to move immediately to the start of the requested track.

Extend the statechart in Figure 8.13 so that it models this behaviour.

8.6 In the ticket machine example of Section 8.10, suppose that the ticket selection buttons are deactivated once a ticket type has been selected, and only reactivated at the end of a transaction. In addition, suppose that once enough money has been entered to pay for the required ticket, the coin entry slot is closed, and only reopened once any ticket and change has been issued. Use entry and exit actions to show this behaviour explicitly on the statechart of Figure 8.20.

8.7 Redraw Figure 8.20 with the activity state removed, and compare the resulting statechart with Figure 8.20 from the point of view of clarity and comprehensibility.

8.8 Alter the statechart of Figure 8.20 so that the availability of change is checked at the start of a transaction and a suitable message displayed, as specified in Section 8.10.

8.9 Redraw the statechart given in Figure Ex8.9, removing all the composite states and replacing all transitions to and from the composite states with equivalent transitions between the remaining states.

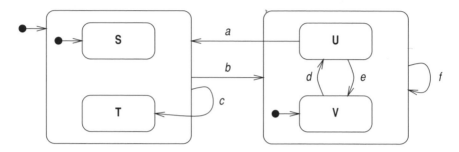

Figure Ex8.9 A statechart using nested states

8.10 Demonstrate that the two statecharts in Figure Ex8.10 are not equivalent in meaning by finding a sequence of events that is accepted by one but not by the other. Assume that sequences start from the initial state shown.

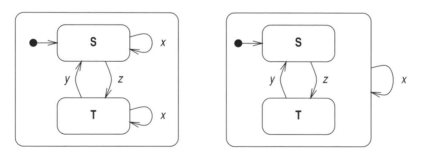

Figure Ex8.10 Two nonequivalent statecharts

8.11 The lights in a lecture theatre are controlled by a panel of three switches, labelled 'On', 'Off' and 'Dim'. 'On' switches the lights on to their full brightness, and 'Off' switches them off. There is also an intermediate level of brightness, used when slides and other projected material are being shown. The 'Dim' switch reduces the lighting level from full to this intermediate level; full brightness can be restored by pressing the 'On' switch again. Draw a state diagram modelling the behaviour of the lighting system in this lecture theatre.

8.12 A window in a window management system can be displayed in one of three states: *maximized*, where it takes up the entire screen; *normal*, where it is displayed as a bordered window with a given size and position on the screen; and *iconized*, where it is displayed as a small icon. When a window is opened, it will be displayed as a normal window, unless *minimize on use* has been selected, in which case it will be displayed as an icon. A normal window and an icon can be maximized; a maximized window and a normal window can be minimized, or reduced to an icon. Maximized windows can be restored to their normal size, and icons can be restored to the size they had before they were minimized. Icons and normal windows can be moved, and normal windows can also be resized. No matter how it is displayed, a window can always be closed. Draw a state diagram expressing these facts about the display of windows.

8.13 A description of the behaviour of an automated telling machine (ATM) is given below. Produce a state diagram describing its behaviour. List any assumptions you have to make as a result of ambiguity, unclarity or incompleteness of the description.

A user begins a transaction at the ATM by entering a bank card. Assuming that the card is readable by the machine, the user is prompted to enter their personal identification number (PIN). Once this number has been entered, a menu is presented to the user containing the following options: show account balance, withdrawal with receipt or withdrawal without receipt. If the user selects one of the withdrawal options, they are prompted to enter an amount of money to withdraw; the amount entered must be a multiple of 10.

The user's PIN is validated when the ATM sends the details of the transaction to the bank's remote computer. If the PIN was invalid, the user is given the option of reentering it, and the selected transaction is retried. This is repeated if the new PIN is also invalid. Once three invalid PINs have been entered, the transaction is terminated and the user's card is retained by the machine.

If a valid PIN was entered, further processing depends on the transaction type selected. For a 'show balance' transaction, the balance is displayed on the screen, and after confirming this, the user is returned to the transaction menu. A withdrawal transaction may fail if the user has exceeded the amount of money that can be withdrawn from the account; in this case an error message is displayed, and after confirmation, the user is returned to the transaction menu. Otherwise, the user's card is returned and the money is issued, followed by the receipt if required.

At any point where user input, other than a simple confirmation, is required, a 'cancel' option is provided. If this is selected, the user's card is returned and their interaction with the ATM terminates.

8.14 A simple digital watch consists of a display showing hours and minutes separated by a flashing colon, and provides two buttons (A and B) which enable the display to be updated.

(*a*) To add two to the number of hours displayed, the following actions should be performed, where button B increments the hours display:

Press A; press B; press B; press A; press A.

Draw a simple statechart showing precisely this sequence of events.

(*b*) In the above interaction, the hours displayed could be incremented by any required number, and the whole interaction could be repeated as often as required. Redraw the statechart to incorporate these generalizations.

(*c*) To increment the number of minutes displayed by the watch, button A can be pressed twice, followed by repeated presses of button B, each of which increases the minutes displayed by 1. Draw a complete statechart for the watch, incorporating updates to both the hours and minutes displayed. Give the states in your statechart meaningful names, and add appropriate actions to any transition labelled 'press B'.

(*d*) The watch is subsequently enhanced to incorporate an alarm, and the following interaction is proposed as a way of setting the time of the alarm:

Press A; press A; press B (repeatedly); press A; press B (repeatedly); press A.

The intention is that the user presses button A twice in quick succession, like a 'double click' with a mouse. Explain how this proposal would introduce non-determinism into the statechart for the digital watch. Show how you could remove the non-determinism by introducing an extra state into the statechart.

8.15 Draw a statechart summarizing the information given in the following description some of the events that can arise in the life cycle of a thread in Java.

> When a thread is created, it does not start running immediately, but is left in the *New Thread* state. When the thread is in this state, it can only be started or stopped. Calling any method besides *start* or *stop* makes no sense, and causes an exception to be raised.
>
> The *start* method causes system resources to be allocated to the thread, and calls the thread's *run* method. At this point the thread is in the *Running* state.
>
> A thread becomes not runnable if either its *sleep* or *suspend* methods are called. The *sleep* method has a parameter specifying the length of time the thread should sleep for; when this time has elapsed the thread starts to run again. If the *suspend* method has been called, the thread only runs again when its *resume* method is called.
>
> A thread can die in two ways. It dies naturally when its *run* method exits normally. A thread can also be killed at any time by calling its *stop* method.

9

CONSTRAINTS

Much of the notation introduced so far in this book has been graphical. Text has been used primarily for naming and labelling model elements, rather than for conveying any formal properties of the system being modelled. The guard conditions written on statecharts are a notable exception to this.

Graphical notations are well suited for displaying structural aspects of systems, but less effective for documenting the fine details of a system's specification. One disadvantage is that graphical notation can quickly become very complex. An example of this is the class diagram in Figure 6.34 where rather complicated notation is required in order to express a fairly straightforward property of the model.

Graphical notations can be supplemented where necessary by textual annotations which state properties that are not implied by the diagrams. Such annotations are known as *constraints*. A constraint is an assertion about a model element, often a class, which states properties that must be satisfied in a legal model of the system.

For example, suppose that a bank is introducing a new type of savings account which pays a preferential rate of interest. However, the balance of the account must remain within the range 0 to £250,000 and a deposit or withdrawal that would take the balance outside this range will be rejected. A class representing savings accounts is shown in Figure 9.1, with the constraint represented informally in a note.

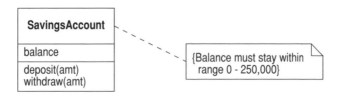

Figure 9.1 An unconstrained savings account

Further situations where constraints are required occur in the diagram editor, whose design was summarized in Figure 4.19. By using a selection tool, the user of the diagram editor can select elements and subsequently move or resize them. Two constraints on this activity are that selected elements must appear on the current diagram, and that an element that is being resized must also be selected. Neither of these properties, however, are guaranteed by the model given in Figure 4.19.

Constraints are written in UML in braces '{' and '}' in or near the model element that they describe. UML defines standard constraints for a handful of common situations. More general constraints can be written either in informal English, in a more formal constraint language, or even using the notation of the target programming language. UML defines a constraint language, called the *Object Constraint Language* or OCL, and this chapter describes the most important features of this language and gives examples of their use.

9.1 STANDARD CONSTRAINTS

In Chapter 7, some of the classifier and association roles on interaction diagrams were provided with the constraints 'new' and 'destroyed' to indicate that objects playing those roles were created or destroyed in the course of an interaction. Examples of this notation appear in Figures 7.9 and 7.11. These diagrams illustrate the convention of writing a constraint in braces and placing it on a diagram in close proximity to the model element being constrained.

'New' and 'destroyed' are simple examples of the standard constraints defined by UML. Two other commonly used standard constraints describe properties of pairs of related associations.

The subset constraint

The subset constraint can be applied to pairs of associations that link the same classes, and states that the set of links which are instances of one association must be a subset of those of another. The constraint is shown by joining the associations with a dependency arrow to which the constraint is attached.

Figure 9.2 shows an example of how this constraint could be used in the context of the diagram editor to specify that an element that is being resized must be one of the elements that is currently selected.

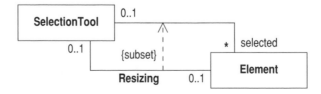

Figure 9.2 The subset constraint

In general, this constraint means that if two objects are linked by an instance of the association at the tail of the dependency arrow, they must also be linked by an instance of the association at the head of the dependency arrow. If a selection tool is being used to resize an element, it will be linked to it by an instance of the 'resizing' association in Figure 9.2. The constraint then requires that it is also linked to it by an instance of the upper association, or in other words that the element is one of the selected elements on the current diagram.

The xor constraint

The xor constraint can be applied to pairs of associations that are connected at one end to the same class. It is used to specify that an instance of the shared class can not participate in both associations at the same time. Figure 9.3 shows an example of the use of the xor constraint to specify that one of the bank's customers cannot hold both a savings account and a deposit account at the same time.

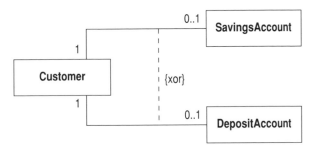

Figure 9.3 The xor constraint

In general, this constraint means that an instance of the class that is connected to both the constrained associations can at any given time participate in a link from one of the associations or the other, but not both. Notice that this means that the multiplicity of the constrained associations must include the zero case.

9.2 THE OBJECT CONSTRAINT LANGUAGE

The standard constraints are useful in particular cases, but in order to handle the arbitrary constraints that can arise in modelling a constraint specification language is required. OCL, the Object Constraint Language, is a text-based formal language which allows completely general constraints to be written for the elements appearing in UML models, particularly in class diagrams.

For example, consider the object diagram in Figure 9.4 which shows an impossible state of the diagram editor, where the element that is currently selected belongs to the 'wrong' diagram, namely a diagram which is not the one that the selection tool is working on. This diagram is a legitimate instance of the diagram editor as specified in Figure 4.19, however, so a constraint needs to be defined to rule it out.

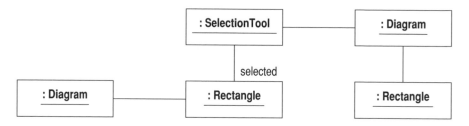

Figure 9.4 An impossible situation

Stated informally, the constraint that needs to be added to the class diagram in Figure 4.19 is that selected elements must belong to the diagram that the selection tool is linked to. We can define this constraint as a property of the selection tool class. Imagine taking an arbitrary instance of this class, and first identifying the diagram it is linked to. Then, for each selected element linked to the tool, we can identify the diagram that that element belongs to. The required constraint is then that in all these cases we should arrive at the same diagram instance.

This example suggests that a constraint language such as OCL has to provide three essential capabilities.

1. The ability to specify which model element is being constrained. This is known as the *context* of the constraint, and is discussed in Section 9.3.
2. The ability to navigate through a model to identify other objects which may be relevant to the constraint being defined. This is done by means of *navigation expressions* which are discussed in Section 9.4.
3. The ability to make assertions about the relationships between the context object and any objects retrieved by means of navigation expressions. These assertions are similar to the boolean expressions used in programming languages but, as discussed in Section 9.6, they are more expressive.

9.3 THE CONTEXT OF A CONSTRAINT

Every OCL constraint has a *context*, which is simply the model element that is being constrained. Very often, the context of a constraint will be a class. When giving a constraint, its context must be made clear. If context is a class, this can be done by writing the constraint in the class symbol near the element constrained. For example, Figure 9.5 shows the account class from Figure 9.1 with a constraint added to specify that an account's balance must fall within the specified limits.

Constraints can also be shown as notes attached to the appropriate model element. This was illustrated, with an informal version of the constraint, in Figure 9.1. It is purely a question of style which method of presenting a constraint is chosen.

This constraint asserts that in all instances of the savings account class, at all times, the value stored in the balance attribute must be greater than 0 and less than £250,000. This constraint is an example of a *class invariant*, discussed further in Section 9.7.

Figure 9.5 A simple constraint

Constraints can also be written in textual form, instead of being shown on a diagram. In this case, the context needs to be explicitly recorded. An alternative way of writing the constraint shown in Figure 9.5 is the following.

```
SavingsAccount
self.balance > 0 and self.balance < 250000
```

The keyword 'self' in the textual form of the constraint simply refers to the current context object. Its presence is unnecessary in this case, as constraints are always evaluated in this context anyway. Its use can make constraints easier to read, however, and it will often be inserted in constraints in the remainder of this chapter.

This constraint also illustrates the OCL notation for accessing the features of an object, namely to write the feature name separated by a dot from an expression which denotes the object. This notation is clearly chosen to resemble the notation used in languages such as Java and C++ for accessing features of classes.

9.4 NAVIGATION EXPRESSIONS

The use of constraints is not limited to stating the invariants of classes considered in isolation. As the discussion of the situation depicted in Figure 9.2 illustrated, many constraints place restrictions on the relationships that can exist between model elements. In order to do this, OCL must provide ways of referring to the objects that are linked to a given context object.

Informally, these linked objects are located by starting from a context object and then following links to gain access to other objects. As this process involves traversing part of the network of objects, the expressions that denote objects are sometimes known as *navigation expressions*. Most of the complexity of OCL arises from the details of the expressions that are needed to denote navigation across the various forms of association defined in UML.

The class diagram in Figure 9.6 will be used to illustrate the OCL notation for forming navigation expressions. This diagram models some information that might be maintained by a personnel department in a large company. The company is modelled as an aggregate of a number of departments. Each employee in the company is allocated to a department. A self-association on the employee class shows who in the company is managed by whom. A qualified association allows individual employees to be accessed by a unique payroll number.

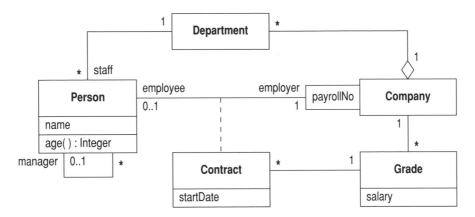

Figure 9.6 A simple model of a personnel system

The association between the person and company classes represents the relationship of a person working for the company. Further details about an employee's contract of employment are recorded by defining this relationship as an association class, 'Contract'. This class records the date on which the employee started work, and maintains an association with a 'grade' class, instances of which record the salary associated with a particular grade within the organization.

Following links

The basic form of navigation involves following links from one object to another. This is specified by giving the names of the associations that are to be traversed. To show navigation, role names on the association end opposite the context object are written after the name of that object, using the dot notation for attributes that was shown above. The value of such an expression is taken to be the set of objects that are currently linked to the object through the specified link.

For example, given the classes and associations shown in Figure 9.6, the following navigation expression denotes the employees working in a department at the time the expression is evaluated.

```
Department
self.staff
```

If an association has no role name, the name of the class at the further end of the association is used instead, with a lower-case initial letter. Given the diagram in Figure 9.6, the following expression refers to the set of all departments in the company. This example also illustrates that there is no difference between aggregations and ordinary associations as far as navigation expressions are concerned.

```
Company
self.department
```

The class name cannot be used in this way if there is any danger of ambiguity, for example if there are two associations between a pair of classes. In this case, suitable role names must be added to the associations to allow the required navigation expressions to be formed unambiguously.

Collections

A navigation expression denotes the objects that are retrieved by following the specified links from the context object. Depending on the multiplicities of the associations traversed, however, the number of such objects may vary.

For example, both the expressions above will in general retrieve more than one object, namely all the staff in a department and the set of departments in a company. In contrast, the following expressions, which describe the department and manager of an employee, cannot return more than one object, given the definition of the relevant associations. The second may return no objects, in the case that a person has no manager.

```
Person
self.department
```

```
Person
self.manager
```

In general, in OCL a navigation expression that can return more than one object is said to return a *collection*, whereas others simply return single objects. As OCL allows single objects to be treated as collections wherever necessary, the simplest approach is to think of every navigation as returning a collection of objects. The detailed properties of collections are important in some situations, however, and they are discussed further in Section 9.5.

Iterated traversal

Navigation expressions are not limited to following a single association. More complicated paths through a diagram can be described by writing a sequence of role or class names, separated by dots. For example, the following expression is one way of denoting all the people who work for a company.

```
Company
self.department.staff
```

We can think of expressions like this as being evaluated in a step-by-step manner. Firstly, the collection consisting of all the departments in the company is retrieved. Then, for each of these departments, the collection of all the people working in the department is retrieved. These collections of people are then merged together to form a large collection containing everybody who works for the company. This large collection is the value returned by the expression.

Traversing qualified associations

Qualified associations can be used in navigation just as well as ordinary ones, but they provide an additional capacity for locating individual objects. When navigating towards the qualifier, there is no difference between a qualified and an unqualified association. For example, the following expression denotes the company that a person works for.

```
Person
self.employer
```

When navigating in the opposite direction, however, the qualifier provides a way of picking out a particular employee whose payroll number is known. The following expression denotes the employee, if there is one, whose payroll number is 314159.

```
Company
self.employee[314159]
```

This notation can be freely combined with subsequent navigation or selection of attributes. For example, the following expression returns the manager of the employee with payroll number 314159.

```
Company
self.employee[314159].manager
```

Using association classes

We can navigate from an instance of an association class to the objects at the ends of the association, using role names or class names as normal. For example, the following expression denotes the set of all employees at a particular grade.

```
Grade
self.contract.employee
```

To navigate in the other direction, the name of the association class can be used like a role name to direct the navigation. For example, the following expression denotes the grade of a particular employee.

```
Person
self.contract.grade
```

9.5 OBJECTS AND COLLECTIONS

OCL is designed so that in many situations the distinction between individual objects and collections, or between different kinds of collections, can be ignored. There are occasions, however, where failure to understand these distinctions can have serious consequences. This section describes some of the different types defined by OCL, including the collection types, and the most important operations available.

Operations on objects

Apart from collections, the types available in OCL consist of *basic types* representing boolean values, real and integer numbers and strings, and *model types* corresponding to classes defined in the UML model for which constraints are being written. The basic types are fairly standard, and will not be explicitly discussed here.

Model types have attributes and operations defined for them in the UML model. These are written in OCL after an expression designating an object of the model type, separated by a dot. For example, the first of the following expressions denotes the age of an employee, and the second denotes the employee's salary.

```
Person
self.age()
self.contract.grade.salary
```

A natural extension of the notation for navigation expressions allows collections of attribute values to be constructed. For example, the following expression denotes the collection containing of the names of the employees belonging to a particular department.

```
Department
self.staff.name
```

Different types of collection

Suppose that in the organization described by the model in Figure 9.6, an operation is to be defined enabling departments to calculate their salary bill. One way of doing this would be to form a collection containing the grade objects corresponding to each staff member in the department, and then to add up the values of the salary attribute in each of these to arrive at the total. It would be natural to write the following navigation expression to represent the collection of grade objects for the employees in the department.

```
Department
staff.contract.grade
```

However, consider what would happen if the department contained two or more employees on the same grade. If this was the case, the same grade object would be reached many times, once for each employee on that grade. The question now arises, how many occurrences of the grade object will there be in the collection returned by the navigation expression above?

The answer to this question could make a big difference to the total salary bill that is calculated. If the collection is like a mathematical set, in which duplicate objects cannot appear, each grade object will appear only once, no matter how many employees the department contains at that grade. If this is the case, the total salary that is calculated will obviously be too low.

What is required in this example is a form of collection which can contain duplicate items, so that grade objects can be stored once for each employee at that grade, and the correct salary bill worked out. Such a collection is known as a *bag*.

OCL specifies that whenever more than one association with a multiplicity greater than one is traversed, the collection that is returned is in fact a bag, not a set. This rule applies here, as both the department to person and contract to grade associations that are traversed in the expression above have a multiplicity greater than one, in one direction or the other.

In this case, then, the semantics of OCL ensure that the expression returns the required collection. Suppose, on the other hand, that the requirement had been to print a report listing the different grades that were represented in the department. In this case, a set would have been the preferred type of collection, as we do not care how many employees there are at each grade. To deal with this situation, OCL provides an operation, described below, which converts a bag to a set.

Operations on collections

OCL defines a number of basic operations on collections of all types. One of these is an operation 'sum', which adds together all the elements in the collection and returns the total. Using this operation, the total salary bill for a department could be defined as shown below. Notice that the symbol '->' is used in OCL to indicate that a collection operation is being applied.

```
Department
staff.contract.grade.salary->sum()
```

Another useful operation returns the size of a collection. This could be combined with the 'asSet' operation, which converts a bag to a set, to return the number of distinct grades that are represented within a department, as follows.

```
Department
staff.contract.grade->asSet()->size
```

All the navigation expressions we have considered so far have returned a collection consisting of all the objects that are available as a result of the specified navigation. Sometimes, however, it is necessary to consider only a subset of the objects returned. For example, a particular constraint might apply not to all the employees in a company, but only to those whose salary is greater than £50,000.

This particular example could be handled if it was possible to form a new collection by picking out the required employees from the larger collection returned by a simple navigation. OCL provides a number of operations on collections to perform such tasks. Here for example is a navigation expression returning the collection consisting of all employees in a company with a salary greater than £50,000.

```
Company
employee->select(p:Person | p.contract.grade.salary > 50000)
```

The term 'employee' at the start of this expression represents a simple navigation which retrieves all the company's employees. This is followed by a 'select' operation which applies a boolean expression to each object in this intermediate collection. The collection returned as a result of the whole expression contains only those objects in the intermediate collection for which the boolean expression returns the value true.

The notation for the select operation includes the declaration of a 'local variable' which provides a context for navigation in the boolean expression. In this case, the intermediate collection formed is a collection of instances of the model type 'Person', so a variable of this type is defined and used as the context object in the following expression. The declaration of this variable, and its use at the start of the nested navigation is often unnecessary, as the type of the objects in the intermediate collection can be worked out from the first part of the expression.

The result of a select operation is a collection which can perfectly well serve as a basis for further navigation. For example, the expression below retrieves the managers of the highly paid employees, and also illustrates the omission of the local variable in the select operation.

```
Company
employee->select(contract.grade.salary > 50000).manager
```

Another useful operation on collections is the 'collect' operation. This takes a navigation expression as its argument and returns a bag consisting of the values of the expression for each object in the original collection. For example, the following expression returns the ages of all the employees in a department. As with the select operation, the local variable is optional, but is included here for clarity.

```
Department
staff->collect(p:Person | p.age())
```

The collect operation is not limited to calling operations from the model, but can perform additional calculations if required. For example, the following expression uses a collect expression to calculate the company's salary bill after applying a 10% pay rise to all employees.

```
Company
contract.grade->collect(salary * 1.1)->sum()
```

A particularly simple form of the collect operation collects together the values of a single attribute belonging to all the objects in a collection. In this case, a natural shorthand form, which has already been used earlier in this chapter, is permitted. The following two expressions are equivalent ways of returning the names of all the employees in a department.

```
Department
self.staff->collect(name)
self.staff.name
```

9.6 CONSTRAINTS

Navigation expressions allow us to write expressions which refer to any subset of the data stored in a model. As such, they might prove useful as the foundation for a UML oriented query language, but they do not by themselves allow us to state desired properties of the data. This is the role of constraints, which in OCL are constructed by combining navigation expressions with various boolean operators.

This section describes the various forms that constraints in OCL can take. Firstly, there are a number of basic types of constraint, which apply directly to either objects or collections. Secondly, there are a number of boolean operators which can be used to combine constraints to express more complex properties. Finally, there are what might be called 'iterative constraints': these apply a constraint recursively to all the elements of a collection, and correspond to the quantifiers of first-order predicate logic.

Basic constraints

The simplest forms of constraints are those formed by using relational operators to compare two data items. In OCL, both objects and collections can be compared for equality or inequality using the operators '=' and '<>' respectively, and the standard operators are available for testing numeric values. Examples of these have been given earlier, in Section 9.3.

Given the ability to write navigation expressions that refer to data items anywhere in the model, quite a wide range of constraints can be formalized using just equality tests. For example, the constraint that the department an employee works for should be part of the company that the employee works for can be reformulated as an assertion that the same company is obtained if you navigate either directly from the employee to the company, or indirectly from the employee to the department and from there to the company. This can be formalized as follows.

```
Person
self.employer = self.department.company
```

There are a number of basic constraints that apply to collections only. Essentially, these are generalizations of properties of sets that are familiar from elementary mathematics. For example, it is possible to test whether a collection is empty by using the constraint 'isEmpty', although strictly speaking it is unnecessary, as the assertion that a collection is empty is the same as the assertion that its size is zero.

Universal properties of a model, such as the assertion that all employees are aged 18 or over, can often be formalized by defining a collection which contains all the exceptions to the property, and asserting that it is empty. The following constraints illustrate two equivalent ways of doing this.

```
Company
employee->select(age() < 18)->isEmpty
employee->select(age() < 18)->size = 0
```

Two operations allow constraints to be written which make assertions about the membership of collections. The 'include' operation is true if a specified object is a member of a collection. For example, a rather basic integrity property of the system is that every employee's grade is one of the set of grades linked to that employee's company, as expressed by the following constraint.

```
Person
employer.grade->includes(contract.grade)
```

The 'includesAll' operation is similar, but takes a collection as its argument rather than a single object. It therefore corresponds to a subset operator for collections. As in the previous example, a common use for this operation is to make basic assertions about consistency between various associations in a model. The following OCL constraint states that the staff of a department are all employees of the company the department belongs to.

```
Department
company.employee->includesAll(staff)
```

Combining constraints

Constraints can be combined using the boolean operators 'and', 'or', 'xor' and 'not'. An example of constraint using 'and' was given in Section 9.3. OCL differs from most programming languages in defining a boolean operator representing implication. For example, suppose the company has a policy that every employee over the age of 50 must receive a salary of at least £25,000. This could be described in OCL as follows.

```
Person
self.age() > 50 implies self.contract.grade.salary > 25000
```

Iterative constraints

Iterative constraints resemble iterative operators such as 'select' in that they are defined over collections, and return a result which is determined by applying a boolean expression to every element in the collection. Rather than returning a new collection, however, they return a boolean value which depends on the results obtained for each individual element.

For example, the operator 'forAll' returns true if the specified boolean expression is true for every member of the collection it is applied to, and otherwise it returns false. A simple use of 'forAll' is the following OCL constraint which states that there is at least one employee appointed at every grade in the company.

```
Company
self.grade->forAll(g | not g.contract->isEmpty())
```

Complementary to 'forAll' is the operator 'exists', which returns true if the boolean expression is true for at least one of the elements in the collection, and false if it is false for all elements of the collection. A simple use of 'exists' is the following OCL constraint which states that every department has a head, in the sense that the department contains an employee who has no manager.

```
Department
staff->exists(e | e.manager->isEmpty())
```

It is easy to assume that it is necessary to use 'forAll' in order to write a constraint that applies to all instances of a class. In fact this is not the case, as constraints on classes apply to all instances of that class. For example, the following constraint states that for every grade in the company, the salary for that grade is greater than £20,000.

```
Grade
salary > 20000
```

This example shows that in simple cases there is no need to form an explicit collection in order to assert that a given property is true of all the instances of a class. Nevertheless, such a collection can be formed if necessary. OCL defines an operation 'allInstances' which is applied to the name of a type and, as the name suggests, returns the collection consisting of all the instances of that type. Using this operation, the simple constraint above could be rewritten in the following way.

```
Grade
Grade.allInstances->forAll(g | g.salary > 20000)
```

In this simple case the use of 'allInstances' makes the constraint more complex than necessary. There are situations where it is necessary, however. One common example is when a constraint has to systematically compare the values of different instances or a class. For example, the following constraint asserts that no two grades have the same value in their salary attributes.

```
Grade
Grade.allInstances->forAll(g : Grade |
        g <> self implies g.salary <> self.salary)
```

This constraint implicitly applies to every instance of the grade class; as always, the context object is referred to by the term 'self' in the constraint. The constraint compares the context object with every instance of the class, by iterating through the collection formed by applying 'allInstances'. The second line of the constraint states the condition being tested, namely that two distinct instances of the class cannot define the same salary level.

9.7 STEREOTYPED CONSTRAINTS

Constraints are commonly used to state properties of a class and its operations that cannot be represented graphically. These properties include limitations on the possible states of instances of the class, and certain aspects of the operations defined in the class. Because of the widespread use of this method of class specification, the corresponding constraints are explicitly identified by means of stereotypes in UML.

Class invariants

A class invariant is a property of a class that is intended to be true at all times for all instances of the class. In a sense, all the constraints given earlier in this chapter can be viewed as invariants, as they state desired properties of class instances. However, the term 'invariant' is commonly used to refer only to constraints that restrict the possible values of a class's attributes.

For example, in Figure 9.1 a note was used to specify that the balance in a savings account had to be in the range £0 to £250,000. This is a typical example of a simple class invariant, and it can be written either as the simple constraint shown below, or as a stereotyped constraint as shown in Figure 9.7. The use of notes tends to clutter up a class diagram, so in many cases the textual form may be preferable, but the difference between the two ways of representing the invariant is merely stylistic.

```
SavingsAccount
balance > 0 and balance < 250000
```

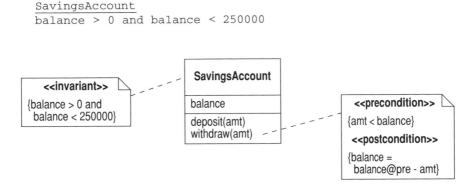

Figure 9.7 Class specification using constraints

Preconditions and postconditions

Even if an invariant is defined for a class, there is no guarantee that the operations of the class will ensure that the invariant is maintained. If the withdrawal operation on the savings account class allowed any amount of money to be withdrawn, for example, it would be very easy for the invariant stating that the balance had to be greater than zero to become invalid.

Preconditions and postconditions are special constraints that can be written for operations. As the names suggest, a precondition is something that must be true just before an operation is called, and a postcondition is something that must be true just after the operation has completed. These constraints should be written in such a way that if they are both true at the appropriate time, the invariant of the class will still be true when the operation has completed.

A precondition is usually expressed as a constraint relating the attributes of a class instance and the actual parameters of the operation being specified. For example, if the withdrawal operation on savings accounts is not to cause the account to become overdrawn, the amount being withdrawn must be less than the current balance of the account. Stated formally, this is the precondition of this operation, and is shown in Figure 9.7 identified by a stereotype.

Postconditions typically specify the effect of an operation by comparing the attribute values before and after execution of the operation. In the case of the withdraw operation, the postcondition is that the balance should have been reduced by exactly the amount specified in the actual parameter of the operation. This constraint is also shown in Figure 9.7.

The formal statement of the postcondition introduces a slight notational problem. The name of an attribute in a constraint denotes the current value of that attribute. Postconditions are evaluated after the execution of an operation, and so the attribute 'balance' in the postcondition of the withdraw operation denotes the balance after the withdrawal has been made. To state the postcondition formally, we need to compare this with the value of the attribute before the operation was called. As Figure 9.7 shows this value is identified in OCL by writing the notation @pre after the attribute name.

Operation specifications can be written textually as well as being shown in a diagram. In this case, however, the context of the constraint is not an object of a given class, but an operation. Also, the labels 'pre' and 'post' are used to identify the stereotyped roles played by these constraints.

```
SavingsAccount::withdraw(amt)
pre: amt < balance
post: balance = balance@pre - amt
```

Design by contract

A specification of an operation using preconditions and postconditions is sometimes thought of as establishing a kind of contract between the caller of the operation and its implementation. In this model, the caller of an operation has the responsibility to ensure that the operation is not called with parameter values that would make the precondition false. The implementation makes a corresponding guarantee that, if the precondition is true, any alteration to the object's state will be such as to ensure that the postcondition is true when the operation terminates.

If both sides of this contract are satisfied, the class invariant will be maintained. This raises the question of what should happen if the contract breaks down: the situation is different depending on whether it is the precondition or the postcondition that fails.

An operation has no control over the parameter values that are passed to it. If it is called with invalid parameters, there may be no way that it can ensure that its postcondition is satisfied on completion. This situation is often thought of as a run-time error, similar to the error that occurs when an attempt is made to divide by zero. When a precondition is not satisfied, the state of the system becomes undefined and the operation may exhibit any behaviour.

It is common for operations which have preconditions to check that the precondition is satisfied before continuing with the body of the operation. If it is not, suitable action can be taken; perhaps an exception might be thrown. In general, drawing attention to the error is a better strategy than carrying on regardless and possibly letting the system's data become corrupted.

If a precondition is satisfied, on the other hand, the only way that a postcondition can fail to be satisfied is if there is an error in the implementation of the operation. In these cases, the remedy is simply to correct the programming error.

9.8 CONSTRAINTS AND GENERALIZATION

Generalization relationships do not give rise to any navigable relationships between objects, and so they do not feature explicitly in constraints. There are some cases, however, where generalization can complicate the writing of constraints by requiring the constraint to make reference to the run-time types of the objects involved.

Consider the basic polymorphic situation shown in Figure 9.8, where a customer can hold any number of accounts, of various different types. Suppose that the bank then imposes a restriction on its customers, stating that at least one of the accounts held must be a current account.

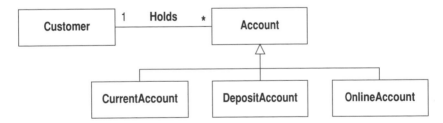

Figure 9.8 Polymorphic account holding

It would be natural to try to formalize this restriction by means of a constraint, but we cannot do this with the OCL notation presented so far in this chapter. Within the context of a customer object, navigation across the association in Figure 9.8 only provides us with a collection of account objects: we need in addition some way of finding out the run-time type of these objects.

OCL defines the operation 'oclIsTypeOf' which takes a type as an argument, and is true only if the actual type of the object is equal to the specified type. Using this operation, the required constraint could be written in the following way.

```
Customer
account->size > 0 implies
  account->select(oclIsTypeOf(CurrentAccount))->size > 1
```

Another use for run-time type information in constraints is to express in textual form the constraint implied by the use of association generalization in Figure 9.9. This diagram shows one way of asserting that only individuals can hold current accounts, and only companies can hold business accounts.

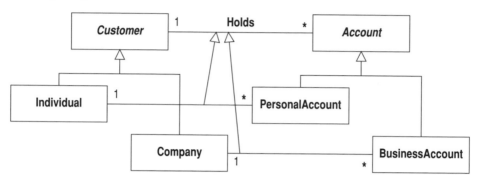

Figure 9.9 Association generalization

The notation for association generalization is visually clumsy and has rather obscure semantics. Often it is preferable to express the same information using OCL. For example, the fact that individuals can only hold current accounts could be expressed in the following constraint.

```
Individual
account->forAll(a | a.oclType = PersonalAccount)
```

The operation 'oclType' that is used in this constraint simply returns the type of a specified object. This constraint therefore asserts that all the accounts held by an individual must be current accounts.

9.9 SUMMARY

- Constraints are assertions about model elements which specify properties that instances of a model must possess.
- Some simple constraints can be represented graphically. UML defines OCL, the Object Constraint Language, for writing more general constraints.
- A constraint in OCL is a boolean expression which asserts certain properties of a specified context object.
- Navigation expressions allow constraints to refer to objects that are linked, directly or indirectly, to the context object. Constraints can therefore also describe desired relationships between objects.

• Class specifications are often written using stereotyped constraints. An invariant describes properties of the class's attributes. Preconditions and postconditions specify the class's operations.

9.10 EXERCISES

9.1 The diagram in Figure 9.6 states that employees of a company can have zero or one managers. Suppose that in fact the company operates a strict line management system whereby every employee apart from the managing director has exactly one manager. Change the diagram so that it models this new situation more accurately.

9.2 Write OCL navigation expressions based on Figure 9.6 for the objects described below. If necessary, add suitable role names to the diagram to avoid ambiguity.
  (*a*) The department that the employee with payroll number 123456 works in.
  (*b*) The department an employee's manager works for.
  (*c*) The employees at a specified grade in a given department.

9.3 Write OCL constraints expressing the following properties of the class diagram in Figure 9.6.
  (*a*) An employee's manager works for the same department as the employee.
  (*b*) Managers earn more than the people they manage.
  (*c*) Every department has a staff member earning at least £100,000.

9.4 What is wrong with the following attempt to write a constraint for the model of Figure 9.6 stating that nobody can be their own manager?

```
Person
self <> self.manager
```

Write a correct OCL constraint for this requirement.

9.5 Write an OCL constraint for the class diagram in Figure 9.1 which states that every account a customer holds has a balance greater than £100.

9.6 Write an OCL constraint for the class diagram in Figure 6.19 which will rule out object structures such as the one shown in Figure 9.4.

9.7 Write an OCL constraint with the same meaning as the subset constraint shown in Figure 9.2. Give a general rule explaining how subset constraints could be replaced by OCL constraints.

9.8 Write an OCL constraint with the same meaning as the xor constraint in Figure 9.3. Give a general rule explaining how xor constraints could be replaced by OCL constraints.

9.9 Show how the multiplicity annotations on the associations in Figure 9.6 could be stated formally in OCL.

9.10 With reference to the class diagram of Figure 6.21, write a navigation expression denoting the companies that a given person works for. Use this navigation expression to write a constraint in OCL specifying that a person can only work for one company.

9.11 With reference to Figure 4.19, write OCL constraints to specify the following properties of the diagram editor.
(*a*) The current diagram is one of the diagrams linked to the diagram editor.
(*b*) The current tool is always linked to the current diagram.

9.12 Write OCL constraints which express the same restriction on the model as the association generalizations used in Figure 6.34.

9.13 With reference to the class diagram of Figure 6.43, write navigation expressions denoting the following.
(*a*) The set of modules that a student is taking.
(*b*) The mark a student gains for a particular modules.
(*c*) The set of modules a student has passed.

9.14 Add an association to Figure 9.6 so that the model can record details of which person is the head of each department. Write a constraint in OCL to express the requirement that the head of each department must be on the staff of the department.

9.15 With reference to Figure 9.7, write a suitable precondition and postcondition for the deposit operation on the savings account class.

10

IMPLEMENTATION STRATEGIES

It is clear from the examples considered earlier in this book that many of the features found in the design models used in UML can be implemented in a very straightforward manner in object-oriented programming languages. For example, the classes in a class diagram can be implemented as classes in Java, generalization as public inheritance, and so on. Many case tools provide a code generation facility by implementing a set of rules such as these.

The fact that the transition from design models to code is so straightforward is a significant benefit of object-oriented design, but nevertheless there are certain features of the design models which do not map directly into programming language structures. This chapter considers the most prominent of these features and discusses various strategies for dealing with their implementation.

The most significant feature of class diagrams which has no direct analogue in programming languages is the association. The implementation of the diagram editor in Chapter 5 gave examples of how simple associations can be implemented using references, and this approach is summarized in Section 10.1 and the following sections. This chapter also describes ways in which more complex types of association, such as qualified associations and association classes, can be implemented.

The information contained in the dynamic models of an application is reflected not in the declarative structure of the implementation, but in the code that implements individual operations. Object interaction diagrams describe the order in which messages are sent in the execution of an operation, and this information is naturally used to guide the implementation of individual operations.

Statecharts, on the other hand, describe constraints that must apply across all the operations of a class, and which can affect the implementation of all a class's operations. It is beneficial to adopt a consistent strategy to ensure that these constraints are correctly reflected in the implementation of the member functions of the class. Section 10.7 discusses various approaches to the implementation of statecharts.

227

10.1 IMPLEMENTING ASSOCIATIONS

Associations describe the properties of the links that exist between objects when a system is running. A link from one object to another informs each object of the identity, or the location, of the other object. Among other things this enables the objects to send messages to each other, using the link as a kind of communication channel. Whatever implementation of links is chosen must support these properties of links. As explained in Section 5.4, references provide the appropriate functionality, and by far the commonest way to implement a simple association is by using references to linked objects.

The major difference between links and references is that links are symmetrical, whereas references only refer in one direction. If two objects are linked, a single link serves as a channel for sending messages in either direction. By using a reference, however, one object can send messages to another, but the other object has no knowledge of the object referring to it, and no way of sending messages back to that object. This implies that if a link has to support message passing in both directions, it will need to be implemented by a pair of references, one in each direction. An illustration of the situation that arises as a result of this was given in Figure 5.9.

The use of two references incurs a considerable implementation overhead as it is crucial for the correctness of the implementation that inverse references are consistently maintained. As explained in Chapter 5, however, the implementation of associations can be simplified in many cases because it often happens that particular links only need to be traversed in one direction. Where this is the case, the association can be implemented by a single reference, pointing in the direction of traversal.

Considerable simplification can therefore be obtained by only implementing links in one direction. On the other hand, if future modifications to the system require an association to be traversed in the other direction as well, significant changes to the program and reformatting of data might be required. Deciding whether to implement an association in just one direction involves a tradeoff between implementation simplicity and the likelihood of future modifications to the association, and this decision can only be taken on a case by case basis.

Section 10.2 discusses how to implement associations when the decision has been taken to maintain the association in only one direction. These are known as *unidirectional* implementations. Section 10.3 discusses *bidirectional* implementations, where it has been decided that the association must be maintained in both directions.

In general there are two distinct aspects to the implementation of associations. Firstly, it is necessary to define the data declarations that will enable the details of actual links to be stored. Usually this will consist of defining data members in one class which can store references to objects of the associated class.

Secondly, it is necessary to consider the means by which these pointers will be manipulated by the rest of the application. In general, the details of the underlying implementation of the association should be hidden from client code. This implies that each class that participates in an association should define a suitable range of interface operations for maintaining the semantics of the associations defined in the class diagram.

10.2 UNIDIRECTIONAL IMPLEMENTATIONS

This section discusses cases where it has been decided that an association only needs to be supported in one direction. This design decision can be shown on a class diagram by writing a navigation arrow on the association to show the required direction of traversal. Different cases arise depending on the multiplicity of the association at the end where the arrowhead is written; the multiplicity at the tail of the arrow has no effect on the implementation of the association. The following sections discuss the cases where the multiplicity of the directed association is 'one', 'optional' and 'many'.

Optional associations

Figure 10.1 shows an association which is only to be implemented unidirectionally. Every account can have a debit card issued for use with the account but as this is an entirely new facility offered by the bank, it is envisaged that many account holders will not immediately take up the chance to have such a card.

Figure 10.1 An optional association

This association can be implemented using a simple reference variable, as shown below. This allows an account object to hold a reference to at most one debit card object. Cases where an account is not linked to a card are modelled by allowing the reference variable to hold the special null reference. This implementation therefore provides exactly the multiplicity requirements specified by the association.

```
public class Account
{
  public DebitCard getCard() {
    return theCard;
  }

  public void setCard(DebitCard card) {
    theCard = card;
  }

  public void removeCard() {
    theCard = null;
  }

  private DebitCard theCard ;
}
```

The operations provided to maintain this link would in practice be derived from a more detailed examination of the relevant application. The code above assumes that a card may be supplied when an account is created. In addition, operations are provided to change the card linked to an account, or to remove a link to a card altogether.

This implementation allows different cards to be linked to an account at different times during its lifetime. Associations with this property are sometimes called *mutable* associations. *Immutable* associations, on the other hand, are those which require that a link to one object cannot subsequently be replaced by a link to a separate object. In this case, this would correspond to the requirement that only one card was ever issued for a particular account.

If the association between accounts and debit cards was intended to be immutable, the alternative declaration of the account class given below might be more appropriate. This provides an operation to add a card to an account, and only allows a card to be added if no card is already held. Once allocated, a card cannot be changed or even removed, and the relevant operations have been removed from the interface.

```
public class Account
{
  public DebitCard getCard() {
    return theCard ;
  }

  public void setCard(DebitCard card) {
    if (theCard != null) {
      // throw ImmutableAssociationError
    }
    theCard = card ;
  }

  private DebitCard theCard ;
}
```

One-to-one associations

This example of an immutable association demonstrates that in general only some of the properties of associations can be implemented directly by providing suitable declarations of data members in the relevant classes. Other semantic features of an association can be enforced by providing only a limited range of operations in the class's interface, or by including code in the implementation of member functions that ensures that the necessary constraints are maintained.

Consider the association shown in Figure 10.2. This association describes a situation where bank accounts must have a guarantor who will underwrite any debts incurred by the account holder. It may frequently be necessary to find the details of the guarantor of an account, but in general it will not be necessary to find the account or accounts that an individual guarantor is responsible for. It has therefore been decided to implement the association only in the direction from account to guarantor.

Figure 10.2 A one-to-one association

Assuming that these constraints are acceptable, the account class could be implemented in the following manner. In this case, the constructor throws an exception if a null reference to a guarantor object is provided, and no operation is provided in the class's interface to update the reference held.

```
public class Account
{
  public Account(Guarantor g) {
    if ( g == null ) {
      // throw NullLinkError
    }
    theGuarantor = g ;
  }

  public Guarantor getGuarantor() {
    return theGuarantor ;
  }

  private Guarantor theGuarantor ;
}
```

This code implements the association between account and guarantor objects as an immutable association. If the association was mutable, so that the guarantor of an account could be changed, a suitable function could be added to this class provided that, like the constructor, it checked that the new guarantor reference was non-null.

Associations with multiplicity 'many'

Figure 10.3 shows an association with multiplicity 'many' for which a unidirectional implementation is required. Each manager within the bank is responsible for looking after a number of accounts, but the model assumes that it is never necessary to find out directly who the manager of any particular account is. The new feature of this association is that a manager object could be linked not just to one, but potentially to many account objects.

Figure 10.3 An association with multiplicity 'many'

In order to implement this association the manager object must maintain multiple pointers, one to each linked account, and hence some suitable data structure must be used to store all the pointers. In addition, it is likely that the interface of the manager class will provide operations to maintain the collection of pointers, for example to add or remove details of particular accounts.

The simplest and most reliable way to implement such an association is to make use of a suitable container class from a class library. For simple implementations in Java, the vector class is a natural choice for this purpose. A skeleton implementation of the manager class using vectors is given below. The class declares a vector of accounts as a private data member, and the functions to add and remove accounts from this collection simply call the corresponding functions defined in the interface of the vector class.

```
public class Manager
{
  public void addAccount(Account acc) {
    theAccounts.addElement(acc) ;
  }

  public void removeAccount(Account acc) {
    theAccounts.removeElement(acc) ;
  }

  private Vector theAccounts ;
}
```

Part of the semantics of a class diagram such as Figure 10.3 is that there can only be at most one link between a manager and any particular account. In this implementation, however, there is no reason why many pointers to the same account object could not be stored in the vector held by the manager. This is a further example of the inability of programming languages to capture in declarations every constraint expressible in UML's class diagrams. A correct implementation of the 'addAccount' function should check that the account being added is not already linked to the manager object.

10.3 BIDIRECTIONAL IMPLEMENTATIONS

If a bidirectional implementation of an association is required, each link could be implemented by a pair of references, as discussed above. The declarations and code required to support such an implementation are essentially the same as those discussed above, the only difference being that suitable fields must be declared in both classes participating in the association.

The extra complexity involved in dealing with bidirectional implementations arises from the need to ensure that at run-time the two pointers implementing a link are kept consistent. This property is often referred to as *referential integrity*. Figure 10.4(*a*) shows the desired situation, where a pair of 'equal and opposite' pointers implement a single link. By contrast, Figure 10.4(*b*) shows the violation of referential integrity.

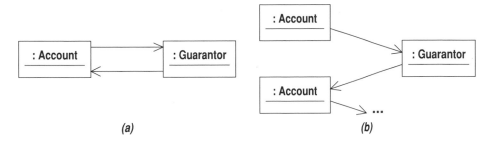

Figure 10.4 Referential integrity and its violation

For the association between accounts and guarantors, the required property can be stated informally as 'the guarantor of an account must guarantee that same account'. Figure 10.4*(b)* violates this: the top account object holds a reference to a guarantor object which in turn holds a reference to a completely different account. These two references cannot be understood as being an implementation of a single link.

It should be clear from this example that referential integrity cannot be ensured by simply giving appropriate definitions of data members in the relevant classes. Such declarations only assert that a reference or references will be held, but give no information about the nature of the objects referred to, or about relationships holding between distinct references. As with certain aspects of unidirectional implementations, the relevant constraints can only be enforced in the code of the operations that maintain the links.

As with unidirectional implementations, not every association needs to support all possible forms of manipulation of links. What behaviour needs to be supported will depend on the details of individual applications, and will be defined by the operational interfaces of the classes participating in the association. This section will consider a few representative cases, and draw attention to the issues that an implementation needs to bear in mind.

One-to-one and optional associations

Figure 10.5 shows the association of Figure 10.1, but with multiplicities added at both ends. Assume that we are now required to provide a bidirectional implementation of this association. We will also assume that the association is immutable in the debit card to account direction, or in other words that once a debit card is linked to an account, it must stay linked to that account until the end of its lifetime. An account, on the other hand, can have different cards associated with it at different times, to cater for situations where the account holder loses a card, for example.

Figure 10.5 A bidirectional one-to-one association

This association can be thought of as a combination of a mutable and optional association in the left-to-right direction with an immutable association in the other. A simple approach to its implementation would simply combine the implementations of those given in Section 10.2, as shown below. For simplicity, the bodies of the methods in the classes are omitted.

```
public class Account
{
  public DebitCard getCard() { ... }
  public void setCard(DebitCard card) { ... }
  public void removeCard() { ... }

  private DebitCard theCard ;
}

public class DebitCard
{
  public DebitCard(Account a) { ... }
  public Account getAccount() { ... }

  private Account theAccount ;
}
```

This implementation certainly provides the data members necessary to store the bidirectional links, but the operations available maintain the two directions of the link independently. For example, the pointer from the account to the card is set up in the account constructor, and the pointer from card to account in the card constructor.

This division of labour makes it harder than necessary to maintain referential integrity for this association. For example, to create a link between a new debit card and an account two separate operations are required, firstly to create the card and secondly to link it to the account. The link from card to account is created when the card itself is created. Code to implement this might be as follows.

```
Account acc1 = new Account() ;
DebitCard card1 = new DebitCard(acc1) ;
acc1.setCard(card1) ;
```

To ensure that referential integrity is maintained, it is necessary to ensure that these two operations are always performed together. However, as two separate statements are needed, there is a real possibility that one might be omitted, or an erroneous parameter supplied, leading to an inconsistent data structure, as in the following example in which the debit card is initialized with the wrong account.

```
Account acc1 = new Account(), acc2 = new Account() ;
DebitCard card1 = new DebitCard(acc2) ;
acc1.setCard(card1) ;
```

A better solution is to give only one of the classes the responsibility of maintaining the association. A link between two objects could then be created by means of a single function call, and encapsulation could be used to ensure that only trusted functions have the ability to directly manipulate links.

The choice of which class to give the maintenance responsibility to often arises naturally out of other aspects of the overall design. In the current case, it is likely that there would be an operation on the account class to create a new debit card for the account, and this would provide a strong argument for making the account class responsible for maintaining the association. If this was the case, the classes could be defined as follows.

```
public class Account
{
  public DebitCard getCard() {
    return theCard;
  }

  public void addCard() {
    theCard = new DebitCard(this);
  }

  private DebitCard theCard ;
}

public class DebitCard
{
  DebitCard(Account a) { theAccount = a; }

  public Account getAccount() {
    return theAccount;
  }

  private Account theAccount ;
}
```

Debit cards are now actually created by the 'addCard' operation in the account class. The implementation of this operation dynamically creates a new debit card object, passing the address of the current account as an initializer. The constructor in the debit card class uses this initializer to set up the pointer back to the account object creating the card. A single call to the add card operation is now guaranteed to set up a bidirectional link correctly.

In an attempt to ensure that there is no other way of setting up links, the constructor of the debit card class is not declared to be public. The effect of this is to limit the classes that can create debit cards to those in the same package, and to provide some measure of protection against the arbitrary creation of debit cards. The equivalent of the 'friend' mechanism in C++ would be needed to ensure that debit cards could only be created by functions in the account class.

This example is particularly simple because the association was declared to be immutable in one direction. In general, if both directions of an association are mutable, a wide range of situations can arise in which links can be altered, and a correct implementation must ensure that these are all correctly handled.

For example, suppose that a customer could hold many accounts but only one debit card, and had the facility to nominate which account was debited when the card was used. The association between accounts and debit cards would now be mutable in both directions, and it would be reasonable for the card class to provide an operation to change the account that the card was associated with.

The manipulations involved in such an operation are quite involved, however. Firstly, the existing link between the card and its account must be broken. Secondly, a new link must be established between the new account and the card. Finally, this should only happen if the new account is not already linked to a card.

The implementation sketched below follows the strategy given above of allocating the responsibility of manipulating pointers exclusively to the account class. As explained above, this makes consistency easier to guarantee, as there is only one place where changes are being made to links. This means that the card class must call functions in the account class to update pointers, as shown in the implementation of the 'changeAccount' operation given below.

```
public class Account
{
  public DebitCard getCard() { ... }
  public void addCard(DebitCard c) { ... }

  public void removeCard() {
    theCard = null ;
  }

  private DebitCard theCard ;
}

public class DebitCard
{
  public DebitCard(Account a) { ... }
  public Account getAccount() { ... }

  public void changeAccount(Account newacc) {
    if (newacc.getCard() != null) {
      // throw AccountAlreadyHasACard
    }
    theAccount.removeCard() ;
    newacc.addCard(this) ;
  }

  private Account theAccount ;
}
```

Although in this function it might seem more 'efficient' to let the card class directly maintain its pointer data elements, a significant amount of security and robustness can be achieved by delegating that responsibility to the account class, as shown.

One-to-many associations

The bidirectional implementation of associations involving multiplicities of 'many' raises no significantly different problems from those discussed above. For example, Figure 10.6 shows an association specifying that customers can hold many accounts, each of which is held by a single customer.

Figure 10.6 Customers holding accounts

As before, the customer class could contain a data member to store a collection of pointers to accounts, and additionally each account should store a single pointer to a customer. It would seem most sensible to give the customer class the responsibility of maintaining the links of this association, though in practice this decision would only be made in the light of the total processing requirements of the system.

Immutable associations

Suppose that the association between accounts and guarantors was intended to be immutable, and needed to be traversed in both directions. Figure 10.7 shows the relevant class diagram which preserves the restriction that each guarantor can only guarantee one account.

Figure 10.7 An immutable one-to-one association

As before, each class could define a data member holding a reference to an object of the other class. The class declarations might be as follows.

```
public class Account
{
   public Account(Guarantor g)      { theGuarantor = g; }
   public Guarantor getGuarantor()  { return theGuarantor; }

   private Guarantor theGuarantor ;
}
```

```
public class Guarantor
{
    public Guarantor(Account a) { theAccount = a; }
    public Account getAccount() { return theAccount; }

    private Account theAccount ;
}
```

These declarations seem to introduce a certain circularity. When an account is created, it must be supplied with an already existing guarantor object, and likewise when a guarantor is created it must be supplied with an already existing account. It might be thought that this could be achieved by creating the two objects simultaneously, as shown in the following code.

```
Account a   = new Account(new Guarantor(a)) ;
Guarantor g = a.getGuarantor() ;
```

However, although an analogous approach works in C++, this is not legal Java code, as the object 'a' has not been initialized by the time it is used in the constructor of the guarantor class. In order to create the required link, one of the objects must be created using a default constructor and the link subsequently established with a suitable 'set' operation. It would then be necessary to check explicitly that the constraints on the association were maintained at all times.

10.4 IMPLEMENTING QUALIFIERS

The previous sections have addressed some of the issues involved in the implementation of simple associations. Some of the additional features of associations defined by UML cannot be handled in such a simple way, however. This section considers one of these, namely the concept of a qualified association. There are certain features of qualified associations that distinguish them from ordinary associations, and which need to be considered carefully in any implementation.

As explained in Section 6.12, a qualifier is a piece of data which can be used as a key to pick out one of a set of objects. For example, Figure 10.8 shows an association modelling the fact that a bank can maintain many different accounts. Each account is identifiable by a single piece of data, namely the account number, and this attribute is shown as a qualifier attached to the bank class. For simplicity, we assume that the association is to be given a unidirectional implementation.

Figure 10.8 A qualified association

The most common use of such an association is to provide efficient access to objects based on the values of the qualifying attributes. This implies that it will often be necessary to provide some kind of data structure which supports such access in the object to which the qualifier is attached.

For example, we may need to retrieve information about accounts given only an account number. If the bank simply held a pointer to each of its accounts, this operation could be implemented by searching through all the pointers until the matching account was found. This could be very slow, however, and a better approach might be to maintain a lookup table mapping account numbers to accounts, as illustrated in Figure 10.9. As account numbers can be ordered, for example, this gives the possibility of using much more efficient search techniques.

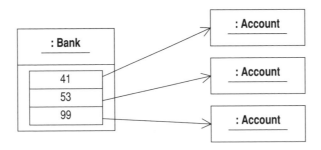

Figure 10.9 How qualifiers can be implemented

This kind of structure is relatively easy to implement, the major issue being to decide how to implement the lookup table. In Java, an obvious and straightforward choice is to use the provided implementation of hash tables. As a unidirectional implementation is being considered, the bank object must have the responsibility of maintaining the association. Operations to add and remove accounts, and to look up an account given its number, could be declared as follows.

```
public class Bank
{
  public void addAccount(Account a) {
    theAccounts.put(new Integer(a.getNumber()), a);
  }
  public void removeAccount(int accno) {
    theAccounts.remove(new Integer(accno));
  }
  public Account lookupAccount(int accno) {
    return (Account) theAccounts.get(new Integer(accno));
  }

  private Hashtable theAccounts ;
}
```

Qualifiers, then, can still be handled using the simple model that implements individual links by references. The implementation given above treats a qualified association in much the same way as an association with multiplicity 'many'. The most significant difference is in the data structure used to hold the multiple pointers at one end of the association. A bidirectional implementation of a qualified association, therefore, does not raise any significantly new problems, and implementation of the association in Figure 10.8 as a bidirectional association is left as an exercise.

10.5 IMPLEMENTING ASSOCIATIONS AS CLASSES

Unlike the situation with qualifiers, it is not possible to handle association classes with a simple implementation of associations based on references. For example, consider the diagram in Figure 10.10 which shows that many students can be registered as taking modules, and that a mark is associated with each such registration. The semantics of this notation were discussed in Section 6.11.

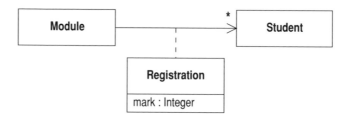

Figure 10.10 An association class

The association class shown in Figure 10.10 needs to be implemented as a class, to provide a place to store the attribute values representing marks. The links corresponding to the association cannot then be implemented as references between the module and student classes, however, otherwise there would be no way of associating the correct mark with a student and module pair.

A common strategy in this case is to transform the association class into a simple class linked to the two original classes with two new associations, as shown in Figure 10.11. In this diagram, the fact that many students can take a module is modelled by stating that the module can be linked to many objects of the registration class, each of which is further linked to a unique student, namely the student for whom the registration applies.

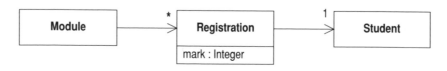

Figure 10.11 Transforming the association into a class

As a result of this transformation, neither of the associations in Figure 10.11 have link attributes and so they can be given straightforward implementations using references. The way in which these associations should be manipulated by client code repays some thought, however.

The original association shown in Figure 10.10 would naturally have been maintained by the module class, which might provide operations to add a link to a student and to record a mark stored for a student. Despite the fact that the association is now being implemented as a class, the interface presented to client code should remain unchanged. This implies that the module class must maintain both the registration class in Figure 10.11 and also the two new associations, and therefore that the operation to add a student to a module must create a new object and two new links. A possible outline implementation for this operation is shown below.

The implementation of the registration class is very simple. It must store a reference to the linked student object and the mark gained by that student. As this class is manipulated exclusively by the module class, we do not bother to provide an operational interface for it.

```
class Registration
{
  Registration(Student st) { student = st; mark = 0; }

  private Student student ;
  private int mark ;
}
```

The relevant parts of the definition of the module class are sketched out below. The very simple implementation given in this example does not perform any of the validation discussed above.

```
public class Module
{
  public void enrol(Student st)
    { registrations.addElement(new Registration(st)); }

  private Vector registrations ;
}
```

Implementing an association as a class is clearly a strategy that is required whenever a class diagram contains link attributes or associations modelled as classes. It is not limited to these cases, however, and in certain situations it might be quite appropriate to implement a general many-to-many association as a class. This might be the case if it was envisaged that there was a possibility of link attributes being added at some later date. A simple pointer-based implementation would not cope at all well with such a change, whereas if the association had been implemented as a class, it would then be almost trivial to add link attributes.

A further consideration in the implementation of this association is that the two class diagrams in Figure 10.10 and Figure 10.11 in fact have slightly different meanings. Figure 10.10 states that a student can only take a module once, as only one link is permitted between any given pair of module and student objects. With Figure 10.11 on the other hand, there is nothing to prevent a student being linked to the same module many times, through the mediation of different registration instances. An implementation of Figure 10.11 should bear this in mind, and check that the appropriate constraints are satisfied.

As in previous cases, bidirectional implementations of associations which are implemented as classes add only complexity to the situation, and not any new conceptual issues. The bidirectional implementation of Figure 10.11 is therefore left as an exercise.

10.6 IMPLEMENTING CONSTRAINTS

Section 9.7 explained how stereotyped constraints can be used to specify certain desirable properties of a class. Class invariants describe relationships that must between the attribute values of an instance of the class, and preconditions and postconditions specify what must be true before and after an operation is called. Often the robustness of an implementation can be increased by including code in the class which checks these conditions at the appropriate times.

In particular, all the preconditions that are specified for an operation should be explicitly checked in an implementation. Preconditions state properties of an operation's parameters that must be satisfied if the operation is to be able to run to completion successfully. However, it is the responsibility of the caller of the operation to ensure that the precondition is satisfied when an operation is called. When the operation is called, it is simply provided with parameter values with no guarantee that they are sensible.

If an operation does not check its parameter values, then, there is a danger that erroneous or meaningless values will go undetected, resulting in unpredictable run-time errors. A better strategy is for an operation to check its precondition and perhaps to raise an exception if a violation of the precondition is detected. The following example provides a possible implementation of the withdraw operation of the savings account class specified in Section 9.7.

```
public class SavingsAccount
{
  public void withdraw(double amt) {
    if (amt >= balance) {
      // throw PreconditionUnsatisfied
    }
    balance -= amt ;
  }

  private double balance ;
}
```

A postcondition was also given for this operation, specifying that the result of the operation was to deduct the amount given from the balance of the account. It might seem logical to check at the end of the operation that the postcondition is satisfied, but in practice this would often involve duplicating much of the effort put into the implementation of the operation, and it is rarely done.

If a class has a non-trivial invariant, it can sometimes be worthwhile writing an operation in the class which checks that the invariant is satisfied. This operation can then be called at suitable times to ensure that instances' attribute values are in a legal state. For example, this could be checked at the end of every operation which changed the state of an instance, such as the withdraw operation shown above.

In general, any constraint can be checked a run-time by writing code which will validate the current state of the model. However, the overheads of such checking can be significant, and except for the case of precondition checking, constraints are rarely implemented explicitly.

10.7 IMPLEMENTING STATECHARTS

The information contained in the statecharts for the tool classes of the diagram editor was used to structure the implementation of the member functions of the classes in a fairly mechanical way. This ensured that all the information contained in the statecharts was in fact accurately reflected in the resulting code. The strategy that was used there is summarized in outline below, and a more extensive discussion of it with examples of the resulting code can be found in Chapter 5.

A basic implementation strategy

This approach models the different states in the statechart explicitly by means of an enumeration in the class to which the statechart applies, or some equivalent technique. The current state that an object is in is recorded by a special data member of the class which can only take on values from this enumeration.

Member functions which can have different effects depending on the state of the object are implemented as switch statements, each case of which represents one possible state of the object. The implementation of each case corresponds to a single transition on the statechart. It should check any applicable conditions, perform any actions, and if necessary change the state of the object by assigning a new value to the data member which records the current state.

This implementation is simple and generally applicable, but also has a few disadvantages. Firstly, it does not provide much flexibility in the case where a new state is added to the statechart. In principle, the implementation of every member function of the class would have to be updated in such a case, even if they were quite unaffected by the change. Secondly, the strategy assumes that most functions have some effect in the majority of the states of the object. If this is not the case, the switch statements will be full of 'empty cases', and the implementation will contain a lot of redundant code.

An alternative approach

An alternative implementation of statecharts can avoid these problems, at the cost of adopting a slightly more sophisticated approach to the representation of individual states. Rather than representing the current state of an object by the value of a data member in the object itself, this approach represents states as objects. Each instance of the class described by the statechart maintains a pointer to its current state, which is an instance of one of the state classes. To allow different states to be referred to by the same pointer, the state classes are arranged in a generalization hierarchy.

A class diagram illustrating the structure of this implementation is given in Figure 10.12, which shows the classes that would be declared to implement the creation tool class from the diagram editor.

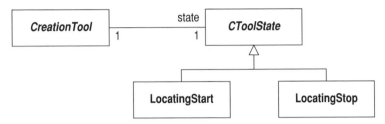

Figure 10.12 Representing states with classes

A field in the creation tool class will hold a reference to an object of type 'CToolState'. This is an abstract class, so at run-time the object referred to will be an instance of one of the subclasses 'LocatingStart' or 'LocatingStop'. In this way, a creation tool always holds a reference to an object representing its current state.

The classes representing states provide implementations of the operations declared in the creation tool interface. When a creation tool receives a message, it simply passes it on to the object representing its current state, which contains a suitable implementation. A partial definition of the creation tool class could be given as follows.

```
public class CreationTool
{
  public void press() {
    state.press();
  }

  private CToolState state ;
}
```

The interface of the 'CToolState' class must include all the messages that will be passed on from tools. In general, these will be be redefined in the subclasses to provide state-specific behaviour. Default implementations can be provided in 'CToolState', however, so that individual states need only define those operations which evoke some interesting behaviour in that state. The following code gives a suitable, partial declaration of the 'CToolState' class.

```
public abstract class CToolState
{
  public abstract void press() ;
}
```

Subclasses that represent individual states must now redefine the operations that interest them. In the case of 'press', the press event can be detected in the 'LocatingStart' state, and in response the tool should change state. A possible definition of the function is given below. For reasons that are discussed below, only pseudocode implementations of the functions are given.

```
public class LocatingStart extends CToolState
{
  public void press() {
    set start position to current ;
    draw faint image of shape ;
    set current state to 'LocatingStop' ;
  }
}
```

As the press event cannot be received in the 'LocatingStop' state, as the mouse button is already depressed, no definition of this function is required in the class 'LocatingStop'. The default implementation of the function inherited from 'CToolState' is quite adequate.

The difference between the two implementations of the statechart can be described in very general terms as follows. Any implementation must be sensitive to the fact that an object can be in different states at different times, and that the effect of operations is dependent on the current state. The simple implementation makes this all explicit, and the programmer must write switch statements to detect the current state of the object. In the more sophisticated implementation outlined above, detection of the current state is performed implicitly by the dynamic binding performed when a virtual function from the general 'CToolState' class is called.

The sophisticated implementation has several advantages over the simple one. For example, the classes that represent individual states only need to define the operations that are relevant to them, and can inherit default implementations of the others from the general state class. This can considerably simplify the implementation of a statechart, especially in the case where many operations are only applicable in a small subset of the object's states.

The sophisticated approach is also more maintainable than the simple one. For example, if the statechart is extended to include extra states, these can simply be added as new subclasses of the general state class, and existing code which is not relevant to the change will be unaffected. This contrasts with the simple implementation, where adding a state requires the implementation of every member function to be updated.

There are costs associated with the sophisticated approach, however, which mostly stem from the fact that the implementation of the member functions of the state classes often needs to update the state of the object itself.

For example, the implementation of the press operation in the locating start state shown above must first update the start position attribute of the creation tool. Then a member function of the creation tool must be called to draw a faint image of the new shape. Finally, the current state of the tool must be changed. This requires deleting the current state object, and creating a new one to represent the new state of the tool.

In order to make all these effects possible, the creation tool class must provide in its interface methods to enable state objects to update certain aspects of the tool. This in turn means that the state classes must hold a reference to the tool enabling these functions to be called. The association in Figure 10.12 between the creation tool and 'CToolState' classes therefore requires a bidirectional implementation.

As an example of what is required we will consider how to change the state of a creation tool in this style of implementation. Firstly, the creation tool class must provide a method which changes its current state.

```
public class CreationTool
{
  public void press() { }

  void changeState(CToolState s) {
    state = s;
  }

  private CToolState state ;
}
```

This method must be called by instances of the state classes. A reference to the current tool must therefore be maintained by the root class 'CToolState', which can also provide a function to update the state of the tool. This function need not be declared to be public, as it is only intended to be called by specialized state classes and does not form part of the interface available to clients.

```
public abstract class CToolState
{
  public CToolState(CreationTool t) {
    tool = t ;
  }

  void changeState(CToolState s) {
    tool.changeState(s);
  }

  CreationTool tool ;
}
```

If as a result of detecting a particular event the tool needs to change state, the last action in the method implementing that event should be a call to the function that changes the state of the tool.

```
public class LocatingStart extends CToolState
{
  public LocatingStart(CreationTool t) {
    super(t) ;
  }

  public void press() {
    // As before
    changeState(new LocatingStop(tool)) ;
  }
}
```

The sophisticated implementation of statecharts outlined here therefore provides considerable benefits, but at the cost of significantly complicating the implementation of the classes involved. As so often in design, the decision of which implementation to adopt can only be made on a case-by-case basis, depending on the relevant factors in a particular project.

10.8 PERSISTENCY

One notable omission in the design of the diagram editor presented in Chapter 5 was the lack of any discussion of how to save data between invocations of the program. The usefulness of the program will be rather limited if it is not possible to save diagrams to disk and to continue working on them at a later date.

Persistent data is data which has a longer lifetime than the program that created it. In the context of an object-oriented program, this means that it must be possible to save the objects created in one run of a program and to reload them at a later date. The user should not have to create all the data used by a program from scratch every time the program is run.

Persistency is provided by enabling data to be stored on a permanent storage medium. Virtually every significant program requires persistent data, and the most common techniques used are to store data in files or to make use of a back-end database system. The remainder of this chapter will discuss the ways in which these techniques are applied in the context of object-oriented programs.

Identifying persistent data

A preliminary problem is that it may not always be clear from a model exactly what data needs to be persistent. Models in UML are not restricted to describing permanent data, or database schemas, and as a result a single model can combine persistent and transient data.

The only notation that UML provides for persistency is a tagged value 'persistence'. This has the two values 'persistent' and 'transient' and can be applied to classes, associations and attributes.

For example, the diagram and element classes in the diagram editor need to be persistent: this is the data that the user would expect to be able to save and reload at a later date. The tool class, on the other hand, does not need to be persistent. Tools represent transient features of the user's interaction with the editor, and it would not be felt to be a major shortcoming if the tool that was being last used was not available when the program was restarted. Figure 10.13 shows part of the class diagram for the diagram editor showing the persistency of various model elements.

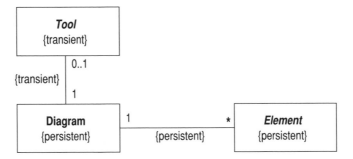

Figure 10.13 Persistent and transient classes

The primary unit of persistency is the class. Associations between two persistent classes are normally persistent, so that information about the links between persistent objects is stored. Conversely, an association between a persistent and a transient class will be transient, as the instances at one end of the association are not being stored. Attributes normally have the same persistence value as their enclosing class, though it is sometimes natural to have a transient attribute within a persistent class.

Dealing with object identities

A significant problem in making the data in an object model persistent is that much information is represented structurally, as links between objects, rather than explicitly as attributes within those objects. When an object-oriented program is running, the identities of linked objects are often represented by references, as explained earlier in this chapter.

However, references are intrinsically transient, and the persistency of an object model cannot be obtained simply by copying the values of these references to disk. The problem is that references are normally implemented using the address of the object referred to in memory, and therefore an object's identity depends on where free memory happened to be available when it was created.

An object may be created at address x, and this address could be saved in another object as a reference to the first object. Suppose now that these two objects are saved to disk. When they are read back and recreated, it is extremely unlikely that the first object will be created at address x. In this case, however, the second object will contain a dangling reference: the link between the two objects has been lost and run-time errors will occur if an attempt is made to navigate across the link.

Some object-oriented languages, notably Smalltalk, get round this problem by storing the entire memory image of the system in binary form. A more common approach, however, is to adopt some form of encoding whereby references and object identities are stored in such a way that they can be consistently recreated when data is read back, even if objects are then located at different addresses.

Serialization

Serialization is a generic term used for mechanisms which enable objects and object structures to be converted into a portable form, removing the volatility created by object addresses. In Java, for example, object serialization provides the ability to read and write objects from streams. By connecting these streams to files, objects can be saved persistently, but the mechanism is of wider applicability, enabling among other things objects to be sent to remote machines through a socket interface.

Serialization is provided in Java by means of an interface called 'Serializable'. This interface defines no methods, so in order to make a class serializable it is sufficient to declare that it implements this interface. Once this has been done, the methods 'writeObject' and 'readObject' can be used to transfer objects to and from streams, and persistence can then easily be implemented.

Serialization therefore provides a convenient and straightforward way of making data persistent. It is most appropriate when the amount of data involved is relatively small. If larger amounts of data are to be stored, serialization may no longer be appropriate. For one thing, it may not be possible for all the data to be stored in memory at one time. In such cases the obvious alternative is to use a database system to support an application, and this is discussed in the next section.

10.9 INTERFACING TO DATABASES

For many applications, the only adequate solution to providing persistency of large amounts of data is to make use of an existing database system. As well as being able to handle effectively unlimited amounts of data, databases provide a number of valuable services, such as support for multiple users, which cannot realistically be implemented afresh for every application. Like the application frameworks discussed in Chapter 5, databases shield application programmers from a large number of low-level concerns which are common to many applications.

Object-oriented databases provide seamless database support for applications designed using object-oriented methods. However, affordable object-oriented databases are not at the time of writing easily accessible or widely used, and instead it is very common for object-oriented applications to be written that make use of a back-end relational database. This approach can create significant problems because the relational model of data is in some ways quite different from the object model. This section will consider some of the implications of this mismatch; the discussion will assume some familiarity with the terminology and concepts of the relational model of data.

Suppose that we have a class diagram describing the data model of an application, containing a number of persistent classes related by associations and generalization relationships. To provide database support for this application, we will have to create a relational database schema enabling the same information to be stored. This activity involves translating one notation into another, and is similar in principle to that of implementing a model in a programming language: we need to find a way of expressing each UML construct using the concepts and notations of the target environment.

Representing classes

It is natural to represent classes by tables in a relational database. The attributes of the class become the columns in the corresponding table, and when the database is populated, each row in the table represents the data corresponding to a single instance of the class.

A potential problem here is that relational databases have no notion of identity. It is impossible for two rows of a table to store the same values for all of their attributes. In many cases, one or more keys are identified for a table: if this is the case, no two rows can share the same values for the fields that make up the key.

The situation with the object model is quite different. As discussed in Section 6.3, it is quite possible for distinct objects to have the same value for each of their attributes. Further, even if a class does possess an 'identifying attribute', the uniqueness of this attribute is not part of the model, but can only be asserted by means of a constraint.

In general, then, an implementation of a class as a relational table should provide a key. If the class already possesses a uniquely identifying attribute, this attribute can be made the key, and the relational model will automatically enforce the constraint that no two instances of the class have the same value of the attribute. If the class possesses no such attribute, a new key attribute should be created, and a unique value generated for each instance of the class. This attribute is in a sense the implementation of the object's identity, and its inclusion in the table preserves the semantic property that two instances could have the same value for all their other attributes.

Representing associations

Associations can be translated into relational schemas in a number of ways. In the simplest case, a unidirectional link from object X to object Y can be implemented by storing the key value of Y in the row of the table corresponding to X. This is the relational equivalent of one object holding a reference to another; the embedded reference is known as a *foreign key* in relational database terminology.

As a general solution to the implementation of associations, however, this approach only works in cases where the multiplicity of the association is at most one. If the database being used does not permit null values, the multiplicity will be further restricted to be exactly one. Fields in relational tables cannot hold multiple values, however, so it is impossible for one row to hold multiple references to linked objects, and this approach cannot be used for associations in general.

A generally applicable technique is to represent an association by a separate table. Each row in this table corresponds to a link between two objects, and could simply consist of the keys of the two objects to be linked. The relational constraint that two rows of a table cannot have the same values for all their fields means that only one link can exist between a given pair of objects. As explained in Section 6.4, however, this property is shared by associations in the object model, so at this point the two models are consistent.

This approach can be easily generalized to cope with association classes. An association class is essentially an association with attributes, and these attributes can simply be implemented as additional fields in the table representing the association. Tables which represent associations have a key made up of the joint key values of the related classes. This key could itself appear in a table representing another association, thus enabling the implementation of association classes which themselves participate in additional associations.

Representing generalization

Implementing generalizations in relational databases is slightly problematic, as there is no single feature or technique which provides the required semantics. The most straightforward approach is to represent both the superclass and the subclass in the generalization relation as tables, with attributes of each class defined in the corresponding table.

A consequence of this approach is that an instance of a subclass will be represented in the database by rows in two separate tables. The row in the superclass table will define those parts of the object's state that are defined in the superclass, and attributes added in the subclass will be stored in the subclass table. To relate these two rows together, it is necessary that the keys of both tables should be defined in the same way, and that the two rows should share the same key value.

There is sometimes a performance penalty to pay for storing details of an object across two separate tables. One approach to avoiding this is to represent each subclass as a table containing all the attributes of the class, including inherited attributes. This involves replicating the definition of superclass attributes, and doesn't model the commonality between the various subclasses.

An alternative possibility is to represent the entire generalization hierarchy as a single table. This means that the table will contain attributes from all the subclasses. Some of these, of course, will not be used in some cases, and will therefore have to be capable of storing null values.

Interfacing to relational databases

Once an object-oriented data model has been implemented as a relational database, it is necessary to write the code which provides the system's functionality. This code must be able to read and write data from the database, interpreting it where necessary in terms of the model used by the program.

To achieve this, programming environments typically support an interface which allows programmers to abstract away from the details of individual databases, and enables an application to work with a variety of databases or data sources. A typical example of such an interface is the Java Database Connectivity (JDBC) API which enables Java programmers to write programs which interface to relational databases.

Essentially, an API like JDBC enables programmers to manipulate a database by constructing commands in the database query language SQL, executing them on the database, and then dealing with the data that is returned as a result. The details of this interface lie outside the scope of this book, however, and will not be considered further here. Further information on this topic can be obtained from the book's web site.

10.10 SUMMARY

- A simple strategy for implementing associations uses references to model links. Implementations can be either unidirectional or bidirectional, depending on how the association needs to be navigated.
- Not all the semantic properties of associations can be captured by data declarations. Further precision can be obtained by limiting the functions available to manipulate links and by ensuring that they check and maintain any relevant constraints.
- Bidirectional implementations of associations need to maintain the referential integrity of the references implementing a link. A strategy for robustness is to assign the responsibility of maintaining references to only one of the classes involved.
- Qualified associations can be implemented by providing some form of index to map qualifiers onto the objects they identify.
- Association classes should be implemented as classes. This involves introducing additional associations connecting the association class to the original classes.
- Implementing an association as a class is a general strategy for the implementation of associations which can increase the ability of a system to withstand future modifications, at the expense of a more complex implementation now.
- Constraints in a model can be explicitly checked in code, but often it is only worth doing this for the preconditions of operations.
- A sophisticated technique for implementing statecharts was described, which represented each state by a class. This offers considerable benefits, at the cost of a significantly more complex implementation.
- Persistent data is data which must be preserved after the program which created it has finished running. Providing persistence for object structures is not easy, because of the use of references to implement links between objects.
- Small amounts of data can be saved using the technique of serialization, provided by many object-oriented programming libraries.
- Alternatively, applications can make use of a back-end database. Although object models can be implemented as relation database schemas, problems can arise caused by incompatibilities between the two notations, particularly in connection with generalization.

10.11 EXERCISES

10.1 Implement the 'addAccount' method in the manager class in Section 10.2 so that multiple references to the same account are not stored in the vector.

10.2 Provide bidirectional implementations of the associations shown in Figures 10.8 and 10.10.

10.3 Complete the implementation of the savings account class that was discussed in Section 10.6. Provide a class constructor, and an implementation of the deposit operation which checks a suitable precondition. Provide a function to check the class invariant and include calls to this function at suitable places in the class.

10.4 Complete the reimplementation of the tool classes in the diagram editor to use the sophisticated implementation of statecharts discussed in Section 10.7.

10.5 Using serialization, design and implement an extension to the diagram editor program which will enable diagrams to be saved to disk and later reloaded. (In Java, this will require recoding the program as an application rather than an applet.)

11

DESIGN PRAGMATICS

A common assumption is that design is a self-contained activity which should be carried out without any concern for the eventual implementation of the design. This idealized situation rarely corresponds to the reality of the software development process, however. In practice it is common for issues related to the implementation of the system to have a backwards effect on the design.

For example, decisions about which programming language to use on a project are often made early in the life cycle. Because of differences between programming languages, certain design solutions may work better in some languages than in others. If the target language is known, it is natural and sensible to take this into account when designing the system.

This chapter considers a number of situations where programming language issues have an impact on design concerns. The first of these is the issue of the physical design of a system. This refers to the way in which a system is packaged into physical components, such as files of executable code. Poor physical design can significantly impair the quality of a system, so it is important to be aware of ways in which decisions about a system's logical design can affect its physical design.

Secondly, the topic of reverse engineering is briefly considered. This is the activity of producing design documentation from existing code. To some extent, this is simply a matter of applying the implementation rules that were discussed in Chapters 5 and 10, but the problem also arises of dealing with programming language constructs for which no equivalent exists in UML. A related matter is the inclusion into UML of constructs which, though not an essential part of the object model, are widely used in object-oriented programming languages.

Finally, an example is given to illustrate some of the ways in which a design might evolve. It is common to start with a rather high-level model which concentrates on application specific features, and as the development progresses to integrate this with lower-level aspects, or to tune the model for specific performance characteristics.

11.1 PHYSICAL DESIGN

The greatest emphasis in the literature on object-oriented design is placed on the *logical design* of programs. From this perspective, a program simply consists of a collection of interrelated classes. These classes are typically thought of as being all on the same level, and little consideration is given to structure or grouping within this set of classes.

The classes in a design also have a parallel *physical* existence, however. Firstly, they are implemented in the target programming language and stored as files of source code. Subsequently, these source files are compiled to produce files of object code, which themselves can be interpreted by the Java run-time system, perhaps, or in other languages linked with other files to produce a file of executable code.

The physical design of a system can have a significant effect on its overall quality, and in particular on certain of the non-functional qualities of the system such as performance, testability and maintainability. As properties of the logical design of a program can affect its physical design, it is important for developers to be aware of the ways in which logical design can affect physical design, in order to be able to avoid these problems.

Problems of poor physical design

A minimal approach to physical design would be to put the code for the entire system into a single source file. This would result in large source files which were easily be read or maintained. Even worse, any change to the program, however trivial, would mean that the entire program had to be recompiled. This leads to a significant wastage of time, particularly on large projects, where the cost of compilation can be a significant factor in the overall cost of development.

If the text of a program is divided between a number of source files, however, the effect of a change can be limited to the recompilation of a small part of the program. This practice brings great benefits in terms of making the program easier to read and maintain, and also shortens development time. When a change is made, only those files which have been affected need to be recompiled.

There are many different ways in which a program could be split into files, however, and some are better than others. Many of the problems that arise stem from cyclic dependencies between mutually referring classes, as in the following example.

```
public class X          public class Y
{                       {
   . . .                   . . .
   private Y theY ;        private X theX ;
}                       }
```

These classes are mutually dependent, each requiring the other to be available before it can be compiled, executed or tested. A number of problems can arise from such pairs of dependent classes, including the following.

1. The classes cannot be tested independently.
2. To understand one class fully, it is also necessary to understand the other.
3. This situation can lead to significant added complexity in coding, particularly in deciding a policy for the creation and destruction of objects belonging to these two classes.

Components

The basic unit of physical design is usually taken to be not a class, but a *component*. The definition of components depends on the environment of the system. Different definitions are appropriate for different languages, and in the context of a complete system components may comprise not only files of code but also database systems, libraries, web pages and many other things.

For the remainder of this section we will confine our attention to environments using the Java language, and define a component to be a file of Java source code. Figure 11.1 shows UML's notation for a component representing the source file holding the implementation of the part class from the stock control system in Chapter 2.

Figure 11.1 A component

The component is labelled with the name of the source file it represents, not simply the class defined within it. The small rectangles on the left hand side of the icon represent the public interface of the component, crossing the component boundary.

Dependencies

The basic relationship between components is a usage dependency, denoting the fact that one component 'depends upon' another. This relationship between components is shown in Figure 11.2.

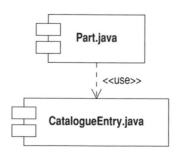

Figure 11.2 A usage dependency between two components

This diagram shows that the implementation of the part class depends on the implementation of the catalogue entry class. The stereotype 'use' on the dependency is the default annotation and can be omitted.

A usage dependency models the fact that one component makes use of the services provided by another, and cannot function correctly in their absence. Particular cases where dependencies can arise are considered in detail below. One consequence of a usage dependency is that when a component is modified, any other components that depend upon it may also have to be modified, as there is in general no guarantee that those aspects of the component that give rise to the dependency have not been changed.

The dependency relationship is transitive: if component A depends on B and B depends on C, then A also depends on C, as shown in Figure 11.3. It is common not to show the derived dependency between A and C, however.

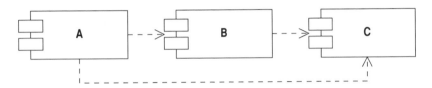

Figure 11.3 The transitivity of dependencies

Where dependencies come from

In general, dependencies between components derive from properties of the logical design of the system. For example, a generalization relationship between two classes generates a corresponding dependency between the classes, as shown in Figure 11.4.

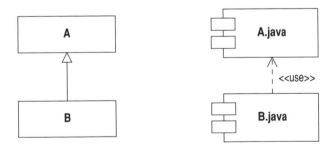

Figure 11.4 A dependency based on generalization

The reason for this is that subclasses in general expect to have access to and to make use of the features that are inherited from their superclasses. There is therefore a usage dependency from subclass to superclass. A further symptom of this is that changes to superclasses may in general affect the subclass, if any features inherited from the superclass have been altered.

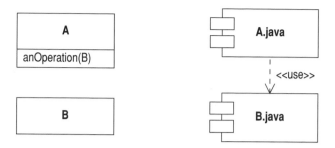

Figure 11.5 A uses B in its interface

Another source of dependencies is where a class B, say, is used in the interface of an operation of class A, as shown in Figure 11.5. The manifestation of this dependency in source code is shown below.

```
public class A {

    public void anOperation( B theB ) {
        ...
    }
}
```

This form of dependency is sometimes known as 'using in the interface' because the parameters of a public method form part of the interface of the class A, in this case. The expectation in this case is that the implementation of the operation will make use of features defined in the interface of class B, and any change to this interface might affect the implementation of this operation.

A third source of dependencies is where a class A contains an attribute whose type is that of another class. In UML, classes are not generally used as attribute types, so this form of dependency will normally arise from the implementation of a navigable association, as shown in Figure 11.6.

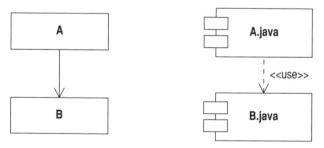

Figure 11.6 A uses B in its implementation

An example of this type of dependency, sometimes known as 'using in the implementation', is shown below. In general, class A may make use of any feature in the interface of class B, and to be vulnerable to changes in that interface.

```
public class A {
  ...
    private B aLink ;
}
```

Dependency graphs

Once the dependencies between the components in a system have been identified, they can be presented in a dependency graph showing the components and the usage dependencies between them. For example, Figure 11.7 shows the dependency graph for the stock control program discussed in Chapter 2.

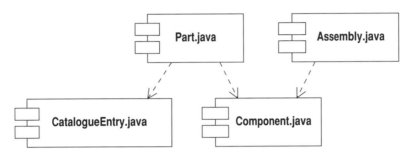

Figure 11.7 The dependency graph for the stock control program

Physical hierarchy

The graph in Figure 11.7 was drawn with all the dependencies pointing downwards. This suggests that components with no dependencies are in a sense simpler, or at a lower level, than those with many dependencies.

Where possible, the design of systems ought to be carried out in such a way that the dependency graph contains no cycles, or loops. In other words, we want to avoid the situation where a pair of components have a mutual dependency, as shown in Figure 11.8.

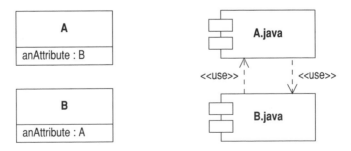

Figure 11.8 A dependency cycle

If a system has a non-cyclic dependency graph, its components can be visited 'bottom-up' in such a way that it is only necessary to consider one new component at a time. This is important for testing purposes: it means that the system can be tested incrementally, one component at a time. It also has benefits for understanding the program: when learning a new system it is only necessary to consider one new component at a time.

11.2 INTERFACES

An interface in UML is a named set of operations. Interfaces are used to characterize the behaviour of an entity such as a class, or a component. Essentially, interfaces generalize the notion of interface as found in Java. The notation for an interface uses the same graphic symbol as a class, but includes a stereotype to identify the classifier as an interface, as Figure 11.9 shows.

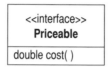

Figure 11.9 An interface

Generalization relationships can exist between interfaces, where one interface is defined as a specialized 'subinterface' of another. The relationship between interfaces and classes is one of realization, where a class implements an interface. This means that the class declares, or inherits from other classes, all the operations that are defined in the interface. Figure 11.10 shows the notation for realization, stating that the part class from the stock control example realizes the 'priceable' interface defined in Figure 11.9.

Figure 11.10 A class realizing an interface

An alternative notation for realization is shown in Figure 11.11. The interface is represented by a small circle, labelled with the name of the interface, and is linked by a line to the class that is realizing it.

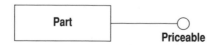

Figure 11.11 An alternative notation for realization of an interface

Components are said to conform to interfaces, meaning that the component supports all the operations defined in the interface. The notation for this is the same as in Figure 11.11, where the interface is represented by a small circle attached to the component icon. One useful application of this is to show explicitly which features of a component give rise to a dependency. Figure 11.12 shows that the part class depends only on the cost function defined in the catalogue entry class.

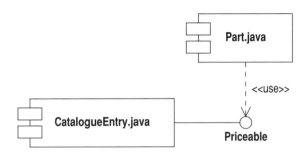

Figure 11.12 Dependency on an interface

In the case of a dependency between classes, this information can be attached to the role name at one end of an association. Using this notation, Figure 11.13 shows the same information as Figure 11.12. The interface is here being used as an *interface specifier*, to assign a 'type' to the role name. This type indicates which features of the class adjacent to the role name are used as a result of the association shown.

Figure 11.13 Using an interface specifier

11.3 REVERSE ENGINEERING

In many situations, such as when large amounts of legacy code are being dealt with, there may exist large amounts of undocumented code which have to be modified or maintained. In these situations, abstract design documentation can be useful for becoming familiar with the code and ensuring that important functional properties of the code are preserved.

The process of generating design documentation from undocumented source code is known as *reverse engineering*. It amounts to spotting in the code applications of various strategies for implementing design features, and then diagramming the resulting features in UML. Many modern CASE tools provide the facility to do this, in addition to the easier task of generating code from a design.

To illustrate reverse engineering, the following code extracts constitute a simple model of some aspects of a Unix-like file system. Firstly, a class representing nodes in the file system is declared.

```
public abstract class Node
{
  protected Node(String n) {
    name = n;
  }

  public String getName() {
    return name ;
  }

  public Node getChild(int i) {
    return null ;
  }

  public void adopt(Node n) {}

  private String name ;
}
```

This can be modelled as a UML class containing one attribute and three operations, as shown in Figure 11.14. This diagram also illustrates the notation UML adopts to show access levels to features of classes.

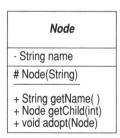

Figure 11.14 The node class

The symbols '+', '#' and ' - ' are used to represent access levels of public, protected and private respectively. The concept of access level has little application in design, and the semantics of these notions tend to be rather language dependent, but the notation is provided in order to enable more comprehensive documentation of code.

Files and directories are represented as subclasses of 'Node'. The example code given here does not attempt to model file contents, but simply shows the constructor of the file class.

```
public class File extends Node
{
  public File(String name) {
    super(name) ;
  }
}
```

To define directories we must define a data structure which will hold references to all the nodes that are currently stored in that directory. In the implementation below, a vector is used to store this.

```
public class Directory extends Node
{
  public Directory(String n) {
    super(n);
  }

  public Node getChild(int i) {
    return i < nodes.size()? (Node)nodes.elementAt(i): null ;
  }

  public void adopt(Node n) {
    nodes.addElement(n) ;
  }

  private Vector nodes ;
}
```

Although this could be modelled as an attribute of the class, it probably captures the intent of the code better to model it as an association between the directory and node classes, as shown in Figure 11.15 which gives a complete class diagram corresponding to the code given in this section.

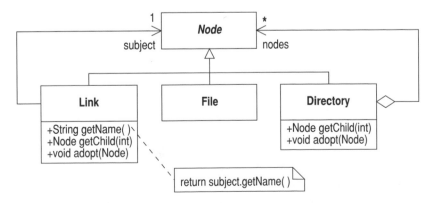

Figure 11.15 A model of files, directories and links

It is presumably a requirement of the system that the file system must not contain cycles, so this association is in fact shown as an aggregation. It is also shown to be navigable in only one direction, as this is all the code provides, and is labelled with a role name identical to the name of the field used to implement the association.

A final type of node is a link, which can act as a surrogate for some other node, the *subject* of the node. A reference to the subject is held in the link class and, as with directory contents, this is modelled as an association in Figure 11.15. The implementations of the link operations are trivial, and one of them has been given as a note in Figure 11.15.

```
public class Link extends Node
{
  public Link(Node n) {
    subject = n;
  }

  public String getName() {
    return subject.getName();
  }

  public Node getChild(int i) {
    return subject.getChild(i) ;
  }

  public void adopt(Node n) {
    subject.adopt(n) ;
  }

  private Node subject ;
}
```

11.4 TEMPLATES

A template is a parameterized model element. The name and some of the notation for templates in UML are borrowed from C++. The commonest use of UML templates is likely to be to document C++ templates as part of an exercise in reverse engineering.

Templates are commonly used to define container classes. A container class is a data structure such as a list, set or tree which can hold many data items. The code that defines the data structure is independent of the actual type of data that is stored, but languages without templates make it difficult to express the required level of generality.

For example, it is easy to write code to implement a list of integers, say. This code can be reused to provide a list of strings by physically copying the source code and editing it to refer to strings rather than integers, but there are many limitations with this approach. Not least among these is that we now have two copies of the code to maintain, and any modification to the data structure code will have to be made in multiple places.

The traditional object-oriented solution to this problem is to define data structures which can hold objects of a root class in the class hierarchy. Java uses the 'Object' class for this purpose, and data structures such as vectors are defined to hold references to instances of 'Object'. As every class in Java is a descendant of 'Object', this means that in virtue of polymorphism, any type of data can be stored in the data structure.

A limitation of this approach is that it does not guarantee that only strings are stored in a vector of strings. Careless programming could lead to any other kind of data being stored in the vector, and because knowledge of the run-time type of the objects in the vector is lost, this kind of error can be hard to recover from.

Practical uses of classes like 'Vector' make use of wrapper functions to guarantee that all objects inserted in the vector are of a single class, and so can be safely cast back to their original type when they are removed from the vector. An example of this approach can be found in the code that adds and removes elements from diagrams in the diagram editor example.

The solution to this problem using templates takes a different approach, allowing languages to define a data structure in terms of elements of an undefined type T, say. To use such a data structure, a programmer has to specify what type to substitute for T in an application of the data structure. This process is very reminiscent of ordinary parameter binding, so type parameters like T are known as *template parameters*.

A template class in UML is notated like an ordinary class, except that the template parameters are shown in a dashed rectangle in one corner of the class icon. A class that is formed from the template can be shown as being dependent on the template, and a stereotype on the dependency gives information about the binding of the template parameters. Figure 11.16 gives examples of both these notations.

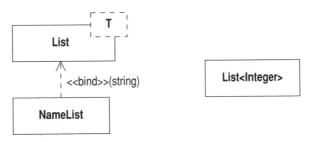

Figure 11.16 Notations for template classes

Figure 11.16 also shows the notation for denoting an 'anonymous' instantiation of the template, where the new class is not given its own name but simply referred to as a 'list of integers', say. This notation is identical to that employed in C++.

11.5 OPTIMIZATION OF DESIGN MODELS

In some circumstances, design models need to be transformed to make them suitable for implementation.

For example, a common form of transformation was described in Section 10.5 where an association is transformed into a class to make it easier to implement. In other cases, modifications might be carried out to simplify a model, or to ensure that the resulting implementation has particular performance characteristics.

The process of carrying out changes to a model which are specifically intended to describe properties of the desired implementation is here called *design optimization*. There are no hard and fast rules governing the process of design optimization. In order to give an introduction to what is involved in the process the rest of this section will consider a single example in some detail, and characterize the various optimizations that are applied. The list is in no sense exhaustive, however.

An important point to notice is that design optimization introduces no new notation. As we have seen, any class diagram can be implemented in a fairly direct manner in Java or similar languages. The process of optimization simply adjusts the model so that the ensuing implementation has certain desirable properties.

It is obviously important that any changes made to the diagram preserve the semantics of the model, and this will be informally discussed for particular cases below. In the absence of tool support, however, it is the designer's responsibility to ensure that any optimizations do not affect the meaning of the model. The identification of transformations that can be safely carried out is currently an active research area.

A simple simulation

The system described here performs a simple simulation of a colony of animals. The universe the animals exist in consists of a grid of cells, each identified by its position. The exact shape and layout of the cells is not important in what follows; for simplicity the universe can be imagined to be like a very large chess board.

Each cell can contain a certain number of food items. The simulation does not distinguish different types of food. Food items appear randomly in cells, rather like plants growing, and once they have appeared, they remain in their cell until they are eaten. The grid is populated by animals of a certain species. The animals move around the grid from cell to cell, and when they find themselves in a cell which contains food, they not unreasonably eat it.

Basic models for the simulation

The objects mentioned above and their relationships are described in the class diagram of Figure 11.17. This diagram simply states that the grid is made up of a collection of cells, indexed by their position, and that each cell can contain an unspecified number of animals and food items.

Whether or not this basic diagram forms an adequate basis for implementation cannot be judged without considering some details of the processing that the model has to support. Throughout this book the interplay between static and dynamic modelling has been stressed as being a fundamental feature of object-oriented design, and this applies just as strongly when optimizing designs.

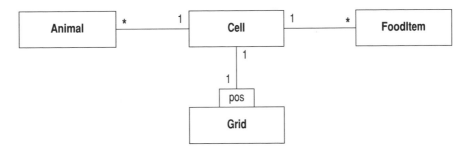

Figure 11.17 A basic class diagram for the simulation

The execution of the simulation is controlled by a clock. Every time the clock ticks, new food items may come into existence in cells and animals may eat what they find in their current cells and move into a new cell. Thus the basic interactions within the simulation involve sending messages to animals and cells at every clock tick to trigger evolution of the system.

A naive implementation might attempt to have the clock send individual messages to every animal and cell. This would be undesirable in that it would require the clock to know about virtually every entity in the simulation. A better solution would be to route clock tick messages through the grid for forwarding on to cells and animals. An interaction diagram that reflects this decision is shown in Figure 11.18.

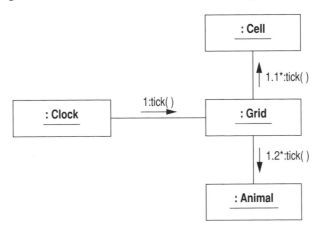

Figure 11.18 Processing a clock tick

Introducing a derived association

Figure 11.18 shows that the grid must send messages both to cells and to bugs. Access from the grid to cells is supported by the qualified association shown in Figure 11.17. There is, however, no association which supports the direct sending of messages from the grid to animals shown in Figure 11.18.

The class diagram and the object interaction diagram are therefore inconsistent, and some modifications must be made to the design. An alternative to having the grid send 'tick' messages directly to the animals would be for the grid to iterate through all cells looking for those which contained animals.

In a large simulation, however, there might be very many empty cells and only a relatively small number of occupied ones. Rather than iterating through a collection of cells only to ignore most of them, it is therefore likely to be more efficient to continue to send messages directly to animals.

In order to support this, the class diagram must be modified to incorporate an association linking grid and animal classes. The revised form of the class diagram is shown in Figure 11.19.

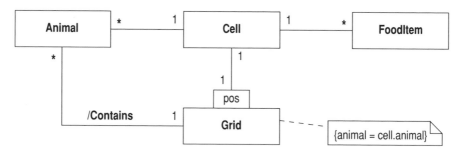

Figure 11.19 Class diagram with derived association

Notice that the new association is a *derived* association, as shown by the diagonal slash preceding its name. A derived element in a model is one whose properties are already implicitly present. Adding a derived element therefore adds no new information, but simply makes explicit information that was already available. In this case, the intention is that the grid is linked to precisely those animals which are reachable by traversing the associations from grid to cell and from cell to animal, as stated by the constrain attached to the grid class.

Derived associations are frequently introduced in design optimization to provide more efficient access paths to data than are provided by existing associations. They do however introduce a redundancy into the system's data model and there may be a processing overhead in ensuring that consistency is maintained between the various ways in which a piece of information is stored.

Replacing a link by an attribute

In Figure 11.19 the information about where on the grid an animal is provided by means of a link between the animal and its cell. This could well turn out to be inconvenient to implement, as it implies that whenever an animal moves it will have to ensure that the link to its existing cell is broken and a link to the new cell created.

The only function of the link is to record the location of animals. It is no longer used as a channel for passing messages to animals, as that job is now performed by the derived association discussed above.

To avoid the overhead of maintaining the link, therefore, it could be replaced by an attribute in the animal class which explicitly stores the position of the animal on the grid, as shown in Figure 11.20.

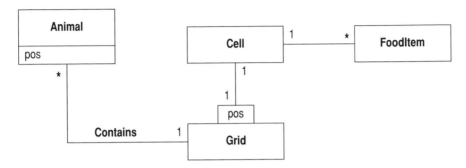

Figure 11.20 Replacing an association with an attribute

The reason that the animal needs to know its position is so that the appropriate cell can be informed that the food in it has been eaten. In the absence of a direct link between an animal and its cell, this interaction must be carried out as shown in Figure 11.21.

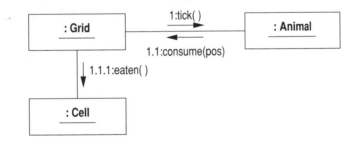

Figure 11.21 Eating food

Removing the link between animals and cells has therefore simplified the process of an animal moving at the cost of an extra message in the interaction in Figure 11.21. This kind of tradeoff occurs repeatedly in design optimization, and is one of the reasons why no firm rules can be given as to how to go about it. Only in the context of an individual system can it be determined what kinds of optimization are necessary.

Removing passive classes

The food item class does not seem to play any role in the simulation. The only important property of food items is how many of them there are in any given cell. If food items are modelled by a separate class, the only way a cell can discover the number of food items it contains is by counting the links to food item instances. As the food item class is not used for any other purpose, we can remove it and simply record the number of food items as an attribute of the cell class, as shown in Figure 11.22.

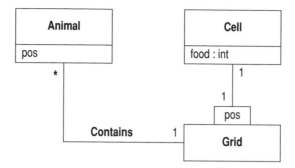

Figure 11.22 Removing a passive class

These optimizations, which do not exhaust the possibilities for this system, have considerably altered the original form of the diagram given in Figure 11.17. Nevertheless, the two models describe the same situation, while clearly suggesting different implementation possibilities. This simple example emphasizes a point made earlier, that a model that accurately describes a given situation may not provide a suitable basis for an efficient implementation. Designers of object-oriented programs can expect to have to carry out significant amounts of design optimization in the course of developing a system.

11.6 SUMMARY

- Physical design deals with the components in a system and the relationships between them. Poor physical design can have a significant impact on the quality of a system.
- Usage dependencies are generated by a number of design features, such as generalization, and one class using another in its interface or its implementation.
- A dependency graph shows the components in a system and the dependencies between them. The basic principle of good physical design is to avoid cycles in a system's dependency graph.
- Interfaces represent sets of operations which are used to characterize the behaviour of other model elements, notably classes, which are able to realize or implement interfaces.
- Reverse engineering is the activity of producing design documentation for existing code. It is of importance when dealing with legacy code. One approach is to apply in reverse the rules used for generating code from a design.
- Templates are parameterized model elements, modelled on the template feature of the C++ language. Templates can be instantiated by providing actual values for the template parameters.
- Strategies for design optimization were discussed, including the introduction of derived model elements, the substitution of an attribute for an association, and the removal of passive classes.

11.7 EXERCISES

11.1 Identify the dependencies between components in the implementation of the diagram editor, and draw the corresponding dependency graph.

11.2 Draw a component diagram for the diagram editor, showing all the source files in the system and the uses relations between them. Suppose that a new kind of element was added to the system. List the modules in the system that would be affected by such a change, and in each case state whether the effect of the change would be limited to recompilation of the module, or whether changes to the source code would also be required. How could the effects of such a change be minimized?

11.3 The following code is a simple function which makes use of the classes defined in the example in Section 11.3.

```
public void test()
{
  Node root = new Directory("")  ;
  Node temp = new Directory("dir")  ;
  Node file = new File("file1")  ;

  root.adopt(temp)  ;
  temp.adopt(file)  ;
  root.adopt(new Link(file))  ;
  root.adopt(new File("file2"))  ;
}
```

Draw a collaboration diagram showing the objects and links that would be created when this code was executed, and the messages that are sent.

11.4 What is wrong with the design fragment shown in Figure Ex11.4?

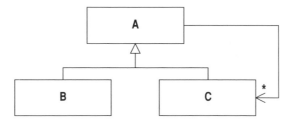

Figure Ex11.4

12

PRINCIPLES AND PATTERNS

In order to make effective use of a design notation such as UML, it is not sufficient simply to have a good grasp of the syntax and semantics of the various diagram types. The mere use of a formal notation does not ensure that good use will be made of it, and it is equally possible to express both good and bad designs in UML.

It is, of course, hard to characterize in purely formal terms the differences between good and bad designs, and it is probably impossible to do this with any degree of completeness. It is also very hard to make methodological recommendations which will ensure that designers produce only good designs. Nevertheless, a large amount of experience of object-oriented modelling and design has now been gained, and with this experience some of the properties that can make a design successful or not are becoming better understood.

The knowledge accumulated by the community of object-oriented designers falls into two distinct categories. Firstly, a number of widely accepted high-level principles have been identified. These principles describe particular properties that designs ought to have, or alternatively ought to avoid. The rationale for such principles is to point out characteristics of designs that experience has shown to have predictable consequences for the systems based on them.

These high-level principles are valuable, but provide little guidance to a designer trying to come up with a model for a particular application. To address these situations, it is necessary to document a different kind of design knowledge, more concerned with specific problems, and strategies for overcoming them. Recent work on *design patterns* attempts to meet this need by identifying common modelling problems and providing verified solutions for them.

This chapter discusses a number of well known and widely accepted principles of object-oriented design, and then introduces the concept of design patterns. The use of patterns is illustrated by considering possible modifications to the stock control program presented in Chapter 2.

12.1 THE OPEN–CLOSED PRINCIPLE

The open–closed principle was enunciated by Bertrand Meyer in 1988 in the influential book *Object Oriented Software Construction*. This principle is concerned with the effects of change within a system, and in particular with maximizing the extent to which modules can be insulated from changes to other modules which they use.

Consider the situation where one module in a system makes use of the services provided by another. It is usual to call the first module the *client* and the second the *supplier*. Although the concepts involved apply more widely, this chapter will consider in detail only the relationship between classes. This can be modelled as a usage dependency in UML, and the general situation is shown in Figure 12.1.

Figure 12.1 A usage dependency between client and supplier classes

A module is said to be *closed* if it is not subject to further change. This means that it can be freely used by client modules without the worry that future changes to the module will necessitate changes to the clients. Closing a module is desirable because it means that it can then be used as a stable component of the system which is not subject to further change which may adversely affect the rest of the design.

A module is *open*, in Meyer's terminology, if it is still available for extension. Extending a module means adding to its capabilities, or enlarging its functionality. Having open modules is desirable, because this will make it possible to extend and modify the system. As system requirements are seldom stable, the ability to extend modules easily is an important aspect of keeping maintenance costs down.

The open–closed principle states that developers should try to produce modules that are simultaneously open and closed. As indicated above, there are significant benefits to be gained from both open and closed modules. The principle seems rather paradoxical, however, because it is hard to see how a single module can be both open and closed at the same time.

If the definition of 'open' was that it should be possible to change a module, then there would be a clear contradiction between a module being open and its being closed. However, the definition of 'open' only states that a module should be available for extension. In order to avoid contradiction, then, it is necessary to find a way in which modules can be extended without being changed.

A general solution to this problem is to distinguish between the *interface* and the *implementation* of a module. If these two aspects of a module could be separated in such a way that client modules only depend on the interfaces of their suppliers, then the implementations of modules could be modified without affecting clients in any way. Object-oriented programming languages provide a number of ways in which the interface of a class can be distinguished from its implementation, and in the remainder of this section these are briefly described and evaluated as suitable mechanisms for supporting the requirements of the open–closed principle.

Data abstraction

The use of data abstraction is intended to separate the interface of a data type or class from its implementation by making the implementation details inaccessible to client code. It might therefore be thought to enable the construction of modules that are simultaneously open and closed. Data abstraction is provided in object-oriented programming languages by assigning to each feature of a class an *access level*, such as 'public' or 'private'. Figure 12.2 shows the generic client–supplier relationship with typical access levels defined for the features of the supplier class.

Figure 12.2 Client–supplier relationship using data abstraction

Access levels are also known as *visibilities* in UML, and they indicate which features of a class can be 'seen' by clients. In Figure 12.2, the operation in the supplier class is declared to be public, and hence visible to the client, whereas the attribute is private and invisible.

From a client's point of view, the interface of a class is simply those features which are visible. It follows that invisible features can be changed, removed or added to without effect on clients, provided that the visible interface is preserved. In Java, for example, the supplier class in Figure 12.2 could be implemented as follows.

```
public class Supplier
{
  public void operation() {
    // Implementation of operation
  }

  private int attribute ;
}
```

The implementation of the public method in this class can be changed without having any effect on clients and, similarly, private fields can be added or removed as required to support the implementation of the methods of the class. What must be preserved to avoid having to make changes to clients is the visible interface consisting of the name and signature of the public methods of the class.

However, this approach to the implementation of the open–closed principle has a number of limitations. In the first place, the client module is technically not even closed, as modifications to the system require changes to the code in the client class. This might be treated as a violation of the letter rather than the spirit of the principle if its more substantial goals were achieved, but there are further, more substantial, problems with the data abstraction approach.

Firstly, although it is the case in Java that private fields can be added to classes without any effect on clients, this is not the case in all programming environments. In C++, for example, a class definition is typically split between a header file, which is physically incorporated into the client module, and an implementation file. Any change to a header file, such as the addition of a new field, requires client modules to be recompiled, even if the change is invisible to them. It would be preferable if an implementation of the open–closed principle could be found that was language independent.

Secondly, in the data abstraction approach the interface required by client modules is left implicit. Clients can make use of all features of the supplier that are visible to them, but need not do so. In practice, different clients of a module may make use of different subsets of the visible interface of a module. This makes it difficult to know exactly what changes to a module will affect a given client. Both documentation and maintainability would be improved by an approach which explicitly documented the interface required by a client module.

Abstract interface classes

An alternative approach to the implementation of the open–closed principle is to use an *abstract interface class*. A class diagram showing the general structure of the design using this technique is shown in Figure 12.3.

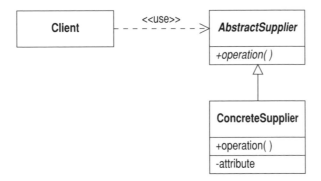

Figure 12.3 Client–supplier relationship using an abstract interface class

Here the abstract supplier class defines the interface for the supplier class. As it is an abstract class it defines no attributes. The implementation of the supplier is deferred to a concrete subclass which defines any necessary attributes and implements the functions declared in the abstract class. The client class declares its dependence on the interface class, which contains only those implementation details which it is known will not be subject to modification, if any.

In Java, the abstract supplier class could be declared as an abstract class extended by the concrete supplier. The concrete subclass defines any necessary attributes for the chosen implementation, and defines all the necessary member functions.

```
public abstract class AbstractSupplier
{
  public abstract void operation() ;
}

public class ConcreteSupplier extends AbstractSupplier
{
  public void operation() {
    // Implementation of operation
  }

  private int attribute ;
}
```

From the point of view of the open–closed principle, the important thing about this implementation is the effect on the dependency relationships between the three classes. As explained in Chapter 11, a generalization relationship induces a dependency between the subclass and the superclass. The usage dependencies between three classes in Figure 12.3 are therefore those shown in Figure 12.4.

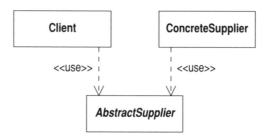

Figure 12.4 Dependencies with abstract interface class

Figure 12.4 makes it clear that the client class has no dependency on the concrete supplier class. A consequence of this is that any aspect of the concrete class can be changed without having any effect on the client module.

It should be remembered that we are talking about compile-time dependencies. Typically, at run-time the client would hold or manipulate a reference to an instance of a concrete supplier class, but through a field declared to hold a reference to an abstract supplier. Thanks to the polymorphic properties of references, such a field is not restricted to holding references to instances of the abstract supplier class.

The abstract supplier class is therefore an example of a module which is open, at least in the sense that it can be extended by the addition of further subclasses. These extra subclasses might provide alternative implementations of the interface, or might add features that were not previously present in the system. For example, the element class in the diagram editor exhibits this feature of extensibility. Further subclasses could be added to it to enable the editor to manipulate new kinds of shapes, but this would not affect any of the client modules, such as the drawing class or the selection tool.

Is the abstract supplier class also closed? It is certainly more closed than the supplier class in Figure 12.2, in that typical changes to the implementation of supplier objects will be made to its concrete subclasses rather than to the abstract supplier itself. However, changes to the interface may be required as the system evolves, and these will require changes to the abstract class. It may be asked if there is any way of closing a module against such changes, and this issue will be considered in the Section 12.3.

The use of abstract interface classes, as exemplified in Figure 12.3, is a fundamental technique in object-oriented design, and examples of its use will appear repeatedly in the patterns examined later in this chapter.

12.2 NO CONCRETE SUPERCLASSES

Section 12.1 has discussed the utility of abstract interface classes in providing software modules which satisfy the open–closed principle. A related principle states that all subclasses in generalization relationships should be concrete, or conversely that all non-leaf classes in a generalization hierarchy should be abstract. This principle can be summarized in the slogan 'no concrete superclasses'.

The rationale for this principle can best be appreciated by means of an example. Suppose that a bank is implementing classes to model different types of account, as in the examples considered in Section 6.6, and that in the initial version of the model only one class is defined, representing current accounts, which have the normal withdraw and deposit operations.

Subsequently the bank introduces savings accounts, which add the facility to pay interest on the balance in an account. As these new accounts share most of their functionality with current accounts, the decision is taken to define the savings account class as a specialization of the current account class, so that the shared functionality can be inherited. This situation is shown in Figure 12.5.

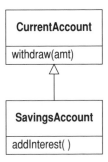

Figure 12.5 An example of a concrete superclass

This design is clearly a violation of the 'no concrete superclasses' principle, as the current account class in Figure 12.5 is both concrete and a superclass. Violation of this principle can lead to significant problems as a design evolves, as the following development of the example above will illustrate.

For example, suppose that the withdrawal operation that was originally defined did not permit accounts to become overdrawn. This restriction made the bank's current accounts unpopular with customers, however, so the decision is made to allow overdrafts on current accounts but not on savings accounts. It is not easy, however, to modify the design of Figure 12.5 to provide this functionality.

It would not be correct, for example, simply to modify the withdrawal operation defined in the current account class to permit overdrafts. As this operation is inherited by the savings account class, this would have the incorrect consequence of also permitting overdrafts on savings accounts. It would be possible to get round this by overriding the operation in the savings account class, to provide the original functionality, but this is rather an artificial solution. More seriously, it would have the consequence of replicating the code that actually performed the withdrawal in both classes. This may be trivial in this case, but in general, code replication is a strong sign of a design error.

Another possibility would be to define the withdrawal operation in the current account class in such a way that it checked the run-time type of the account the withdrawal was being made from, and then chose an appropriate course of action. In outline, the implementation of the operation might be as follows.

```
public class CurrentAccount
{
  void withdraw(double amt) {
    if (this instanceof SavingsAccount) {
      // Check if becoming overdrawn
    }
    balance -= amt ;
  }
}
```

This style of programming has a number of serious drawbacks, however, including the fact that the superclass 'CurrentAccount' makes explicit reference to its subclasses. This means that when a new subclass is added, the code in the current account class will in general have to change, making it impossible for the current account class to be closed, in Meyer's sense. For this reason, among others, recourse to this style of programming is also taken as evidence of shortcomings in the design of a system.

Similar problems arise if a function has to be defined on current accounts only. For example, suppose the bank wants to add the capability for cheques to be cashed against a current account, but that this facility is not available for savings accounts. The only obvious implementation of this function is for it to check the run-time type of its argument, as shown below.

```
void cashCheque( CurrentAccount a ) {
  if (a instanceof SavingsAccount) {
    return ;
  }
  // Cash cheque
}
```

The problems in these cases arise from the fact that the current account class in Figure 12.5 is performing two roles. As a superclass, it is defining the interface which must be implemented by all account objects, but it is also providing a default implementation of that interface. In the cases we have examined, these roles conflict. In particular, this happens when specialized functionality must be associated in some way with instances of the concrete superclass.

A general solution to this sort of problem is to adopt the rule that all superclasses should be abstract. This means that the design shown in Figure 12.5 should be replaced by the one shown in Figure 12.6.

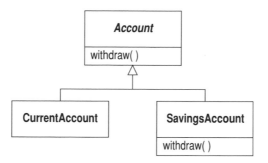

Figure 12.6 Applying the 'no concrete superclasses' rule

Now the withdraw operation in the 'Account' superclass can perform the basic withdrawal, and the code that checks that a savings account is not becoming overdrawn can be placed in the function that overrides it. If necessary, the implementation of the operation in the superclass can be called from the subclass in order to make use of common functionality. Furthermore, as 'SavingsAccount' is no longer a subclass of 'CurrentAccount', instances of the subclass can no longer be passed to functions like 'cashCheque', above, and there is no need for that function to check the run-time type of its arguments.

12.3 DECOUPLE THE INTERFACE HIERARCHY

Suppose that an abstract interface class has been implemented along the lines shown in Figure 12.3. A modification request is then received, to add a function to the interface provided by the abstract supplier class, to satisfy the requirements of a new client class.

The design shown in Figure 12.3 seems to offer no alternative to adding this function directly to the abstract supplier class. There are serious problems with this approach, however. Firstly, the aim is to close the abstract supplier, and hence it should not be modified. Secondly, it is possible that such a change may lead to further changes to existing clients, at least to the extent of forcing them all to be recompiled. Thirdly, the new function will have to be implemented in all existing concrete supplier classes, or a default implementation provided by the abstract supplier.

These problems can be avoided by defining abstract suppliers not as a base class in a hierarchy of supplier classes, but as an interface. If this is done, concrete supplier classes are no longer subclasses of abstract supplier, but instead provide realizations of the interface it defines. The new design, an alternative to that shown in Figure 12.3, is shown in Figure 12.7.

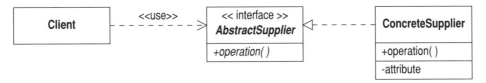

Figure 12.7 Using an interface

Now it is possible to handle the request to extend the abstract supplier interface to deal with the requirements of the new client without modifying the interface itself. Instead, a new interface can be defined which is a specialization of the abstract supplier interface. The new client uses this new interface, and the original client can continue to use the original, unchanged interface. The new interface can itself be realized by a new concrete supplier class. The abstract supplier is unchanged, and so is a contender for being a genuinely closed module. The resulting situation is shown in Figure 12.8.

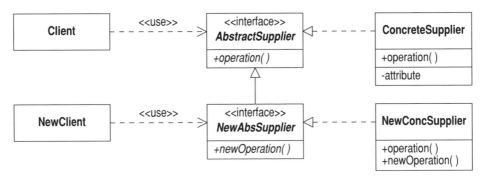

Figure 12.8 Extending an interface by specialization

Notice that Figure 12.8 does not show a generalization relationship between the concrete supplier and new concrete supplier classes. One way to implement new concrete supplier would be to inherit the implementation of abstract supplier's functions from concrete supplier (at the risk of running foul of the no concrete superclasses rule), but alternative implementations are possible. For example, a reference to an instance of concrete supplier could be included in the new concrete supplier class and the appropriate function calls delegated, or everything could simply be re-implemented from scratch. Because client modules are now only indirectly related to concrete suppliers, different suppliers do not need to be related by generalization in order to provide polymorphic client interfaces: this is provided by the generalization between interfaces.

12.4 THE LISKOV SUBSTITUTION PRINCIPLE

If abstract interface classes are used, as described in Section 12.1, then any client module which programs to the interface defined by the abstract interface class will make extensive use of polymorphism. For example, in Figure 12.3 the client class only knows about abstract suppliers. This means that the clients will call supplier operations through a reference of type 'AbstractSupplier', as shown below.

```
AbstractSupplier supplier ;
...
supplier.operation() ;
```

When this code runs, the 'supplier' variable does not contain a reference to an instance of 'AbstractSupplier': as this is an abstract class, it can have no instances. Instead, it will hold a reference to an instance of 'ConcreteSupplier' or some other subclass of the abstract supplier class.

If this kind of polymorphism is not to cause problems in programs, the semantics of the language must ensure that something like the following is true: if a client is expecting to hold a reference to an object of class T, then it will work equally well when provided with a reference to an object of class S, where S is a specialization of T.

The *Liskov substitution principle*, named after the computer scientist Barbara Liskov who gave a classic statement of it in 1987, provides a definition of what it means for one type to be a subtype of another which in effect provides the required guarantee. In this context the principle can be stated as follows.

> Class S is correctly defined as a specialization of class T if the following is true: for each object *s* of class S there is an object *t* of class T such that the behaviour of any program P defined in terms of T is unchanged if *s* is substituted for *t*.

Less formally, this means that instances of a subclass can stand in for instances of a superclass without any effect on client classes or modules. One consequence of this is that associations on superclasses can be considered to be inherited by their subclasses, as it makes no difference to an object at the other end of a link whether it is linked to a subclass object in place of a superclass object.

Although it is formulated in terms of types and subtypes, the Liskov substitution principle effectively defines the meaning of the notion of generalization as used in object-oriented design languages. In UML, the various forms of generalization that are defined, between classes, use cases and actors for example, share the property that instances of the specialized entity in such a relationship can always be substituted for instances of the more general entity.

Exactly what this means will depend on the type of entity being considered. In the case of actors, for example, it means that specialized actors can participate in all the interactions with use cases that are available to the more general actors that they are specializations of, as shown in Figure 3.23.

Generalization between classes can therefore only be correctly used in situations where occurrences of the superclass can be freely substituted by occurrences of the subclass, and where such substitution is undetectable by client modules. If there are any circumstances where a program would behave differently if a subclass object was used in place of a superclass object, then generalization is being used incorrectly.

Programming languages check for substitutability at a syntactic level, and will check that subclasses are defined in such a way that certain classes of error will not occur at run-time, such as an object being sent a message that it does not understand. There is always the possibility that a programmer will implement an operation in a derived class in such a way as to undermine substitutability, however, perhaps by providing an implementation which causes subclass instances to behave in a completely different way from superclass instances.

Attempts have been made in the research literature to characterize a stronger notion of substitutability, which will ensure that subclasses provide behaviour that is in some way compatible with the behaviour defined in superclasses. This requirement has to be carefully phrased, however: it is not appropriate to demand that subclasses provide the same behaviour as superclasses, because in many cases the whole point of defining a subclass is to define specialized behaviour for certain classes of objects. One approach to this problem is to specify relationships between the constraints defined for the classes in a generalization relationship.

12.5 INTERACTIONS DETERMINE STRUCTURE

This example is based on an article by Robert Martin. It illustrates the heuristic used in in the development of the diagram editor, namely that interactions between objects can be used as a basis for identifying structural relationships between the classes that the objects in the design belong to.

Suppose that we are modelling a simple mobile phone whose interface consists of a set of buttons for dialling numbers, a 'send' button for initiating a call, and a 'clear' button for terminating a call. A component known as a 'dialler' interacts with the various buttons, and keeps track of the state of the current call, and the digits that have been dialled so far. A cellular radio deals with the connection to the cellular network, and the telephone has in addition a microphone, a speaker and a display on which the number dialled is shown.

Figure 12.9 shows a naive design for the mobile phone based on this description. This diagram gives an intuitively clear model of the physical structure of the mobile phone. Each component is represented by a class, and aggregation is used to indicate that the various components are parts of the whole assembly, represented by the mobile phone class.

The adequacy of this design can be tested by seeing whether it supports the interactions that implement the required behaviour of the phone. For example, consider the following scenario which describes the basic course of events that might take place when a user is making a call with the phone.

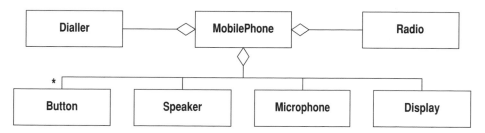

Figure 12.9 A 'physical' model of the mobile phone

1. The user presses buttons to enter the phone number being called.
2. Each digit pressed is added to the display.
3. The user presses the 'send' button.
4. The radio establishes a connection to the network and places the call.
5. The display indicates that the phone is now in use.
6. At the end of the call, the user presses the 'clear' button.
7. The display is cleared.

Figure 12.10 shows a realization of this scenario, up to the point at which the connection is made. When the user presses a button, a message is sent to the dialler giving the information about which digit has been pressed; this digit is then added to the display. When the user presses the send button, the dialler sends the complete number to the radio which places the call and, once a connection is made, updates the display.

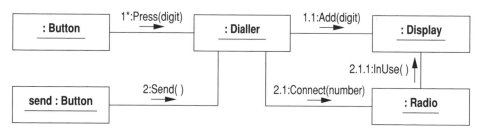

Figure 12.10 Making a call on the mobile phone

It is immediately obvious from these diagrams that the associations on the class diagram in Figure 12.9 do not support the messages that are sent in the course of the interaction shown in Figure 12.10. To obtain a consistent design, either the static model of the mobile phone should be altered, or the realization of the scenario made consistent with the model in Figure 12.9.

In this example, it is probably preferable to adopt the structure implied by the interactions shown in Figure 12.10. A realization of the scenario above could be based on the structure shown in Figure 12.9, but by forcing all the interactions between objects to be routed through the central mobile phone object this approach would lead to a more complex interaction, which forced the phone object to keep track of every detail of what was going on.

A better approach is to adopt a static structure which is modelled on the structure required to support the system's interactions. The model of the mobile phone that is obtained by following this approach is shown in Figure 12.11.

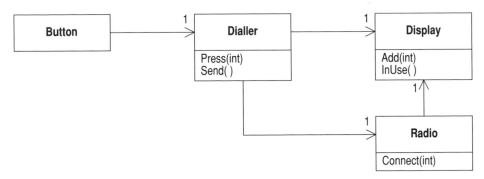

Figure 12.11 A better model of the mobile phone

Perhaps the most striking difference between this model and the one shown above in Figure 12.9 is that there is no longer any need for an object representing the mobile phone itself, and hence the mobile phone class and the aggregation relationships linking it to the various components of the phone no longer appear in the model.

As a result, it could perhaps be claimed that the new model does not represent the real world as well as the original one. However, the notion that there is a 'real world' which can only be correctly modelled in one way is rather over-simplistic. The moral of this example is that the physical relationships between the objects we are modelling may not provide a suitable basis to support the interactions which provide the functionality required of the system. In such cases, it is usually advisable to adopt the static model which best supports the necessary interactions.

12.6 DESIGN PATTERNS

In any design activity, there are certain characteristic problems that occur repeatedly. Different designers will arrive at different solutions to these problems, but as design experience becomes more widely shared among practitioners, it is often the case that a substantial body of knowledge evolves which describes these common problems and methods of solving them. Often the solutions are not altogether obvious, and involve 'tricks of the trade' that are not widely known.

There are obvious advantages to making such knowledge explicit and publicly available. Most important among these, perhaps, is that inexperienced designers can then gain access to a library of techniques that are immediately applicable, thus making the process of developing expertise in the relevant design technique easier. In the case of object-oriented design, *design patterns* have been proposed as a way of codifying the ways in which expert designers tackle and solve particular commonly occurring problems in design.

The classic reference to the subject is the book *Design Patterns* published in 1995 by Erich Gamma, Richard Helm, Ralph Johnson and John Vlissides. This book is widely known by the nickname of the 'gang of four book', and will be referred to as such in the rest of this chapter.

The problems that designers face come at a number of levels. At a very low level, there are problems concerning the details of the interface or implementation of a single class. At the highest level, the problems concern the creation of an overall architecture for a system. Design patterns address an intermediate level of concern, where particular localized properties of a design have to be guaranteed.

Typical problems addressed by design patterns might include the following. How can a design ensure that only one instance of a class is ever created inside a system? How can recursive, tree-like structures be modelled? How can additional functionality be attached to an object dynamically?

The solution to the problem posed by a design pattern is typically expressed as a fragment of an object-oriented design, consisting of a number of interacting classes which, taken together, provide a ready-made solution for the problem raised. A pattern can usually be applied in a great many situations, however, so the solution describes a template, or stereotypical, design which can be adapted and reused as required.

Definition of patterns

A pattern is often defined as 'a solution to a problem in a context'. The solution to a problem in object-oriented design can most succinctly be described by using a formal notation such as a class diagram or an interaction diagram, but this formal representation should not be identified with the pattern, for at least two reasons.

Firstly, many patterns share a similar formal structure, while being designed for use in completely different situations. An integral part of distinguishing one pattern from another is to understand the problem that is being addressed, even if the proposed solutions in two or more cases may seem formally similar.

Secondly, most patterns can be manifested or implemented in a variety of different ways, using class structures or interactions that can differ in detail. Thus designs which are quite different in detail can in fact be applications of the same pattern

The gang of four book defines the following essential elements of a pattern.

1. A *name*. Having a memorable name for a pattern helps designers to remember it. A collection of named patterns also provides a language which permits designers to discuss designs at the level of patterns.
2. The *problem*. This defines the situation in which the pattern is applicable.
3. The *solution*. This describes design elements that address the problem. Often the solution is expressed using suitable formal notation, but as emphasized above, a pattern will usually encompass a number of variations round a common idea.
4. The *consequences*. These are the results and tradeoffs of applying the pattern. Knowledge of the consequences of using a pattern is essential if an informed decision is to be made about whether or not the pattern should be applied in a particular situation.

The concept of a design pattern is therefore rather informal. This informality can make it hard to give unequivocal answers to questions of when two patterns are the same, or whether a design does or does not make use of a given pattern. Many people within the patterns community defend this informality, arguing that a pattern captures a 'design insight' which resists formalization, and which loses its scope for applicability if it is defined too narrowly.

On the other hand, without a clear idea of what actually constitutes the definition of a pattern, it is difficult to tell whether two authors are describing the same pattern, variations on a pattern, or two distinct patterns, for example, or to find a pattern that is applicable to a given situation. These problems are becoming more serious as the published pattern literature expands.

Patterns versus frameworks

Patterns and frameworks are two approaches to the problem of enabling certain elements of designs to be recorded and reused, and as such they are sometimes confused. They differ significantly, however, both in terms of what they provide and how they are intended to be used.

Firstly, patterns and frameworks differ in terms of *size*. A framework defines an architecture for a complete application, or a class of related applications. A pattern, on the other hand, describes a solution to a single design problem, which may be applicable in many applications or frameworks.

Secondly, patterns and frameworks have different *contents*. A pattern is a pure design idea which can be adapted and implemented in various ways in different languages. A framework typically is a mixture of design and code which can be extended in various ways by application programmers.

Thirdly, as a consequence of the second point patterns tend to be more *portable* than frameworks. Frameworks are already implemented, although without necessarily constituting a complete application, and are therefore usually restricted to a single implementation environment. Patterns are language independent, and can be applied in widely differing situations.

A third concept, which also carries connotations of reuse, is that of a 'component'. Components are usually thought of as enabling code reuse, and permitting at most a limited degree of customization. The formula 'frameworks equal components plus patterns' has been used in the literature, but this rather underplays the role of a framework in defining a complete architecture for a system.

12.7 RECURSIVE STRUCTURES

In several examples earlier in the book, we have considered cases where an object has been linked to several objects of related classes, possibly including the object's own class, and has needed to treat them all in a similar manner. An example of this is provided by assemblies in the stock control program considered in Chapter 2.

In this example, an assembly could contain an unspecified number of other objects, some of which were simple parts, and others which were themselves assemblies. These subassemblies could in turn contain further subassemblies in addition to parts, and this nesting of assemblies could continue to whatever level is required. In many ways, however, parts and assemblies were treated in an identical manner, and the classes share aspects of a common interface.

This situation was modelled by introducing a new class to define the common features shared by files and directories. In Chapter 2 this class was called 'Component', and the relevant part of the class diagram describing the structure of components is shown in Figure 12.12.

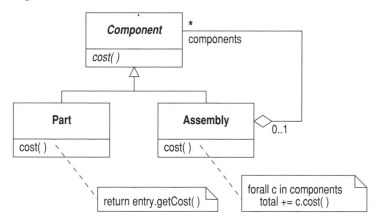

Figure 12.12 Parts and assemblies

'Component' is an abstract class which describes the common features of parts and assemblies. The operation to determine the cost of a component is abstract, and is overridden in each of the subclasses. In the case of parts, the operation retrieves the cost of the part from the associated catalogue entry object (not shown in Figure 12.12). In the case of assemblies, the operation iterates through all the components contained in the assembly, calls the cost operation for each, and returns the sum of the values returned. These properties are shown in the notes attached to the operations in Figure 12.12.

The link between an assembly and the components it contains is modelled by means of an association from the assembly class back to the superclass 'Component'. This states that an assembly can have zero or more components, each of which can be either a part or an assembly. The association in Figure 12.12 differs from that given in Chapter 2 in that an assembly is defined to be an aggregate of its components. As explained in Section 6.9, this guarantees that the assembly has a strict tree structure, and that an assembly can never contain itself, either directly or indirectly.

There are two important semantic properties of parts and assemblies that make the generalization in Figure 12.12 appropriate. Firstly, they share a common interface, which is defined in the common superclass. Secondly, the overall structure of an assembly is a recursively defined tree structure, in which the contents of an assembly can be either parts or other assemblies.

The Composite pattern

The structure exemplified by Figure 12.12 is very common, and its essential properties are captured in the pattern named 'Composite' given in the gang of four book. The intention of the Composite pattern is to 'compose objects into tree structures to represent part–whole hierarchies. Composite lets clients treat individual objects and compositions of objects uniformly'.

The solution presented by a pattern is typically documented in a class diagram which shows how a number of classes can interact together to provide the required functionality. In the case of Composite, the description of the pattern is very similar to its application shown in Figure 12.12, but with more general names given to the participating classes. A slightly simplified version of the structure of the Composite pattern as defined in the gang of four book is shown in Figure 12.13.

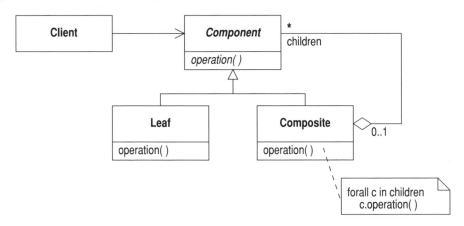

Figure 12.13 The structure of the Composite pattern

This diagram shows that a component of a recursive structure can either be a leaf, which has no subcomponents of its own, or a composite, which can have any number of child components. In the stock control example, the part class corresponds to the 'Leaf' class, and the assembly class to the class called 'Composite'.

The component class defines a uniform interface through which clients can access and manipulate composite structures. In Figure 12.13 this is represented by an abstract operation. This interface must be defined explicitly in each of the subclasses, and normally the implementation of the operation in the composite class will call the operation on each of its children. This is indicated by the note attached to the operation in the composite class.

The class diagram in Figure 12.13, then, defines a generic structure which enables tree-like structures to be built up by programs. A designer who wished to apply this pattern would take this diagram and identify classes in the application corresponding to the leaf and composite classes, and create a common superclass for them. The definition of the operation then provides a reusable implementation of an operation to visit every node in the tree.

Patterns in UML

A design pattern is intended to be a general-purpose design solution which can be reused in many different situations. The classes in Figure 12.13 are not application classes, but are more like placeholders which will be identified with different classes in different applications of the pattern.

To reflect this, patterns are represented in UML as *parameterized collaborations*. The pattern is treated as a single unit, a collaboration, and names of classes in the pattern are defined as parameters, which can be replaced by real class names when the pattern is applied. Figure 12.14 shows the Composite pattern represented in this form.

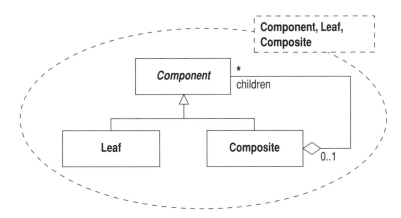

Figure 12.14 The Composite pattern as a parameterized collaboration

One of the advantages of representing patterns in this form is that the application of a pattern can be documented on a class diagram. Figure 12.15 shows a simplified class diagram for the stock control program together with an abstract representation of the Composite pattern. Links from the pattern to classes are labelled with the names of the classes in the pattern, and this documents which classes in the design correspond to particular roles in an instantiation of the pattern.

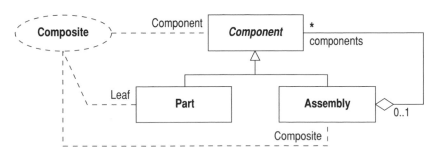

Figure 12.15 Documenting the application of a pattern

12.8 THE STATE AND STRATEGY PATTERNS

The alternative implementation of the information contained in the statechart of a class described in Section 10.7 is an application of a design pattern called 'State' from the gang of four book. The intent of the State pattern is to 'allow an object to alter its behaviour when its internal state changes. The object will appear to change its class'.

The class diagram summarizing the structure of the State pattern is given in Figure 12.16. The 'Context' class represents the entities which display state dependent behaviour. The different states of context objects are represented by classes in the state hierarchy; every context object is linked to exactly one of these at a time, representing its current state.

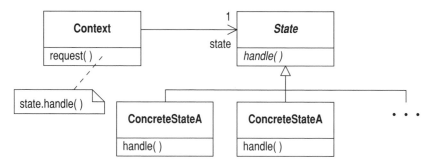

Figure 12.16 The State pattern

When a context object receives a request, it does not attempt to deal with it itself, but instead delegates it to an operation in the state class which will handle it. By providing different implementations of this operation in the subclasses of the state class, the context object appears to be providing dynamically varying behaviour.

A related pattern called 'Strategy', shown in Figure 12.17, allows alternative implementations of an algorithm to be provided in such a way that different instances of a class can support different implementations of the same operation, or even change implementation at run-time. Here, the interface of the context object defines an operation, but the class does not implement it. Rather, the implementation is provided by a linked object of class 'Strategy', to which calls to the operation are delegated. Despite these differences, however, the structure of the Strategy pattern is almost indistinguishable from that of the State pattern, apart from the naming of the classes and operations involved.

Nevertheless, the State and Strategy patterns are thought to be distinct patterns because they are supposed to be addressing different problems. This example illustrates that there is more to a pattern than the diagram giving its structure, but on the other hand it might raise doubts about how patterns are to be distinguished from one another. Perhaps the different states of an object could be thought of as alternative strategies for implementing the object's operations, for example. To complicate the situation still further, the next section considers a family of patterns which are essentially implementations of the same idea, but which are nevertheless structurally distinct.

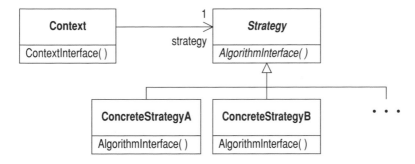

Figure 12.17 The Strategy pattern

12.9 MVC, DOCUMENT/VIEW AND OBSERVER

The basic idea behind the document/view architecture, which was briefly described in Section 5.7, is the separation of the data being used from the user interface through which it is viewed and manipulated. The original source of this idea was the model–view–controller architecture (MVC) defined for Smalltalk programs. This section will briefly describe the structure of MVC, and the way that its key ideas have been used in the document/view architecture and in the Observer pattern.

Models, views and controllers

Figure 12.18 shows the generic structure of an application using the model–view–controller architecture. There is a single *model* object, which stores and maintains the data of interest. Linked to the model are a number of *view* objects, each of which is responsible for displaying the data in a particular way. For example, if the model contained some statistical data, different views might display this either in bar chart or pie chart formats. Also linked to the model are a number of *controllers*, responsible for detecting user input and forwarding it to other objects.

The three components of this architecture communicate by message passing, and Figure 12.18 also shows the details of a typical interaction whereby some action on the part of the user causes the model and its associated views to be updated.

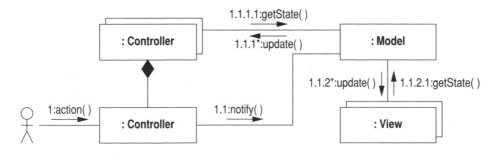

Figure 12.18 A standard interaction cycle in MVC

User input is detected by a specific controller, shown in Figure 12.18 to be one of the set of controllers. In general, user input can change the state of the model, so the controller then sends a notification message to the model informing it of the change. This message, along with others in the interaction, would typically pass some data as arguments which, for clarity, are not shown in Figure 12.18.

When it receives a change notification, the model sends an update message to all the controllers and views linked to it, collectively known as its dependents. On receiving an update message, a dependent will query the model for the latest information about its state, and then redisplay whatever portions of the user interface are affected. Notice that, in general, controllers as well as views can be affected by changes to the model: a simple example might be a menu option that needs to be enabled or disabled.

The benefits of this architecture lie in the clear separation it makes between the code which processes an application's data and that which deals with its user interface. This makes it easy, for example, to develop new types of view without affecting the model. This approach was particularly valuable in the Smalltalk environment, which was one of the first to make large-scale use of graphical user interfaces.

Document/view revisited

The document/view architecture was briefly described in Section 5.7 in connection with the implementation of the diagram editor. Document/view can be viewed as a simplification of the MVC architecture in which documents correspond to models, but views combine the functionality of both the controllers and views of MVC. The structural relationship between the document and view classes, together with some of the operations that cause them to interact, is shown in Figure 12.19.

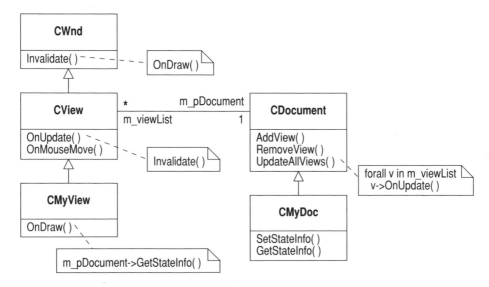

Figure 12.19 The document/view architecture (simplified)

Figure 12.20 shows the details of a typical interaction that would take place in the document/view architecture following a user action such as a mouse move. Notice that this collaboration is drawn using instances rather than roles, to emphasize the fact that the objects participating are instances of the two user-defined classes 'CMyDocument' and 'CMyView', and not simply objects playing the roles of document and view.

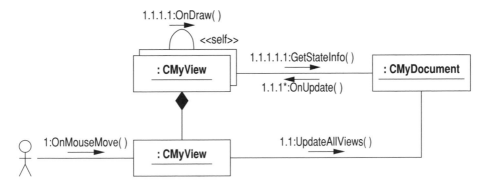

Figure 12.20 A typical document/view interaction

The overall structure of the document/view interaction is similar to the one shown in Figure 12.18 for the MVC architecture. The view that detects the user's action sends the notification message 'UpdateAllViews' to its document. The document then sends an update message to all the views linked to it, including the one that sent the notification. This update message gets translated into a call to the view's 'OnDraw' method, and in the course of executing this a view will typically retrieve information about the current state of its linked document before displaying it.

The Observer pattern

Another variation on this theme of separating model and view is provided by the Observer pattern defined in the gang of four book. This pattern is intended to 'define a one-to-many dependency between objects so that when one object changes state, all its dependents are notified and updated accordingly'. A class diagram showing the classes involved in the pattern is shown in Figure 12.21. This diagram shows the by now familiar relationship between a model, called a subject in this pattern, and a number of views, now known as observers.

The Observer pattern is meant to be applicable in a wider range of circumstances than simply updating a graphical display in response to a user's actions. Observer objects, therefore, do not necessarily have any responsibility for detecting user input, and so the interactions involved in the use of Observer are often simpler than in MVC and document/view. Nevertheless, as Figure 12.22 shows, the basic structure of the interaction is the same as those considered earlier. An unspecified client sends a notification message to the subject which then sends update messages to all its observers; these in turn may then query the state of the subject.

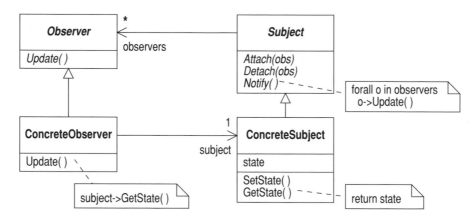

Figure 12.21 The Observer pattern

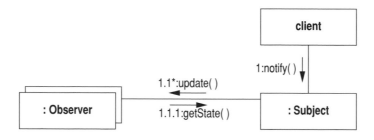

Figure 12.22 Interactions in the Observer pattern

12.10 APPLYING VISITOR TO THE STOCK CONTROL PROGRAM

Suppose there is a requirement to add a function to the stock control program to print out a list of all the parts and subassemblies in an assembly. Such a report is often called a 'parts explosion'. A simple approach might be to add an 'explode' function to the hierarchy, analogous to the existing 'cost' function. The implementation of this function in the part class would print out the details of a simple part, and in the assembly class it would iterate through all the components of the assembly calling 'explode' on each. There are potential problems with this approach, however, including the following.

1. Every class in the hierarchy must be altered to add 'explode'. If the hierarchy was large, this might be an unfeasible, or very expensive operation.
2. The code which controls the iteration through the components of an assembly is repeated in both the 'cost' and 'explode' functions. It would be preferable to avoid this redundancy by having the iteration implemented in a single place.
3. The 'Part' class is part of the model in this application, and yet this proposal makes it directly responsible for producing output. The basic principle of the patterns discussed in the previous section, however, is that user–interface code should be separated from the model, to allow easy modification and extension.

These issues are addressed by the Visitor pattern, whose intent is to 'represent an operation to be performed on the elements of an object structure. Visitor lets you define a new operation without changing the classes of the elements on which it operates'. Visitor therefore provides a method for implementing classes which are simultaneously open and closed, in the sense discussed in Section 12.1.

Visitor works by separating the classes that represent data, the part hierarchy in this example, from operations which can be applied to that data. Operations are represented by classes in a new hierarchy of 'visitors'. The connection between the two is made by defining a single operation in the part hierarchy which 'accepts a visitor'. Figure 12.23 shows how a single operation, to find the cost of a component, can be implemented using this technique.

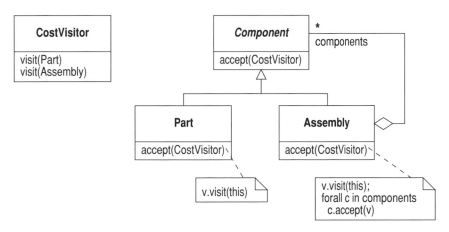

Figure 12.23 Finding the costs of components using Visitor

With this design, a programmer can no longer simply call an operation in the component class to find out the cost of a component. Instead, a cost visitor object must be created, and passed to the component, as follows.

```
CostVisitor visitor = new CostVisitor() ;
int cost = component.accept(visitor) ;
```

What happens when a component accepts a visitor depends on the run-time type of the component. If the component is a part, the job of working out the cost of the part is delegated to a function in the visitor object; to make the required information available, a reference to the part is passed to this function. If the component is an assembly, however, an iteration through all the subcomponents of the assembly is performed, and each subcomponent in turn is asked to accept the visitor. In this way, the visitor object is passed from component to component until every part in the assembly has been visited.

The actual business of working out the cost of the assembly is carried out in the cost visitor object. The definition of this class given below shows how the total cost is preserved as the iteration is being carried out.

```
public class CostVisitor
{
  private int total ;

  public void visit(Part p) {
    total += p.cost() ;
  }

  public void visit(Assembly a) {
    // null implementation
  }
}
```

As this shows, the cost visitor class contains all the code that is specific to working out the cost of a component. The generic code which traverses the part hierarchy, however, appears in the accept function in the assembly class. In order to work out the cost of an assembly, there is nothing to do apart from ensuring that all its components are visited, so the cost visitor class contains no specific code for working out the cost of an assembly. In other cases, however, this function may not be empty, and it has been left in this example to indicate its general role.

Figure 12.24 shows the interactions that take place when the code above is used to work out the cost of a simple assembly consisting of two parts. Notice that every component in the assembly is asked in turn to accept the visitor and in response sends a 'visit' message to the cost visitor, with the component itself as a parameter. Finally, the client object retrieves the total cost of the assembly (this operation is trivial and not shown in the code above).

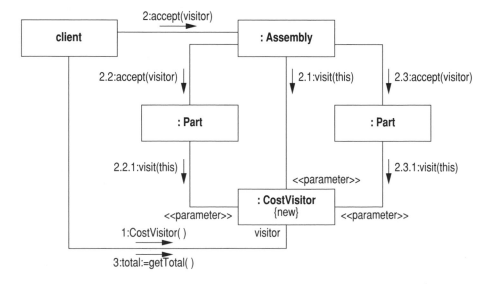

Figure 12.24 Working out the cost of an assembly with visitors

At the cost of making the overall design more complex, then, this use of visitors makes it possible to define new operation on the part hierarchy without changing any of the classes in that hierarchy. All that is required is to define a suitable visitor class, and to pass visitors to components using the 'accept' operation.

In order to complete the design, it is necessary to define an abstract visitor class, so that references to particular types of visitor do not have to be made in the part hierarchy. Classes defining visitors for different types of operation, such as calculating the cost or printing a parts explosion, can then be defined as subclass of the abstract class, as shown in Figure 12.25.

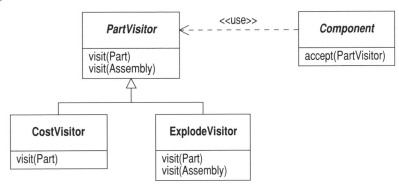

Figure 12.25 The visitor hierarchy

In general, a visitor class must provide an operation corresponding to each class in the hierarchy that is being visited. In Figure 12.25, therefore, the part visitor class provides two overloaded operations to visit parts and assemblies.

Specific visitor classes should override these functions to provide appropriate functionality for each type of component. As it may not be necessary to override every function, null implementations of these are provided in the part visitor class. For example, cost visitors do not need to perform any specific processing when visiting assemblies, so the null function in implementation of this class above could be removed and simply inherited from the superclass.

The use of the Visitor pattern in this case neatly addresses the problems identified above with the proposal to define new functions with new operations in the part hierarchy. Firstly, the classes in the original hierarchy are now untouched when the explode operation is added: all new code is contained in the class 'ExplodeVisitor'. Secondly, the code that controls the iteration through assemblies is kept separate from the code that implements particular operations and is automatically reused for all operations. Finally, user–interface code can be localized in the 'ExplodeVisitor' class, thus preserving a kind of model–view distinction.

The Visitor pattern has limitations of its own, however. For example, references to the classes in the part hierarchy are hard-coded in the visitor classes, which means that if a new part subclass is created, all the visitor classes will have to be modified. The Visitor pattern is most suitable, therefore, when operations are to be added to a relatively stable class hierarchy.

12.11 SUMMARY

- The open–closed principle calls for modules which are simultaneously extensible, and yet immune from change. The use of abstract interface classes is a way of defining classes which have this property.
- Decoupling interface and implementation hierarchies protects classes even further, by allowing the interfaces of existing classes to be changed without affecting existing code.
- In order to prevent any ambiguity between polymorphic and non-polymorphic operations a rule can be adopted that all superclasses in a design should be abstract.
- The Liskov substitution principle provides the definition of interchangeability between instances which is the foundation of the semantics of generalization in UML.
- Static relationships in a design should be based on the interactions they are to support, not on the perceived physical structure of application domain objects.
- Design patterns provide examples of tested solutions to commonly occurring problems in design.
- The separation of a system's data from its presentation to the user is a principle widely applied in object-oriented design, appearing in the MVC and document/view architectures and also in the the Observer pattern.
- The Visitor pattern provides a way to add operations on an existing hierarchy without changing the definitions of the classes in the hierarchy.

12.12 EXERCISES

12.1 Add a new element type to the diagram editor, such as rectangles with rounded corners as displayed by the 'drawRoundRect' method in the Java graphics class, and check that the element class is in fact open and closed in the sense of Section 12.1.

12.2 Implement the structure shown in Figure 12.8, and confirm that the abstract supplier interface is in fact a closed module. An implementation in a language that does not provide interfaces should replace them by abstract classes, and use multiple inheritance where necessary.

12.3 Extend the interaction shown in Figure 12.10 so that it includes the messages sent when the user presses the clear button to terminate a call. Make any necessary changes to the class diagram in Figure 12.11 to keep it consistent with the updated collaboration diagram.

12.4 Write a simulation of the mobile phone based on the design given in Figures 12.10 and 12.11 and the amendments made to these in the previous exercise.

12.5 Use the composite pattern to design an amendment to the diagram editor to allow for 'group elements', as described in Exercise 3.9.

12.6 Draw up a table identifying in detail correspondences between the document/view architecture and Observer, as presented in the class diagrams above. For example, the operation called 'Attach' in Observer corresponds to the one called 'AddView' in document/view. Also, list any significant discrepancies between the two. Discuss the extent to which document/view can be considered to be an instantiation of the Observer pattern.

12.7 One of the implementation considerations for the Observer pattern given in the gang of four book concerns the question of which object should trigger the update operation. Observers will only stay consistent with their subjects if the notification operation is called at appropriate times. This operation should be called whenever the subject's state has changed, but it could be called either by the subject itself, or by the client object that has caused the change. Explain how these two approaches would be applied in MFC, and outline the advantages and disadvantages of each.

12.8 The Java AWT contains a faithful implementation of the Observer pattern in the interface `java.util.Observer` and class `java.util.Observable`. Consult documentation for the Java AWT and document this instantiation of the pattern formally, in class and interaction diagrams, and commenting explicitly on the correspondences and differences between Observer and its Java implementation.

12.9 One weakness of the stock control program is that each individual part is represented by an object. This could lead to a very large number of identical objects being created, with a consequent waste of storage. Consult the definition of the Flyweight pattern in the gang of four book, and apply it to the stock control program to remove this problem.

12.10 In the mobile phone example, instances of the button class need to know what type of button they are so that they can send the appropriate message to the dialler when they are pressed. This means that any application that requires to use a button for a new purpose will have to modify the button class to support the new functionality. However, the button class is potentially a useful reusable component, if it could be turned into a closed module. Investigate how this could be done by applying the Adaptor pattern given in the gang of four book.

13

CAB DISPATCHING SYSTEM

This chapter presents an extended example of object-oriented development. The system described is intended to help a human controller to dispatch a fleet of radio-controlled minicabs efficiently in response to calls from customers.

A basic requirement is that the system should record details of all the drivers currently working and their current locations, and should control the allocation of cabs to new jobs. When a request for a cab is received by the controller the system should automatically allocate a cab to service the request.

In addition to calls which ask for a cab to be dispatched immediately, the system should also be able to handle *prebooked calls*, where the customer asks for a cab to be made available at some time in the future for a particular journey. In this case, the system should automatically dispatch a cab to service the call at the required time without any further intervention from the human controller.

The system will calculate the appropriate fare for each job. Jobs can either be paid for in cash directly to the driver at the end of the journey, or on account. To support the account facility, the system must maintain a list of account customers and arrange for periodic invoices to be generated. The dispatching system is not responsible for maintaining details of the actual accounts; this is to be handled by a separate, manual system for the time being.

13.1 USE CASES

In order to make a start on the design of the system, we can compile a list of use cases. There seem to be three major areas of functionality involved in the system, namely maintaining details of the currently active drivers, handling customer requests, and recording the charges incurred by account customers. The following list of use cases covers the basic functionality required in each area.

1. *Add driver*: whenever a driver starts a new shift, the system must be informed of the fact that the driver is available to be assigned to jobs.
2. *Remove driver*: this is performed when a driver's shift is finished and the driver is no longer available to be assigned to jobs.
3. *Update location*: this use case informs the system of the current location of a driver.
4. *Handle immediate job*: a typical job is generated in response to a phone call from a customer requesting a cab to go from A to B, as soon as possible. This use case involves recording the details of such a job and dispatching a cab to service it.
5. *Log prebooked job*: some customer calls will not request immediate dispatch of a cab, but will book a cab for a specific date and time in the future. This use case simply records the details of such a prebooked job within the system.
6. *Dispatch prebooked job*: When the date and time of a prebooked job comes round, the system should automatically dispatch a cab to service the job.
7. *Add account customer*: to handle details of account jobs, the system must maintain at least a rudimentary database of account customers. This use case allows a new account customer to be added to the system.
8. *Charge job to account*: this use case records the details of a job that is being charged to an account.
9. *Invoice account customer*: this will generate a list of all the outstanding jobs for an account customer. This list will be passed over to the account department to enable an invoice for the customer to be drawn up.

The most important use case seems to be the handling of immediate jobs. This use case will probably account for the majority of transactions with the system. In addition, it seems to involve all the central aspects of the real-world domain being modelled, namely jobs, drivers and the allocation and dispatch of a driver for a particular job. By contrast, use cases such as adding a new driver seem rather simple, and therefore less likely to reveal important aspects of the design of the system. The detailed development of the system therefore begins by examining this use case in detail.

13.2 HANDLING IMMEDIATE JOBS

The basic course of events that takes place when a customer requests a cab to be dispatched immediately is described in the following scenario.

1. A customer contacts the cab firm and requests a cab to go from location A to location B as soon as possible.
2. The system works out the estimated time of arrival (ETA) of a cab at location A, and the controller reports this ETA to the customer.
3. The customer finds the arrival time of the cab acceptable.
4. The controller asks the customer for a contact telephone number, and confirms the job on the system.
5. The system dispatches a cab to carry out the job.

From this description it seems clear that *jobs* are important entities within the system. A job has certain attributes, such as its pickup and delivery locations, and seems to go through various stages from initial request to final confirmation, when a cab is dispatched to carry out the job. In addition, this last fact suggests a relationship between a job and the cab that is dispatched on the job, implying that cabs are also important objects in the system.

Figure 13.1 shows an initial attempt to model these classes and the relationship between them. Optional multiplicity is specified for both ends of this association for the following reasons. Obviously, cabs are not going to be busy the whole time; there will be many occasions when a cab is not assigned to any job. On the other hand, there may be occasions when a job has not got a cab assigned to it; this will be the case when there is no cab available to meet a particular job, for example.

In addition to the pickup and delivery locations, the job class also defines an attribute to hold the phone number recorded when the job is confirmed by the customer. The use case 'update location' implies that the system also needs to record the current location of each cab. This is modelled as an attribute of the cab class. Locations are assumed to be represented by a data type, the definition of which is not considered further at this point.

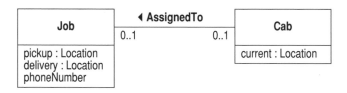

Figure 13.1 Classes representing jobs and cabs

The scenario above suggests that jobs have a characteristic life cycle, in which certain events occur in predictable sequences. For example, a job is always created in response to a customer enquiry, and following this the job can be confirmed and a cab dispatched. This suggests that a statechart could be used to document the progress of jobs. Figure 13.2 shows a preliminary attempt to model the the life cycle of jobs. This statechart shows that jobs are created in response to a customer call, and that confirming a job is a one-off action which moves the job into a new state.

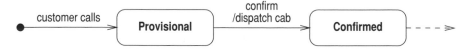

Figure 13.2 The start of the life cycle of a job

Both Figure 13.1 and Figure 13.2 must be understood to be highly provisional. Formal notations are being used here primarily to document in a formal way aspects of the system that have caught our attention so far, and it is very likely that the details shown will change substantially before a final design is produced.

Figure 13.2 indicates that it is not at the moment clear what happens to jobs after they have been confirmed. In particular, the statechart raises questions like 'can a job be cancelled?' and 'how else can a job finish?' which we are not yet in a position to answer. These possibilities will be considered later as extensions, or exceptional cases, of the basic course of events described above.

In the scenario above, the system has two major processing responsibilities, namely to calculate the ETA of a cab at the pickup location of a job, and to dispatch a cab when the job is confirmed. The remainder of this section uses collaboration diagrams to document a preliminary realization of the use case, and from this to deduce additional features of the static model of the system.

Working out the ETA of a cab

Step 2 of the scenario given at the start of this section asserts that the system works out the ETA of a cab at the pick up location of the job. The ability to do this is obviously an important feature of the system, and our design must ensure that this processing requirement can be met.

The ETA that is returned to the controller should be the shortest time that a cab might take to arrive at the pickup location. One way of obtaining this would be to take the minimum of the ETAs of all the cabs in the system. This requires some method of iterating through all the cabs, and so we introduce the notion of a 'pool' which maintains references to all the cabs that are currently active in the system. Figure 13.3 shows how the pool queries each cab in turn for its ETA at the specified location, and then returns the smallest of these times to the controller.

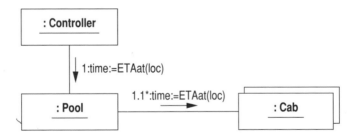

Figure 13.3 Getting the ETA

Figure 13.4 shows the facts about the static model that are required to support the interaction shown in Figure 13.3, namely that the pool administers many cabs.

Figure 13.4 The cab pool

Dispatching cabs

The system must also provide some means of dispatching a cab to a job, and allocating a cab to a job. In many cab firms, the controller would normally be in radio contact with individual drivers. Cab firms are increasingly making use of more sophisticated communication devices, however, such as computers in cabs which display messages sent directly from a central controlling computer. It would be desirable for the design of the cab dispatching system to permit flexibility and extensibility in the way that communications are actually carried out.

Ideally, the appropriate communications strategy would be able to vary on a cab-by-cab basis. To consider two extremes, in the primitive case a message might be sent to the controller asking for the driver to be contacted directly by radio; at the other extreme, the communications might be handled entirely automatically.

Design problems of this kind can often be solved by finding an appropriate pattern to apply. In this case, the 'Strategy' pattern that was briefly discussed in Section 12.8 looks as if it might be appropriate. The intention of this pattern is to 'define a family of algorithms, encapsulate each one, and make them interchangeable. Strategy lets the algorithm vary independently from the clients that use it.'

This suggests the possibility that the different methods of communicating with cabs could be represented by a 'family of algorithms' which could vary from case to case. Figure 13.5 shows how the strategy pattern might be applied to the problem of cab communication.

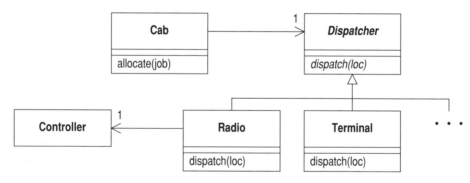

Figure 13.5 Dispatching cabs using the 'Strategy' pattern

By defining an abstract interface for dispatching a cab to a job, this design allows individual cabs to be equipped with different communications devices, but at the same time provides one simple interface through which a cab can be dispatched. Each cab is linked to a single object representing the way that communications from the controller to that cab are actually carried out.

This object supports a very simple interface, namely the ability to dispatch the cab to a particular location. How this interface is supported will vary from case to case. For example, the radio subclass might cause a cab to be dispatched by sending a message instructing the controller to contact the driver by radio. The resulting interaction is illustrated in Figure 13.6.

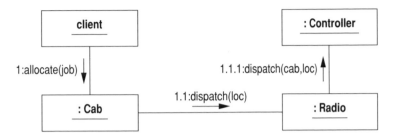

Figure 13.6 Dispatching a cab by radio

By contrast, in the case of a cab containing an onboard terminal, all the details of contacting the remote cab might be handled by the terminal object itself. Detailed modelling of this case is left as an exercise.

Exceptional courses of events

The scenario at the beginning of this section only considered the normal progression of a job. There are a number of alternative courses of events that need to be considered, however, including the following.

1. On learning the ETA of the cab, the customer might not confirm the request.
2. The customer might ring and cancel the cab before it arrives.
3. The driver might not be able to pick up the customer, either because the pickup location or the customer cannot be found, or because the customer cancels the job at that point.

If none of these situations occurs, the driver will confirm that the pickup has taken place. When the job is subsequently completed, this will be reported to the system along with the cab's current location, which need not be the same as the delivery location originally specified for the job.

All these various outcomes can be conveniently summarized by extending the statechart for jobs, as shown in Figure 13.7.

Progress of the design

A class diagram summarizing the classes identified so far and the relationships between them is given in Figure 13.8. An association has been added between the controller and job classes, to reflect the controller's central controlling role in the system, but as very little of the functionality of the system has yet been considered, these decisions must be considered to be highly provisional.

The design presented so far has at least one potentially significant problem, namely that the identity of the cab with the minimum ETA is not recorded, so there is no guarantee that the cab which is dispatched to a job will be the one which reported the minimum ETA.

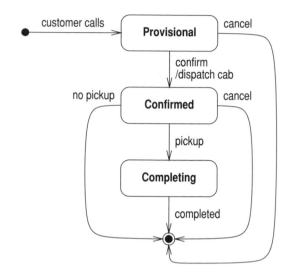

Figure 13.7 Extended statechart for jobs

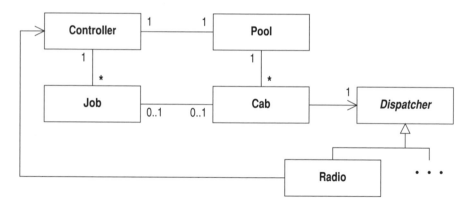

Figure 13.8 Provisional class diagram for the cab dispatching system

This could result in a customer waiting longer than expected for a cab. This also raises the possibility that the driver's shift might finish before the job is confirmed, or that the cab might be assigned to another job. Either of these cases might make it impossible for the system to dispatch a cab which will reach the pickup point in the time promised.

These questions are related to a more general problem that will arise with prebooked jobs, namely, how does the system ensure that a cab will be available to meet a job that has been booked in advance? There seems to be no easy way of ensuring that all available cabs will not be busy with immediate jobs when a prebooked job needs to be handled. No obvious solution presents itself at the moment, so this issue will be left until prebooked jobs have been considered in more detail.

13.3 HANDLING PREBOOKED JOBS

The use case for handling an immediate job has provided a lot of insight into various aspects of the dispatching system, but it has also raised a number of questions which we are not in a position to answer without a broader understanding of the processing requirements of the system. To help achieve this, we will examine further use cases, starting with the use case describing how a prebooked job is logged.

Logging a prebooked job

The basic scenario for this use case is very simple.

1. A customer requests a cab from location A to location B, the pickup to be at a given date and time, and leaves a contact phone number.
2. The system confirms the booking.

One implication of this scenario is that the system must maintain the details of all the prebooked jobs which have not yet become active. We can introduce a job manager class to handle this: the responsibility of the job manager is simply to manage the collection of prebooked jobs known to the system. Prebooked jobs share many properties with ordinary jobs, but have an additional attribute, namely the time of the requested pickup. This is provisionally modelled in Figure 13.9 by making the prebooked job class a specialization of the job class discussed earlier.

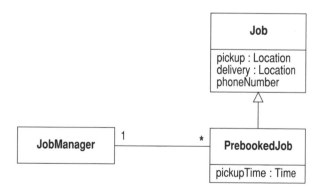

Figure 13.9 The job manager

Dispatching prebooked jobs

A more interesting use case, from the point of view of revealing important aspects of the system's design, is the one for ensuring that a cab is dispatched at the correct time to meet a prebooked job. The scenario for this is very straightforward and simply states that shortly before the pickup time, the system dispatches a cab to the job.

This description begs several questions, however, the most pressing of which is perhaps the following: how does the system ensure that a cab will be available for dispatch at the appropriate time? It is easy to imagine a situation where all the available cabs are occupied with immediate jobs, leaving the system no way of meeting the requirements of the prebooked job.

One way of addressing this problem is as follows. At a certain interval before the pickup time of the job, the system provisionally allocates a cab to the job. This cab is thought of as being on standby ready to carry out the prebooked job. The exact timing of this event will depend on a number of factors both internal and external to the system. These include the number of cabs currently working, how busy the system is, and perhaps how long it would take the controller to make a new cab available if one is needed when all the existing cabs are busy. The calculation of this time interval will not be addressed further at the moment, as the details do not affect the overall dynamic behaviour of the system.

To ensure that a cab is available to meet a prebooked job we can place constraints on what a cab on standby can do. For example, we might say that a cab on standby cannot be used for any other job unless an alternative cab can be found to act as a standby for the prebooked job.

More relaxed constraints could be imagined, such as allowing standby cabs to carry out local jobs that will be finished by the time of the pickup on the prebooked job. For simplicity and safety, however, we will adopt the strong constraint that cabs on standby are not available for any other purpose until they are released by the system.

Details of the process whereby a cab is allocated to a prebooked job are shown in Figure 13.10. The job manager has been given the responsibility of monitoring jobs and detecting when the approaching pickup time of a prebooked job has reached the limit that determines when a cab must be allocated to the job. In Figure 13.10 this is shown by means of the message 'isActive' sent to each job in turn. A true response received in response to this message indicates that it is time to allocate a cab to the job.

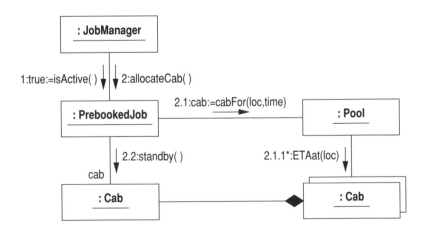

Figure 13.10 Allocating a cab to a prebooked job

In response to this message, the job asks the cab pool for a cab which is capable of reaching the specified location at the given time. The pool interrogates all the available cabs, and assuming that one is found, returns its identity to the job which then sends it a message placing the cab on standby.

At this point it becomes apparent that the treatment of prebooked jobs has addressed an outstanding problem with immediate jobs, namely how to ensure that a cab is available to be dispatched to meet a job. By introducing the concept of a cab on standby, Figure 13.10 seems to offer a solution; there is no reason why, in the case of immediate jobs, the cab with the quickest ETA at the pickup location of a job should not be placed on standby, thus guaranteeing its availability when the job is subsequently confirmed.

This further suggests that the distinction between prebooked and immediate jobs, although important in the real-world operation of the cab firm, does not reflect any significant differences in the way the jobs should be handled by the system. It is worth investigating if it is possible to handle both types of job in exactly the same way, perhaps by thinking of immediate jobs as prebooked jobs with a pickup time equal to the current time. The consequences of adopting this approach are explored in the next section.

13.4 ALLOCATING A CAB TO A JOB

The basic insight gained at the end of the previous section was that the concept of placing a cab on standby to meet a job should apply equally well to both prebooked and immediate jobs. The interaction shown in Figure 13.10 can be generalized to apply to jobs of all sorts. Figure 13.11 shows the interactions by means of which a cab can be allocated to a job, and as a result placed on standby.

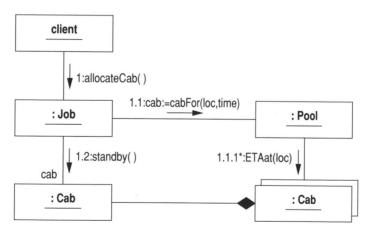

Figure 13.11 Allocating a cab to a job

Important aspects of this interaction are that a job object is created for all jobs known to the system, and that finding a cab and placing it on standby is made a responsibility of the job itself.

The client object will vary depending on the type of job. For prebooked jobs, it is the responsibility of the job manager to initiate allocation of a cab, as shown in Figure 13.10. For immediate jobs, this will be the controller's responsibility, as Figure 13.3 shows. Details of these interactions are given later.

Figure 13.11 assumes that the pool is capable of finding a free cab to meet every request. This is of course an unrealistic assumption, but consideration of the exceptional case where no cab is available will be left as an exercise.

The pool ascertains the availability of cabs by sending the message identified earlier asking for the ETA at a given location. This raises the following considerations. Firstly, the ETA will be calculated by comparing the cab's current location with the pickup location passed as a parameter, and returning the expected travel time from one to the other. This implies that the system must maintain information about travel times. This clearly will not be stored in the cab class. We can assume that the location type supports an operation to calculate journey times, and calculation of the ETA is modelled by sending a message to the location representing the cab's current position.

Secondly, not every cab should be asked for its ETA. Those cabs which are on standby already, or which are busy on a job, are not available to be placed on standby for another job. One way of implementing this would be for the pool to record the status of each cab, and only ask cabs that are currently free for their ETA. This is an over-complex solution, however. As well as imposing extra complexity on the implementation of the pool class, it implies that a cab will somehow have to inform the pool every time its status changes.

An alternative solution is to recognize that cabs have different states, and for cabs to respond to different messages in different ways depending on their state. For example, a cab on standby could respond to an 'ETAat' message by ignoring it, or returning a special value to signal its nonavailability. This implies that a statechart will be necessary to explain the dynamic properties of cabs, and this will be given later.

One consequence of the preceding discussion is that all jobs are now being handled in the same way. It follows that there is no need to define a subclass to represent prebooked jobs, as was shown in Figure 13.9. The distinction between immediate and prebooked jobs rests solely in the way they are treated by the rest of the system.

Allocating prebooked jobs

The allocation of cabs to prebooked jobs is implemented as described in Figure 13.10. Because many of the interactions in that diagram have now been factored out into the separate diagram given in Figure 13.11, the necessary message passing can be shown very simply as in Figure 13.12

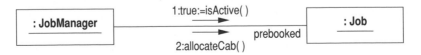

Figure 13.12 Allocation of a prebooked job

As before, we assume that the job manager is capable of detecting when a job becomes active by sending it the message 'isActive'. The mechanism by which it does this is internal to the job manager, and is not considered in detail here. A simple possibility would be for the job manager to poll every job repeatedly; a more sophisticated implementation might maintain a priority queue of jobs ordered by the time of their pickup.

When a job indicates that it is entering the active period, a further message is sent to it to trigger the allocation of a cab, on standby, to that job. The effect of this message has been shown in Figure 13.11 and need not be repeated here.

Allocating immediate jobs

It is now necessary to consider how cabs get allocated to immediate jobs. Figure 13.13 shows an interaction modelling this, based closely on the scenario given at the start of Section 13.2.

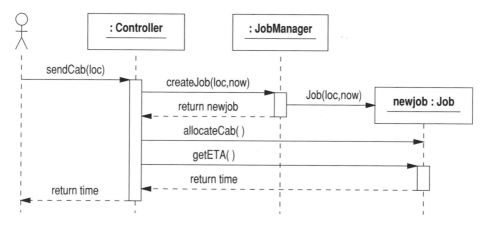

Figure 13.13 Creation and allocation of an immediate job

The initial contact from the customer is modelled by a message received by the controller object, requesting that an immediate job be created. The value returned by that message is the time it will take to get a cab to the pickup location of the job. This is the information that needs to be relayed back to the customer requesting a cab.

In response to this initial message, the controller does the following things. A message is first sent to the job manager requesting that a new job object is created. The identity of this new job is then returned to the controller. As it is an immediate job, a cab must be allocated to the job immediately. Once this has been done, the job is asked for the ETA of its allocated cab at the pickup location. This is the information that the controller must return to the customer, and so it is given as the return value from the initial message.

Creation of prebooked jobs

The final detail that needs to be integrated into the new model is the question of how prebooked jobs get created and entered into the system. This process was described in Section 13.3. All that needs to be done is for the job manager to be informed of the parameters of the new job and to create a new job object. The interaction by which this is achieved is shown in Figure 13.14.

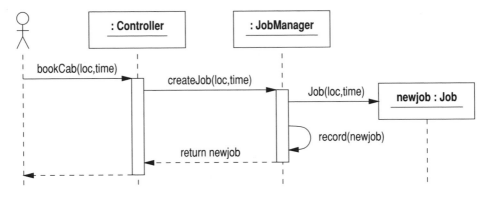

Figure 13.14 Creation of a prebooked job

The initial message triggering creation of a prebooked job is called 'bookCab'. Its parameters specify the pickup location and time of the job. In response to this message, the job manager will create a new job. The controller does not immediately attempt to allocate a cab to this new job, however. This is done later, at the time the job becomes active, by means of the interaction shown in Figure 13.12.

13.5 JOB CONFIRMATION

The previous section has shown how the creation of new jobs and the allocation on standby of a cab to service the job can be handled in a fairly uniform manner for the two types of job. The next stage in processing a job is to dispatch a cab to perform the required pickup, and this section considers how this can be achieved in the two cases.

Dispatch of immediate jobs

A cab is dispatched on an immediate job if the customer finds the ETA of a cab at the pickup location acceptable. This can be modelled by a 'Confirm' message sent to the controller, as shown in Figure 13.15. The effect of this message is to instruct the job to dispatch the cab that is currently allocated to it, and this message is simply forwarded to the linked cab object. The subsequent effect of the dispatch message on the cab will depend on the nature of its dispatcher, and will not be considered in detail here. Figure 13.6 shows one simple possibility.

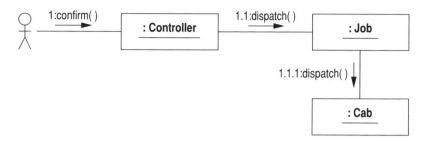

Figure 13.15 Dispatch of an immediate job

This diagram raises the question of how the controller knows which job is to be dispatched. The controller has got a natural connection with one job, namely the immediate job currently being dealt with. This corresponds to the situation of a human controller talking to a customer on the phone. We will make the simplifying assumption that only one such job can be dealt with at a time. This can be modelled by an association between the two classes, as shown in Figure 13.16.

Figure 13.16 The immediate job

The multiplicities on this association imply firstly that the controller will not always be dealing with an immediate job, and secondly that not every job is an immediate job. Prebooked jobs, for example, will never participate in the association shown here.

Dispatch of prebooked jobs

The dispatch of prebooked jobs can be handled internally by the job manager. The cab on standby for the job will take a certain amount of time to reach the pickup location, and this will depend on its current location. It should be dispatched to meet the job when the time taken to reach the pickup is equal to the time remaining until the specified time of the pickup. (In practice, a margin of error might be allowed to cope with unforeseen traffic conditions, but we will not consider this complication here.) This interaction is shown in Figure 13.17.

We can suppose that the job manager repeatedly sends 'CheckDispatch' messages to jobs. In response to such a message, the job will check the current ETA of its allocated cab at the pickup location and if necessary dispatch the cab to meet the job.

Revised statechart for jobs

The interactions considered earlier in this section have indicated that the statechart for jobs given in Figure 13.7 is in fact slightly over-simple. A revised statechart is shown below in Figure 13.18.

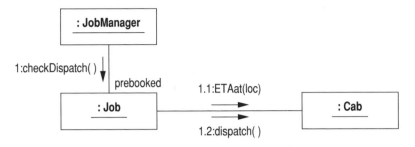

Figure 13.17 Dispatch of a prebooked job

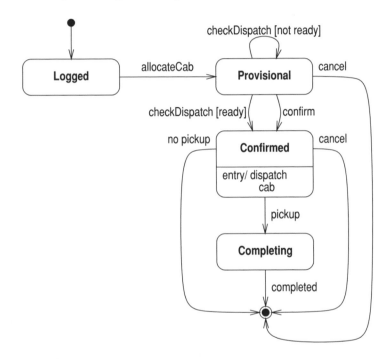

Figure 13.18 Final statechart for jobs

Jobs are created in the 'Logged' state, which simply means that the details of the job have been entered into the system and, in the case of prebooked jobs, that the job manager has knowledge of the job.

The following state, 'Provisional', corresponds to the period when a cab is allocated on standby to the job. Many immediate jobs will progress to this state immediately after creation, as a result of the 'allocateCab' message sent in Figure 13.13 after job creation. Prebooked jobs will remain logged until their pickup time approaches.

When the job is confirmed, it moves into a third state, and as a result of this a cab is dispatched to the pickup location. This happens whenever a job is confirmed, so an entry action on the state is used. Subsequent progression of the job is exactly as before.

13.6 CANCELLING A JOB

Jobs can be cancelled at any time prior to a pickup. This can only happen in response to a direct request from the customer, but there are two slightly different cases to consider. In the case of an immediate job, a customer might decide not to confirm a booking, perhaps because the estimated time of arrival of a cab at the pickup location was too long.

This interaction is shown in Figure 13.19, which has an analogous structure to Figure 13.15. The use of a role name on the link between controller and job objects indicates that the job being cancelled is the one linked by means of the association shown in Figure 13.16, which picks out the job currently being dealt with by the controller.

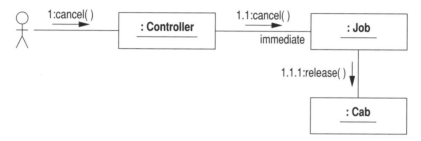

Figure 13.19 Cancelling an immediate job

An important aspect of this interaction is to return the cab to the pool as being available for subsequent jobs. Cabs are placed on standby when they are allocated to a job, as shown in Figure 13.11. The interaction in Figure 13.19 shows how they are subsequently released.

For prebooked jobs we cannot rely on a link to pick out the job to be cancelled: any prebooked job is subject to cancellation at any time. Some information will therefore have to be supplied to help identify the job that is to be cancelled. If we assume that the pickup time and location are sufficient to identify a job, then cancellation could be modelled as shown in Figure 13.20.

The job manager splits the processing required into two stages. It first has to find the job corresponding to the given parameters. This is achieved by means of a separate operation 'FindJob'. The rationale for this is that it is quite likely that other areas of the system will need to be able to identify jobs based on some of their attributes. This was, in fact, identified as one of the key responsibilities of manager objects in the previous chapter. The required functionality is better provided as a separate operation than being integrated into the 'Cancel' operation.

Once the job has been identified, the job manager sends it the cancel message with the same effects as shown in Figure 13.19. If a cab has been allocated to the job, it will be released; otherwise nothing will happen.

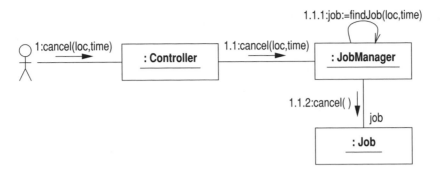

Figure 13.20 Cancelling a prebooked job

13.7 PROGRESSION OF JOBS

Once a job has been dispatched, its further development depends on the detection of events such as 'pickup' shown in Figure 13.18. When a cab arrives at a pickup location it will normally pick up the customer and then proceed to the delivery location. This corresponds to the firing of the transition labelled 'pickup' in Figure 13.18. Alternatively, the cab driver might not be able to find the pickup location, modelled by the 'nopickup' transition, or the customer may cancel the job at that point, as shown by the 'cancel' transition from the 'Confirmed' state.

Whatever happens, the outcome needs to be passed back to the system. Exactly how this is done will depend on the communications strategy adopted by individual cabs. We will assume for simplicity that the driver contacts the controller, identifying the cab in question, and states what event has taken place.

Figure 13.21 shows a generic interaction describing how events from cabs are managed by the system and passed on to the appropriate cab object We assume that cabs are identified by some sort of identifier, perhaps a call sign, and that one of the responsibilities of the pool will be to identify cabs based on the value of this attribute, in much the same way as the job manager identifies jobs in Figure 13.20 based on their time and place of pickup.

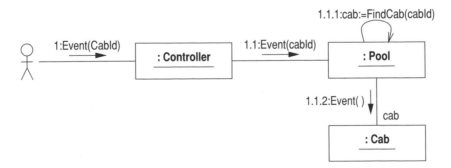

Figure 13.21 Detecting events from cabs

Events detected by a cab cause the job that the cab is servicing to progress through the statechart shown in Figure 13.18. To illustrate this, Figure 13.22 shows the normal progression of a job, receiving first a 'pickup' event and an event stating that the customer has been dropped off and the job completed.

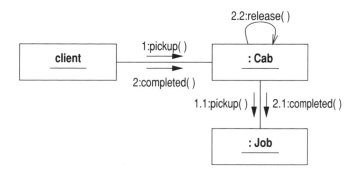

Figure 13.22 Events completing a job

When these events are detected, the cab passes on an appropriate message to the job it is assigned to. In addition, once a job is completed, the cab can be released as it was following the cancellation of a job in Figure 13.19. A 'nopickup' event will be handled in an exactly analogous way. It will be passed on to the job, and will also cause the cab to be released.

13.8 COMPLETING THE STATIC MODEL

In the previous sections, interactions for the most important areas of the cab dispatcher system have been developed. These cover all aspects of the creation and management of jobs, including the assignment of a cab to a job and tracking the subsequent progress of the job. These developments imply that significant changes have to be made to the class diagram given earlier in Figure 13.8. A revised class diagram, supporting all the interactions considered above, is given in Figure 13.23.

Most of the features of this diagram are fairly self-explanatory. The distinction between immediate and prebooked jobs is no longer made by defining specialized classes, but by identifying the jobs in each category by means of their links with other objects. Jobs which are linked to the job manager are prebooked, and a job that is linked to the controller is an immediate job. These distinctions are made clear by the role names attached to each association, and an xor constraint states that a job cannot be both immediate and prebooked.

The fact that both jobs and cabs have to be identified at certain points by certain of their attributes is modelled by defining the identifying attributes as qualifiers on the manager classes. The multiplicity on the association from job manager to job states that it is not possible to have two jobs picking up at the same time and place.

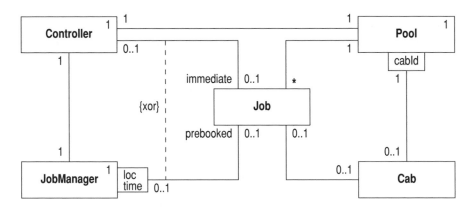

Figure 13.23 Class diagram for the cab dispatching system

Three of the classes in Figure 13.23 are specified only to have one instantiation within the system, namely the controller, the job manager and the cab pool. This reflects the fact that their role is basically to manage the other objects, and to coordinate operations.

The association between pool and job classes is included to support the message shown in Figure 13.11 where a job is made responsible for finding its own cab. This was done by means of a request to the pool object.

The details given in Figure 13.5 about the dispatcher associated with each cab, and the various subclasses of dispatcher, have been omitted from Figure 13.23. A more complete class diagram for the system would have to include these classes, as well as showing the attributes defined for each class. Production of such a diagram is left as an exercise.

13.9 IMPLEMENTATION OVERVIEW

We have now constructed a fairly complete design for the central aspects of the cab dispatcher system. If fully implemented, this would provide a useful and self-contained system and hopefully one that could easily be maintained and extended. This section briefly considers some aspects of the implementation of the system, but the bulk of the work will be left as an exercise.

The discussion above has suggested that the controller object receives messages from external clients. This raises the question of the user interface of the system, and how input from the user is to be detected by the system and forwarded on to the appropriate objects.

In the design presented so far, the controller object has implicitly been given a role as an interface object. Not only is it a target for external messages, but also output from the system, such as the radio messages that inform the controller about the cabs that must be contacted, are sent to this object.

Cycles in the static model

Messages are passed in both directions between instances of the cab and job classes. This implies that the association between those classes may require a bidirectional implementation. Cabs need to report certain events to the jobs that they are servicing, as shown in Figure 13.22, and jobs also send various messages to cabs. There does not seem to be an easy way of redesigning the operations to remove the need for bidirectionality.

Chapter 10 discusses general strategies for implementing bidirectional associations. The important decision that needs to be made is which of the two classes is responsible for maintaining the links. Once the link has been set up, passing messages between the linked objects is unproblematic.

In this case, the link management required is not complicated. A link between a cab and a job is set up as a result of the 'Standby' message sent from a job to a cab in Figure 13.11. This suggests that all the code for maintaining the link should be placed in the job class.

Using singleton objects

Figure 13.23 specifies that three of the classes in the system can only ever have one instance. As is often the case, these classes represent manager objects of various sorts, responsible for looking after a collection of other objects, or for controlling the interaction between the system and its users.

Given this, it can be argued that it is unnecessary for other objects to explicitly maintain references to these objects. For example, the radio class is linked to the controller, but this link would be tiresome to set up and represents an unnecessary overhead in the implementation of the radio class. Furthermore, there will only ever be one controller object, so the link is not necessary to enable a radio object to identify the controller it is communicating with.

A technique for implementing such classes is given by the 'Singleton' pattern. The intention of this pattern is 'to ensure a class has only one instance, and provide a global point of access to it'. Figure 13.24 shows the interface provided by a class which implements a singleton.

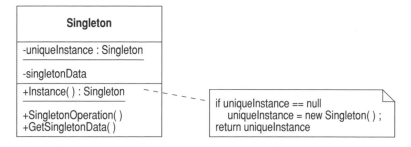

Figure 13.24 A singleton class

The central feature of this pattern is the use of a variable 'uniqueInstance', with class scope, to store a reference to the unique instance of the singleton class. Clients gain access to this object by calling the public 'Instance' operation, which returns the reference. The first time the 'Instance' operation is called, a new singleton instance will be created. Clients have no other way of creating or accessing the unique instance.

Provided that the singleton class is visible to the client, then, there is no need for a permanent link to its instance to be maintained. Whenever necessary, clients can call 'Instance' to obtain a reference to this object, and store it in a local variable. Once this reference has been obtained the other operations, which are only represented in generic form in Figure 13.24, can be called as normal.

Implementation of qualified associations

Two associations in Figure 13.23 are qualified. The implementation of qualified associations was discussed in Section 10.4, and the techniques mentioned there can be applied in these cases.

Locations

The location class is very simple, and apart from identifying discrete positions exists solely to support looking up the time taken to travel between two locations.

A simple implementation of this could assume a fixed set of locations, each representing an area covered by the cab firm, or a popular destination such as an airport. The times taken to travel between these locations could then be stored in a simple static lookup table. When the system was extended to handle charging for trips, this same structure could easily also store the costs of particular journeys.

Constructing cab objects

Whenever a cab object is created, which will take place on the current model whenever a driver starts a new shift, a linked object representing the cab's communications strategy will also need to be created. An alternative to creating a strategy object for each cab would be to store each strategy as a singleton object, and simply link the cab to the appropriate strategy when it was created. This approach is discussed in more detail in connection with the *strategy* pattern in Chapter 12.

Job statechart

Figure 13.18 gives a statechart summarizing the dynamic behaviour of jobs. As in the diagram editor, this statechart can be used to guide the implementation of the job class. The technique introduced for the implementation of statecharts in Chapter 7 could be reapplied here, but in fact there is a subtle difference between the job statechart and those for the tool classes in the diagram editor, which might make a different implementation strategy more appropriate.

In general, the tools in the diagram editor responded to the majority of the messages in their interface at any time. Clearly, the response to a message received in different states varied, but messages such as 'Move' could be sensibly received in any state. In the case of the job class, however, only a small minority of messages are applicable at any given time.

Because of this, a naïve implementation of this statechart using the technique of Chapter 7 would result in a lot of 'empty cases' in the switch statements implementing each message. Although not incorrect, this could lead to large amounts of redundant code, making the resulting program harder to read and maintain. An alternative approach to the implementation of statecharts which can get round this problem is discussed in Section 11.7.

Cab statechart

A statechart for the cab class can also be drawn as shown in Figure 13.25. Although relatively simple, it is important because it indicates certain properties of cabs' behaviour that are not elsewhere documented, such as the fact that a cab that is already on standby cannot be placed on standby again.

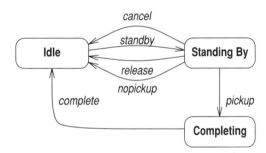

Figure 13.25 Statechart for cabs

13.10 SUMMARY

- This chapter has given a final example of object-oriented design. As before, the strategy adopted has been to make extensive use of object interaction diagrams to design the interactions that implement the required behaviour as specified in use cases and scenarios.
- An interesting point about the design was the way that a distinction, that between immediate and prebooked jobs, which seemed natural and compelling in the real-world system, in fact was of very little importance in the design. Initial design work that made use of this distinction was in fact revised.

13.11 EXERCISES

13.1 Identify a plausible set of actors for the cab dispatcher system described in this chapter, and draw a use case diagram showing the actors and the use cases listed in Section 13.1.

13.2 Consider in more detail how to model communications between the system and cabs equipped with on-board computers. The computer is an external entity which is communicating with the system: should it be modelled as an actor? What use cases does it participate in?

13.3 Construct a complete class diagram for the cab dispatcher system, based on Figure 13.23 but including all the classes mentioned in the chapter and the attributes of each class.

13.4 By considering the details of the interactions presented in this chapter, add navigation information to the class diagram for the system, and define the operations that each class must support.

13.5 Implement the basic cab dispatching system described in this chapter.

13.6 An exceptional course of events that has not been covered in detail in this chapter concerns what happens if the cab pool is unable to satisfy a request for a cab to allocate to a particular job. Decide what should happen in this case, and draw suitable diagrams to document your decisions.

13.7 Extend the design of the cab dispatcher system to incorporate the first three use cases mentioned in Section 13.1, dealing with drivers starting and finishing shifts and cabs reporting their current locations.

13.8 Extend the model of the cab dispatch system so that more than one immediate job can be dealt with simultaneously. This might correspond to the case where a cab office has a number of telephones being answered by more than one human controller.

13.9 Suppose that drivers who are not currently allocated to a job can be flagged down in the street by potential customers and new jobs created as a result of this. Extend the system to incorporate this requirement.

13.10 Extend the cab dispatch system to handle the calculation of fares for journeys. Each job should have a basic fare associated with it. In addition, any changes in the job specification, such as change in delivery location, should be reported back to the system so that a new fare can be calculated.

13.11 Further extend the system to keep track of account customers and the jobs carried out for each customer. As specified in Section 13.1, the system should be able to print out a list of jobs for each account customer. Jobs can be removed from the system once payment has been received.

A

SUMMARY OF NOTATION USED

This appendix summarizes all the graphical notation that has been used in the course of this book. The notation is that defined in the UML User Guide by Booch (1999) and the Reference Manual by Rumbaugh (1999). In cases where the two differ, the latter book has been taken as definitive.

A.1 COMMON NOTATIONS

Notes

Diagrams are made up of *model elements*, which are mostly depicted using a particular form of graphical symbol. *Notes* can be attached to model elements to describe them informally. Notes play a role in UML similar to comments in programming languages. Figure A.1 shows the notation for notes.

Figure A.1 Notation for notes

Standard elements

Stereotypes and *tagged values* provide ways of giving additional information about model elements in cases where no graphical notation is provided. *Constraints* state general properties of model elements that must be maintained.

UML predefines many stereotypes, tagged values and constraints. These are known as *standard elements*. Those which are used in this book are summarized in Table A.1.

Table A.1 Standard elements

	Applies to	Notation

Stereotypes	Link ends	`<<association>>`
		`<<global>>`
		`<<local>>`
		`<<parameter>>`
		`<<self>>`

	Messages	`<<destroy>>`

	Classifiers	`<<type>>`
		`<<enumeration>>`
		`<<interface>>`

	Dependencies	`<<bind>>`
		`<<invariant>>`
		`<<include>>`
		`<<instanceOf>>`
		`<<instantiate>>`
		`<<use>>`

	Constraints	`<<invariant>>`
		`<<precondition>>`
		`<<postcondition>>`

Tagged values	Classes	`persistent` `transient`

Constraints	Roles	`{destroyed}`
		`{new}`
		`{transient}`

	Associations	`{subset}` `{xor}`

Relationships

UML defines four different types of relationship that can hold between model elements. These are summarized in Figure A.2.

Associations connect classes and other classifiers such as actors and use cases. Associations have instances, called links, which connect instances of these classifiers.

Generalization is a relationship between classifiers, which implies that instances of the specialized classifier can be substituted for those of the more general one. Generalization relationships can connect classes, interfaces, actors, use cases and associations.

Realization, or implementation, describes the relationship between a class and an interface that it supports. It also describes the relationship between a use case and an interaction that realizes it, though this is rarely shown on diagrams.

Any other relationship between model elements can be shown as a *dependency*. Dependencies are often labelled with stereotypes to give more information about the type of relationship being shown.

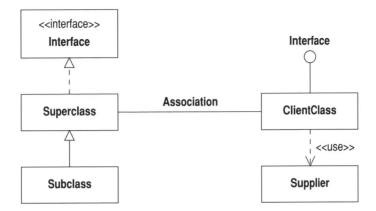

Figure A.2 Types of relationship in UML

Multiplicities

Multiplicities are used in a variety of places in UML to specify how many occurrences of a model element are permitted in a given context. UML uses the symbols shown in Table A.2 to represent the commonest multiplicity constraints.

Table A.2 Common multiplicity constraints in UML

Symbol	Meaning
1	exactly one
0..1	zero or one ("optional")
* (or 0..*)	zero or more ("many")
1..*	one or more

A.2 USE CASE DIAGRAMS

Use case diagrams show the actors who interact with a system and the use cases which define the ways in which such interaction can take place. Actors are linked to the use cases they participate in by an association. Figure A.3 summarizes the notation used on use case diagrams.

Both use cases and actors can be related by generalization. Two stereotyped dependencies can exist between use cases. The 'includes' stereotype is used in the case where one use case 'calls' another at some point in its execution. The 'extends' stereotype is used when a use case allows some optional processing at a given point (the 'extension point'); the optional processing is represented as a separate use case which extends the base case.

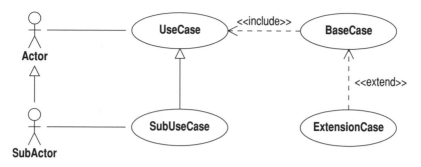

Figure A.3 Use case diagrams

A.3 OBJECT DIAGRAMS

Object diagrams show the individual objects that exist at run-time in a system and the links between them. The basic notation for objects is shown in Figure A.4. The class name must always be shown in an object icon. The object name, attributes and attribute values are optional.

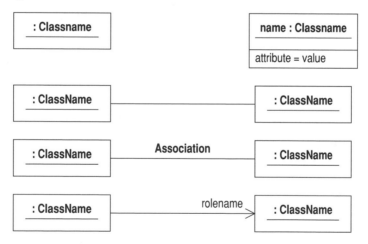

Figure A.4 Notation for objects and links

Objects are connected by links, which can be labelled with any combination of a single link name and role names at either end of the link. Links can be directed to indicate the direction(s) in which they can be navigated. Notation for links is also shown in Figure A.4.

A.4 COLLABORATIONS

Collaborations describe collections of linked objects that can participate in interactions. Notation for collaborations is shown in Figure A.5.

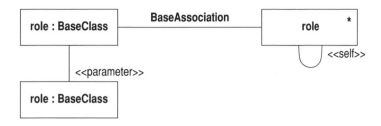

Figure A.5 Notation for collaborations

Collaborations consist of classifier roles linked by association roles. Classifier roles have a name and may have a specified base class. Association roles can have a base association, or may represent one of a number of transient forms of link, such as parameters or local variables. The link an object has to itself can also be shown on a collaboration.

Classifier roles have a default multiplicity of 1. Other multiplicities can be indicated explicitly in the icon. Multiobjects can be used to represent the set of objects playing a particular role. The notation for multiobjects is shown in Figure A.6. Individual instances can be linked to the multiobject using composition.

Figure A.6 Notations for multiobjects

A.5 SEQUENCE DIAGRAMS

Sequence diagrams show an interaction between roles or prototypical objects in a collaboration. The basic notation for sequence diagrams is shown in Figure A.7.

Each role has a lifeline extending below it. Messages are represented by labelled arrows going from one lifeline to another. Messages give rise to activations. At the end of an activation, a return message indicates that the flow of control returns to the calling object. Parameters and return values can be shown on messages. Messages sent to an object by itself give rise to nested activations.

Object creation is shown by a constructor message terminating at the newly created role. This is position at the point in time at which it is created. Object destruction is shown by a stereotyped 'destroy' message. The destroyed object's lifeline terminates at the point of destruction.

actor

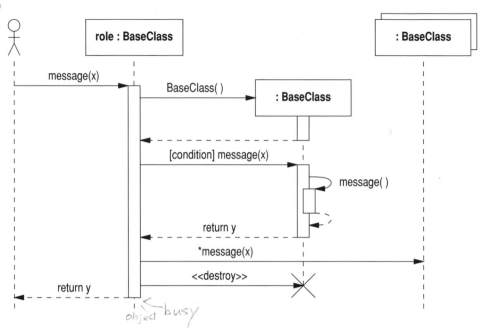

Figure A.7 Notation for sequence diagrams

A.6 COLLABORATION DIAGRAMS

Collaboration diagrams provide an alternative way of showing an interaction between roles or prototypical objects in a collaboration. The basic notation for collaboration diagrams is shown in Figure A.7.

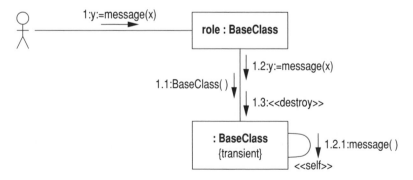

Figure A.8 Notation for collaboration diagrams

Association roles or transient links connect roles. These act as communication channels for messages. Messages are numbered to indicate the sequence in which they are sent. If a hierarchical numbering scheme is used, information about activations can be retrieved from the collaboration diagram.

Object creation and deletion is signified by annotating the affected objects with the properties 'new', 'deleted' or 'transient'.

A.7 CLASS DIAGRAMS

Classes categorize the objects that can exist in a system, and define their shared properties. Class diagrams show the classes in a system and a variety of relationships between those classes. Basic notation for classes is shown in Figure A.9.

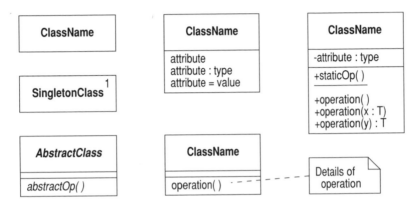

Figure A.9 Basic notation for classes

Classes can be connected by means of associations. An association between two classes implies the possibility of links between instances of the classes. Like links, associations can be directed or undirected, depending on the directions of traversal that the model supports. Notation for associations is shown in Figure A.10.

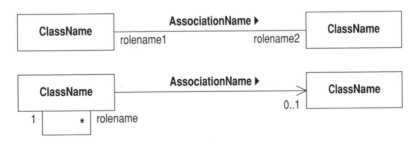

Figure A.10 Notation for associations

Association ends can be annotated to show the multiplicity of the association. This defines how many objects a given object can be linked to.

Classes can also be connection by generalization relationships. A generalization relationship connects one superclass to one or more subclasses.

Attributes and operations of the superclass are inherited by the subclasses, where they can be redefined if necessary, or new features added. Notation for generalization is shown in Figure A.11.

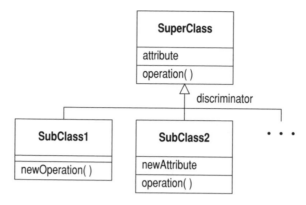

Figure A.11 Notation for generalization

Links as well as objects can have data associated with them, by defining an association class. Qualifiers are a special form of association class attribute which specify that one or more attributes function as a key to enable access to instances of one class from another. Notation for association classes and qualifiers is shown in Figure A.12.

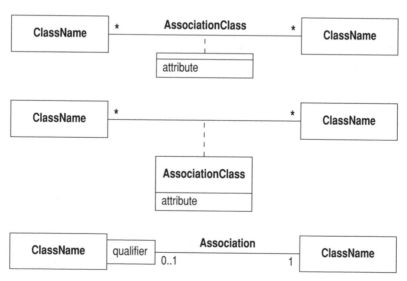

Figure A.12 Notation for association classes and qualifiers

Aggregation models the 'whole–part' relationship between classes. It can be decorated with multiplicity symbols to show various different types of aggregation.

Composition defines a stronger form of the whole–part relationship than simple aggregation. Notation for aggregation and composition is shown in Figure A.13.

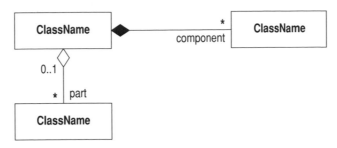

Figure A.13 Notation for aggregation and composition

A composite object can contain classes and associations. If an association lies wholly within the composite, the objects it connects must be parts of the same composite. Objects from different composites can only be connected by an association that crosses the boundary of the composite. The notation for composite objects is shown in Figure A.14.

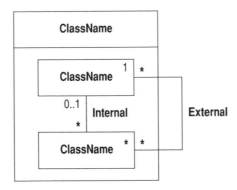

Figure A.14 Notation for composite objects

A.8 STATECHART DIAGRAMS

A statechart can be drawn for any class whose instances respond to messages in different ways depending on their current state. The basic notation for statecharts, shown in Figure A.15 allows the states of an object to be shown, along with the events the object can detect and the transitions between states consequent on detecting an event.

Transitions between states can be made conditional on the truth of certain properties, and a statechart can also show the actions performed by an object as a result of carrying out a certain transition. Notation for this is also shown in Figure A.15.

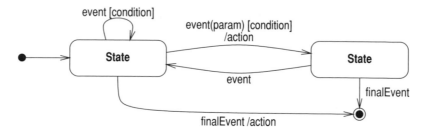

Figure A.15 Notation for states, events and transitions

The internal structure of state can be specified to show attributes of the object that are relevant to that state, and also the operations that an object performs while entering, exiting from or remaining in a state. Notation for the internal structure of a state is shown in Figure A.16.

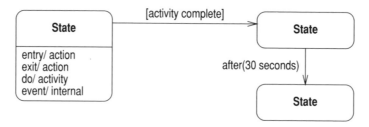

Figure A.16 Notation for the internal structure of a state

In order to simplify complex statecharts, states can be grouped together into *superstates*. This can cut down on the number of transitions shown, as a transition from a superstate is by definition equivalent to a set of transitions, one from each of its substates. Notation for nested states is shown in Figure A.17.

A.9 COMPONENT DIAGRAMS

Figure A.18 shows the notation for components and the interfaces they realize, and how to express a usage dependency between two components.

A.10 TEMPLATES

A number of model elements can be parameterized, and represented as templates. Templates can then be instantiated by binding a suitable model element to the template parameter. Figure A.19 shows the notation for templates and two ways of showing template instantiation.

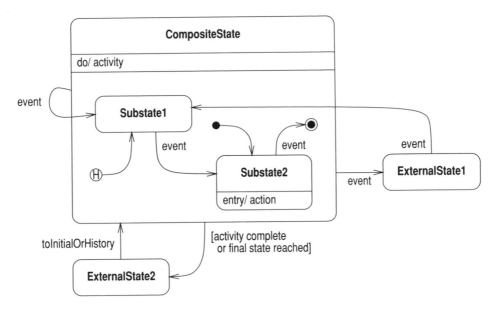

Figure A.17 Notation for composite states

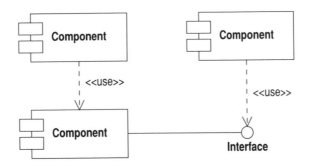

Figure A.18 Notation for components and dependencies

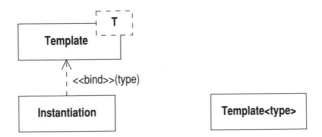

Figure A.19 Templates and template instantiation

REFERENCES

The principal references for UML are the User Guide, by Booch, Rumbaugh and Jacobson (1999) and the Reference Manual, by Rumbaugh, Jacobson and Booch (1999). Definitive documentation of the latest version of UML is available from the web site of the Rational Software Corporation (http://www.rational.com).

Many books describe UML from the perspectives of systems analysis and development methodologies. Suitable books to read after completing this one would include those by Bennet *et al.*, Fowler, and Pooley and Stevens.

The original books written by the developers of UML are good sources of background information about object-oriented modelling and the development of the language. The classic descriptions of these are contained in the books by James Rumbaugh and others (1991), Grady Booch (1994) and Ivar Jacobson and others (1992). The excellent book by Robert Martin (1995) describes the Booch method from a programming perspective similar to the one adopted in this book.

Although UML is not tied to any particular development methodology, it is often associated with the *Unified Software Development Process* defined by Jacobson, Booch and Rumbaugh (1999). More general accounts of software development and the role of design in the process can be found in Sommerville (1992) and Pressman (1997).

A following references provide more detailed coverage of some of the topics introduced in this book. OCL is described in detail by Warmer and Kleppe (1999). The book by Blaha and Premerlani (1998) contains a comprehensive account of object-oriented design for database applications. The classic source for material on design patterns is the 'gang of four' book by Erich Gamma and others (1995). For C++ users, a very thorough treatment of the issues of physical design is provided by Lakos (1996).

334

Bennett, S., McRobb, S. and Farmer, R. (1999), *Object-Oriented Systems Analysis and Design using UML*, McGraw-Hill, London.

Blaha, M. and Premerlani, W. (1998), *Object-Oriented Modeling and Design for Database Applications*, Prentice-Hall, Upper Saddle River, NJ.

Booch, G. (1994), *Object-Oriented Analysis and Design with Applications (Second Edition)*, Benjamin Cummings, Redwood City CA.

Booch, G., Rumbaugh, J. and Jacobson, I. (1999), *The Unified Modeling Language User Guide*, Addison-Wesley, Reading MA.

Fowler, M. and Scott, K. (1997), *UML Distilled: Applying the Standard Object Modeling Language*, Addison-Wesley, Reading MA.

Gamma, E., Helm, R., Johnson, R. and Vlissides, J. (1995), *Design Patterns*, Addison-Wesley, Reading MA.

Jacobson, I., Christerson, M., Johnsson, P. and Övergaard, G. (1992), *Object-Oriented Software Engineering*, Addison-Wesley, Reading MA.

Jacobson, I., Booch, G., Rumbaugh, J. (1999), *The Unified Software Development Process*, Addison-Wesley, Reading MA.

Lakos, J. (1996), *Large-Scale C++ Software Design*, Addison-Wesley, Reading MA.

Martin, R. (1995), *Designing Object-Oriented C++ Applications Using the Booch Method*, Prentice Hall, Englewood Cliffs NJ.

Meyer, B. (1988), *Object-Oriented Software Construction*, Prentice-Hall, London.

Pooley, R. and Stevens, S. (1999), *Using UML*, Addison-Wesley, Reading MA.

Pressman, R. S. (1997), *Software Engineering: A Practitioner's Approach, 4th Edition, European Adaptation*, McGraw-Hill, London.

Rumbaugh, J., Blaha, M., Premerlani, W., Eddy, F. and Lorensen, W. (1991), *Object-Oriented Modeling and Design*, Prentice Hall, Englewood Cliffs NJ.

Rumbaugh, J., Jacobson, I. and Booch, G. (1999), *The Unified Modeling Language Reference Manual*, Addison-Wesley, Reading MA.

Sommerville, I. (1992), *Software Engineering (Fourth edition)*, Addison-Wesley, Reading MA.

Warmer, J. and Kleppe A. (1999), *The Object Constraint Language*, Addison-Wesley, Reading MA.

Wirfs-Brock, R., Wilkerson, B. and Wiener, L. (1991), *Designing Object-Oriented Software*, Prentice Hall, Englewood Cliffs NJ.

INDEX